For the Many or the Few

American Politics and Political Economy

A series edited by Benjamin I. Page

For the Many or the Few

The Initiative, Public Policy, and American Democracy

John G. Matsusaka

The University of Chicago Press
Chicago & London

John G. Matsusaka is professor in the Marshall School of Business at the University of Southern California and president of the Initiative & Referendum Institute.

The University of Chicago Press, Chicago 60637
The University of Chicago Press, Ltd., London

Printed in the United States of America

13 12 11 10 09 08 07 06 05 04   5 4 3 2 1

ISBN (cloth): 0-226-51081-6

Library of Congress Cataloging-in-Publication Data

Matsusaka, John G.
For the many or the few : the initiative, public policy, and American democracy / John G. Matsusaka.
p. cm. — (American politics and political economy)
Includes bibliographical references and index.
ISBN 0-226-51081-6 (cloth : alk. paper)
1. Referendum—United States. 2. United States—Politics and government. 3. Democracy—United States. 4. Fiscal policy—United States. I. Title. II. Series.
JF494.M38 2004
328.273—dc22

2004001839

∞ The paper used in this publication meets the minimum requirements of the American National Standard for Information Sciences—Permanence of Paper for Printed Library Materials, ANSI Z39.48-1992.

To my parents

CONTENTS

PREFACE

I happen to have spent most of my life in states where citizens have the right to propose and pass laws without the consent of their elected representatives. Most Americans are in the same boat; about 70 percent of us live in a city or state where this option—called the "initiative process"—is available. The polls say people like having this right, and most would even add it to the U.S. Constitution if they could. Yet there has always been an undercurrent of concern about the initiative process, especially about the role of money. Money can place a measure, virtually any measure it seems, on the ballot, and money provides access to the costly media where issues are debated.

Over time, I formed opinions about these and other issues pertaining to the initiative process. Like most people, my opinions were based on casual intuition and impressions from watching initiative campaigns in the news. About ten years ago, however, I started thinking more seriously about how the initiative affects public policy, and whether the initiative was a wise or foolish way to make public decisions. I realized it would take systematic and objective evidence that went beyond my simple intuitions and anecdotes if I wanted to really understand the initiative process. So, as researchers tend to do, I looked to the literature.

The literature is significant, comprising hundreds if not thousands of books, articles, monographs, and pamphlets written over the last hundred years by academics, policymakers, journalists, and activists. I found that most of the writers fall into one of two camps. One camp consists of critics of the initiative process, who argue that although the initiative has a populist veneer, it is actually a tool for the wealthy few to subvert public policy. A good example is David Broder, the prize-winning columnist at the *Washington Post,* who recently concluded in *Democracy Derailed: Initiative Campaigns and the Power of Money* that "the experience with the initiative process at the state level in the last two decades is that wealthy individuals and special interests . . . have learned all too well how to subvert the process to their own purposes" (2000, 243). In the other camp are supporters of the initiative, who argue that special interests have *already* subverted the state legislatures, and that the initiative is a way for the majority to regain control. According to Dane Waters, founder of the Initiative & Referendum Institute, a nonpartisan think tank, in the *Initiative and Referendum Almanac,* "for a century, the initiative and referendum process has been THE critical tool to check the power of unresponsive and unaccountable government at the national, state and local level" (2003, xix).

The debate over whose interests are advanced by the initiative process—the many or a special interest few—is perhaps the central point of contention concerning the process, and any attempt to evaluate the process must confront this issue. What I found surprising about the debate, as I looked deeper into it, was how little it had advanced despite one hundred years of discussion. Broder's conclusion, for example, is just an updating of the anti-initiative arguments of pamphleteers a century ago: "[The initiative] provides a device through which 'special interests' can secure their ends with far greater ease than they can under the representative system, when they have familiarized themselves with its tricks and when the general public have become wearied of the numerous petitions and elections peculiar to the system," wrote James Boyle in 1912 in *The Initiative and Referendum: Its Follies, Fallacies, and Failures* (28–29). And Waters's defense of the initiative is scarcely different from the one offered in 1900 by Frank Parsons in *Direct Legislation: The Veto Power in the Hands of the People:* "[The initiative] only can destroy the private monopoly of legislative power and establish public ownership of the government" (1900, 23).

People often fail to reach agreement when the point of contention is inherently subjective. But this debate involves nothing more than objective facts: either special interests are empowered by the initiative process or they are not. A dispute that essentially hinges on matters of fact should be amenable to resolution by careful examination of the evidence. Yet the literature I discovered showed a preoccupation with advocacy not inquiry, and a reliance on a priori arguments, opinions, anecdotes (Proposition 13 is a favorite), and excerpts from *Federalist* no. 10. Careful empirical research that treated contending arguments as testable hypotheses and compared them to data were nowhere to be found. And no attempt had been made to tap even a tiny fraction of the huge amount of data produced over the last hundred years.

In short, I found a good deal of rhetoric in the literature, but could not find the facts that would resolve whether the initiative serves the many or the few. The facts I needed were out there buried in the data, waiting to be discovered. So I set off to dig them out. The end result of that effort (more than ten years later!) is this book. As will be seen, the book is not about building a case for or against the initiative. Rather, my goal is to establish some facts about the initiative: how does it affect policy, and who does this benefit? I believe we need to understand the facts before we can go about evaluating the process (and I also believe that facts are much more interesting and useful to a reader than an author's personal views).

The basic approach is simple to describe. First, I assemble and analyze tax and spending data spanning one hundred years for all of the states and 4,700 or so cities—essentially all data currently available—to determine what the initiative does to policy. Second, I examine opinion data to see what tax and spending policies the majority actually wants. Finally, I compare the policies brought about by the initiative with the expressed preferences of the voters and ask: Does the initiative give the majority policies it likes or dislikes? In this simple way, we can learn whether the initiative benefits the many or the few. If the initiative promotes majority rule, then most people should approve of the policies it brings about; if the initiative allows narrow interests to subvert the process, then most people should disapprove of the policies it induces.

The evidence turns out to tell a remarkably consistent story. For every policy I am able to examine, the initiative pushes policy in the direction a majority of people say they want to go. I am unable to find *any* evidence that the majority dislikes the policy changes caused by the initiative, as implied by the special interest subversion view. This does not, in my opinion, establish that the initiative is a wise or desirable way to make public decisions—there are other issues that await examination, particularly the possibility that majority rule undermines the rights of numerical minorities—but it does go a long way toward rejecting the view that the initiative process allows special interests to subvert the policy process. Indeed, a century of tax and spending data tell us (as clearly as any data can) that the initiative process has made American government the servant of the many and not the few.

The core of this book was written during a sabbatical in the 2000–2001 school year. I would like to acknowledge the generous financial support of the Earhart Foundation, the Stigler Center at the University of Chicago (where I spent two quarters as the John M. Olin Visiting Professor of Economics), and my home institution, the University of Southern California. This book is the culmination of more than ten years of research on the initiative process. I could not have completed a project of this scope without a great deal of help in getting around intellectual roadblocks, and although it would be impractical to itemize all of my debts, I would be remiss if I failed to acknowledge the numerous contributions of colleagues at the University of Chicago and USC, especially Tom Gilligan, and the comments of workshop participants at George Mason University, the Hoover Institution at Stanford University, University of California–Berkeley, University of California–Irvine, the University of Chicago, USC, and the Public Choice Society Meetings. Larry Kenny, Eugene Matsusaka, and two anonymous reviewers read the entire manuscript and gave me invaluable feedback on how to clarify and improve the arguments. Jaffer Qamar read multiple versions of the manuscript in painstaking detail, and his uncompromising feedback helped me avoid countless mistakes in exposition and substance. Natalia Moskvitina provided reliable and energetic research assistance in a project that required inordinate attention to details. Finally, I would like to thank my wife, Jia, for her advice, encouragement, support, and patience with my long hours, and Elise and Theo for inspiration.

> When we consider the extent to which [political] pressure is made effective today by the greedy and highly organized few, rather than by the mere normally interested and unorganized many, a legislative system which may have been safe once comes to look decidedly defective.
>
> —Lewis Jerome Johnson, *The Initiative and Referendum* (1909)

CHAPTER 1 An American Institution

The initiative process embodies the simple idea that ordinary citizens should have the right to propose and pass laws without the consent of their elected representatives. Support for this idea is deep and enduring. The initiative has been a part of state and local government for more than one hundred years now, making it an older institution than universal women's suffrage, term limits for the president, direct election of U.S. senators, the federal income tax, and social security. None of its popular luster has diminished over time. Opinion polls consistently reveal strong support for the initiative process at all levels of government—even the federal—from residents of both initiative and noninitiative states. As of 2003, twenty-four states and about half of all cities provided for the initiative. All told, about two hundred million Americans, some 70 percent of the population, live in either a city or state with the initiative, and by most indications the numbers are growing.

Yet despite its enduring popularity, the initiative continues to trouble some thoughtful observers. They question whether voters are sufficiently informed to decide complicated policy issues, and whether the initiative ultimately promotes democracy or works to the advantage of rich special interests who use it to hijack the policy process. As David Broder recently argued in *Democracy Derailed,* "the experience with the initiative process at the state level in the last two decades is that wealthy individuals and special interests—the targets of the Populists and Progressives who brought us the initiative a century ago—have learned all too well how to subvert the process to their own purposes" (2000, 243).

This is not, of course, the view of the majority of the public that strongly supports the initiative. They believe that special interests subvert the *legislative* process in the state capitals, and that the initiative is a way for the majority to reassert its will. For example, M. Dane Waters, founder of the Initiative & Referendum Institute, a nonpartisan think tank, argues in the *Initiative and Referendum Almanac* that, "for a century, the initiative and referendum process has been THE critical tool to check the power of unresponsive and unaccountable government at the national, state and local level" (2003, xix).

The different views stem from fundamentally different beliefs about who benefits from the initiative process. Initiative defenders believe the process makes government more responsive to the public, while critics believe it makes government more responsive to special interests. Which of these beliefs is correct is a matter of fact, not a matter of theory or principle. To a large extent, then, the different assessments of the initiative process hinge on an empirical question: *what does the initiative do to public policy, and who does this benefit?* The only way to address such a question is to determine the facts. That is what I attempt to do in this book. The book examines a huge amount of data on tax and spending policies of states and their local governments from 1957 to 2000 and select years in the first half of the twentieth century, and from over four thousand cities in the last two decades. With so much data it is possible to draw a fairly clear picture of how the initiative process changed fiscal policies in the twentieth century. I also examine a significant amount of opinion data to see what policies the majority of people wanted. By comparing public opinion to actual policies, we can determine whether the initiative advanced the interests of a majority or empowered narrow special interests.

You might wonder whether such an intensive look at the data is necessary. After all, everyone has heard of Proposition 13—don't we already know what the initiative does? It is true that California's famous Proposition 13 in 1978 cut property taxes, and triggered a reduction in other taxes and spending in California and other states. The problem is that there were also initiatives that *increased* taxes and spending, pushing policy in the opposite direction of Proposition 13. For example, California's Proposition 108 in 1990 appropriated $2 billion for public transit, and Proposition 99 in 1988 increased tobacco taxes by $600 million a year. There is no such thing as a "typical" initiative, and the diversity of initiatives makes it inappropriate and misleading to generalize about the process from specific examples. Since the effect of the initiative cumulates over many measures and many years, the net effect can only be seen by "adding up" all of the individual effects. This is one reason the book analyzes so much data instead of focusing on a handful of measures.

You might also think that someone, somewhere, must have supplied the relevant facts already. To be sure, the initiative has attracted the attention of numerous scholars over the years. I count more than one hundred books and articles in the last two decades alone. These studies have provided a great deal of descriptive information about voter information, initiative campaigns, and use of the initiative. Yet with exceedingly few exceptions that I will discuss later in the book, they have not attempted to document the effect of the initiative by looking at actual policies across states and across time. And none of the existing work makes use of anything more than a small fraction of the available data. The limited empirical scope of previous work is easy to explain: until about ten years ago when low-cost computing first became available, it was simply not practicable to work with data sets that were anywhere near the size of those used in this book.

The main findings are easy to summarize. First, over the last three decades, the initiative has had a significant impact on state and local governments. States with the initiative spent and taxed less than states without the initiative, they decentralized spending from state to local government, and they raised more money from user fees and less from taxes. Second, opinion surveys throughout the period show that a majority of people supported each of these policy changes: the voters wanted less spending, more local disbursement of funds, and greater reliance on user fees compared to broad-based taxes. The facts, then, do not support the view that the initiative process allows special interests to distort policies away from what the public wants. The initiative appears to promote the interests of the many rather than the few.

It takes quite a bit of work to reach these conclusions. In the rest of this chapter, I provide background information on the initiative—its history and current use—partly to dispel some misconceptions. Then I discuss some important lessons from the previous literature, and explain the empirical approach of the book.

A Brief History of the Initiative

A recurring misconception about the initiative is that it is a new and exotic form of government. For example, Broder's book begins: "At the start of a new century—and millennium—a new form of government is spreading in the United States." In fact, the initiative is an old form of government—it has been used in the United States for more than one hundred years, roughly half of the life of the Republic—and its "spread" in the United States took place very early in the *twentieth* century. And it is not exotic: the initiative is now (and has been for decades) part of state and local government for a majority of the population. American democracy has been extremely successful, and we naturally venerate those parts of it that have stood the test of time while raising a skeptical eye to innovations. One purpose of the short history that follows is to clear away some common misunderstandings that make it difficult to take an objective look at the initiative.

The initiative was first incorporated into a state constitution in 1898, when South Dakota took the step. To put things in perspective, the initiative process is older than such newfangled ideas as universal women's suffrage, direct election of U.S. senators, the federal income tax, social security, and the one-person one-vote principle. A great burst of adoption activity followed in South Dakota's wake, propelled by the Progressive movement. By 1918, nineteen other states had amended their constitutions to provide the initiative. These initiative states were home to 33 million people, roughly one-third of total population of the country at the time. When Mississippi adopted the initiative (for a second time) in 1992, it brought the number of initiative states to twenty-four. As of the 2000 census, these twenty-four initiative states (and the District of Columbia, which also has the initiative) were home to 136 million Americans, just shy of half the population. Figure 1.1 identifies the states that currently provide for the initiative, and appendix 1 describes in detail the key legal procedures in each initiative state. The initiative enjoys the greatest popularity in the West, but can be found in all regions of the country, from the South (Arkansas, Florida) to the Northeast (Maine, Massachusetts) to the Midwest (Michigan, Ohio).

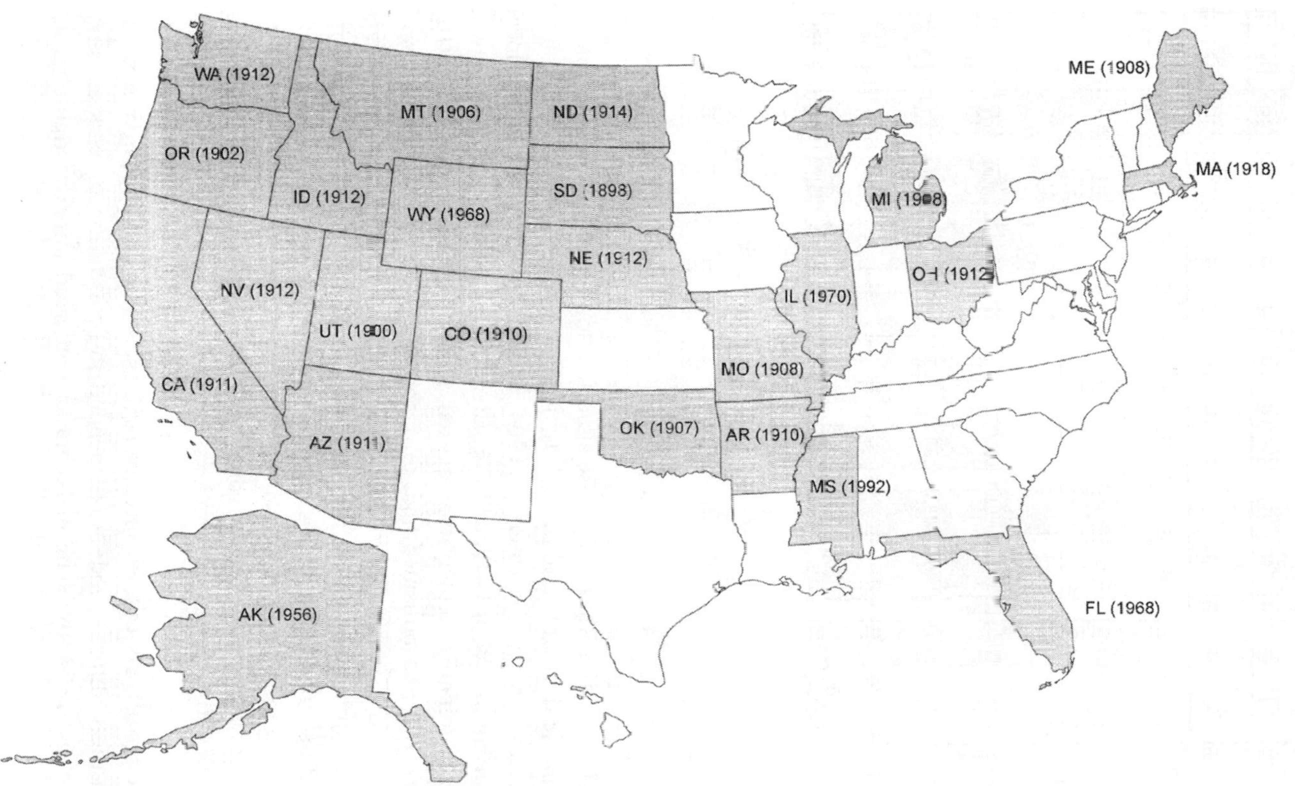

Figure 1.1 States with the Initiative. (Year of adoption is shown in parentheses.)

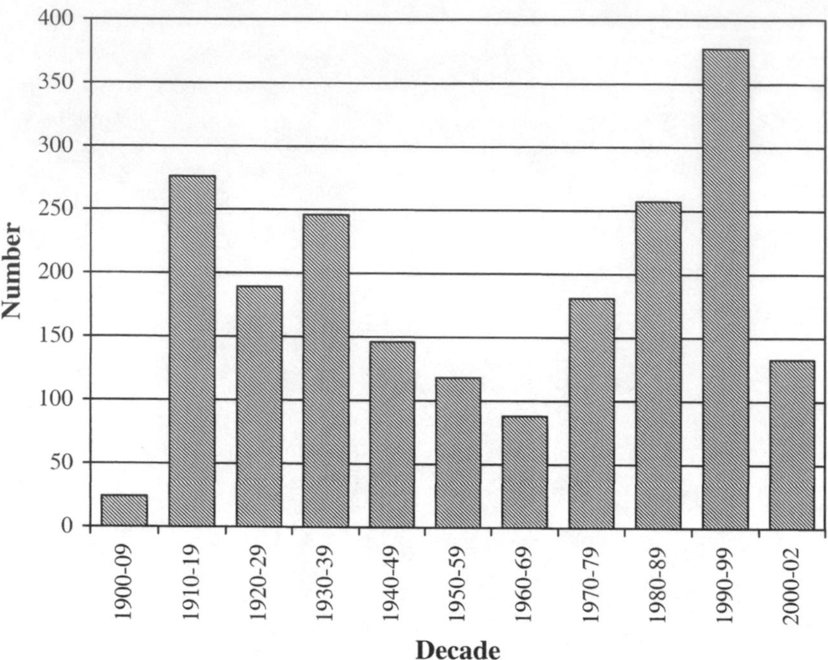

Figure 1.2 Number of Initiatives by Decade.

The initiative was put into use almost as soon as it became available; it did not lie dormant until the 1970s, as is sometimes suggested. The first measures reached the voters in 1904, a direct primary law and a local option liquor law in Oregon (both passed.) The following decades saw a burst of initiative activity that peaked with 276 measures in the 1910s (figure 1.2) and remained high through the 1930s. For reasons not well understood, the number of propositions then went into a three-decade decline, bottoming out with 88 measures in the 1960s. Initiative activity picked up again in the 1970s (also for reasons not well understood), and continued to increase as the century came to a close. In 1996, a record 93 initiatives were put before the voters, and the overall total of 378 measures for the 1990s eclipsed the previous record from the 1910s.

At the local level, cities and other governments began to adopt the initiative process about the same time as the states. It first appeared in 1893, when the California code was amended to provide the process in every county. In 1897, the state of Nebraska conferred initiative rights on all cities and municipal subdivisions in the state. The first cities to incorporate the initiative in their charters were San Francisco and Vallejo in California in 1898. By 1911, all or substantially all municipalities in ten states had been granted initiative rights, and individual cities in at least nine other states had adopted the initiative: state law granted the initiative to all cities in Colorado, Montana, Nebraska, Oklahoma, Oregon, South Dakota, and Utah, and to most cities in California, Ohio, and Wisconsin. Individual cities had the initiative in Florida (including Miami), Massachusetts, Michigan (including Detroit and Grand Rapids), Minnesota, Nevada (including Reno), North Carolina, Texas (including Austin, Dallas, and Forth Worth), Washington (including Tacoma and Spokane), and West Virginia. The process was actively used in some cities: by 1940, 33 initiatives had come before voters in Detroit, 51 in Los Angeles, and 55 in San Francisco.[1]

There is no systematic evidence on how the initiative spread through American cities after the Progressive movement crested. Beginning in 1981, however, the International City/County Manager Association (ICMA) began surveying its some-odd 5,000 member cities at five-year intervals to determine how many had the initiative. Of the cities that responded to the survey in 1986 (the most recent year with reliable data), 50 percent had the initiative. These cities had a combined population of 66 million in 1986, far exceeding the 27 million people who lived in cities that reported not having the initiative. Figure 1.3 shows the fraction of cities in each region that reported having the initiative. Again we see that the initiative is most popular in the West, but not a stranger to any region of the country.

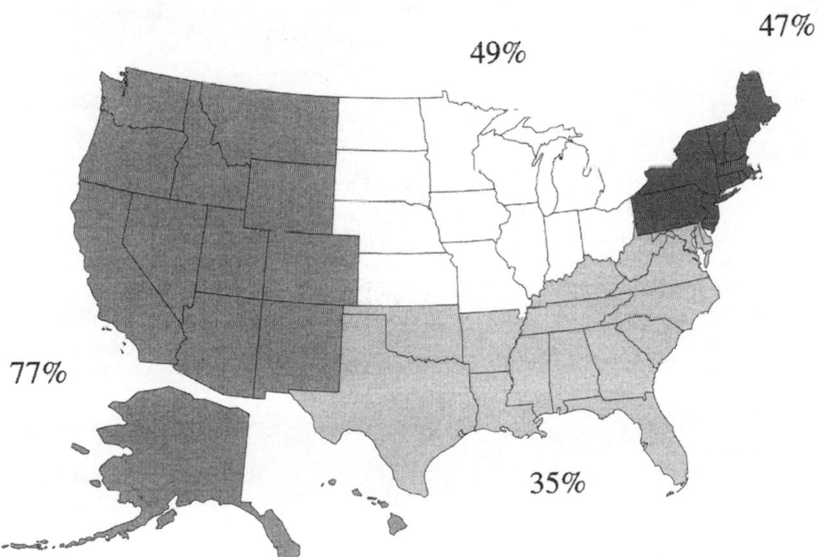

Figure 1.3 Percentage of Cities Providing the Initiative by Region, 1986.

The initiative is especially prevalent in the largest cities. Table 1.1 lists the twenty largest cities in 2000, and whether or not they had the initiative (appendix 2 details their procedures). Among the twenty largest cities, fifteen provided the initiative. Of the 117 cities in the ICMA survey with more than 100,000 residents, 80 percent had the initiative in 1986. Since large cities are more likely to allow the initiative, it turns out that in all regions of the country, more people live in a city with the initiative than a city without it (even though there are fewer initiative cities).

Is the initiative exotic? One way to answer this question is to count the number of people who live in a state or city with the initiative. The exact number cannot be calculated because the ICMA survey includes only half of all cities. However, we can get a ballpark figure for 1986 by supposing that the initiative is as common for cities missing from the ICMA survey as those that are in the sample. Under this assumption, the estimate for 1986 is that 169 million Americans lived in a city or state with the initiative, 71 percent of the total population. Put differently, only 29 percent of the population had no access at all to the initiative. It seems fair to say that the initiative is a normal rather than exceptional feature of political life for most Americans.

Another way to gauge the importance of the initiative process is by the amount of money spent on ballot proposition campaigns. In 1998, roughly

Table 1.1 Initiative Availability in the Twenty Largest Cities, 2000

City	Population, 2000	Initiative available?
New York, NY	8,008,278	Yes
Los Angeles, CA	3,694,820	Yes
Chicago, IL	2,896,016	No
Houston, TX	1,953,631	Yes
Philadelphia, PA	1,517,550	No
Phoenix, AZ	1,321,045	Yes
San Diego, CA	1,223,400	Yes
Dallas, TX	1,188,580	Yes
San Antonio, TX	1,144,646	Yes
Detroit, MI	951,270	Yes
San Jose, CA	894,943	Yes
Indianapolis, IN	791,926	No
San Francisco, CA	776,733	Yes
Jacksonville, FL	735,617	Yes
Columbus, OH	711,470	Yes
Austin, TX	656,562	Yes
Baltimore, MD	651,154	Yes
Memphis, TN	650,100	No
Milwaukee, WI	596,974	Yes
Boston, MA	589,141	No

Note: Appendix 2 provides more detail.

$400 million was spent nationally on proposition campaigns. To put this in perspective, the 2000 presidential campaigns (primary and general elections, all parties) spent $326 million, and the federal House and Senate elections of 1998 spent $740 million. Expenditure on propositions is even more impressive considering that proposition contests only take place in part of the country, unlike the nationwide presidential and congressional campaigns.

The initiative is not unusual outside the United States either. The Swiss have been using initiatives to set policy at national, state, and local levels since the middle of the nineteenth century. Italy uses a form of the referendum that is very close to an initiative. The provinces of British Columbia and Saskatchewan brought the initiative to Canada in the 1990s. Among the fifteen successor states to the Soviet Union, six provide for the initiative in their new constitutions.[2] If we consider referendums more generally (meaning a popular vote on an issue, not necessarily originating with a citizen petition), it turns out that at least 96 countries have had a national vote to resolve some public issue at one time or another in their history. The only established democracies that have never had a national referendum are India, Israel, Japan, the Netherlands, and the United States (Butler and Ranney 1994).

Voter Competence, Money, and Majority Rule

Most research on the initiative process focuses on two issues, voter competence and the role of money. It is important to understand what we currently know about these two issues, and how they are related to the main issue in this book.

The "voter competence" question asks whether voters are capable of making the right decision in the initiative process.[3] There is reason to be skeptical. Many voters do not understand the petitions they sign. Few read the actual text of the measures they vote on. And most people fail miserably when quizzed about the details of any given measure. Based on evidence of this sort, Magleby (1984, 197–98) colorfully concluded:

> Some voters will be able to master the initiative process, but those with less than graduate-school reading ability will be unable to read and understand the voter's handbook or the actual description of the measure printed on the ballot. Those who have not learned about the measure before entering the booth will play a form of electoral roulette, casting affirmative and negative votes at random, or will decide not to vote on the measures at all. The majority of the ballot measures are decided by voters

> who cannot comprehend the printed description, who have only heard about the measure from a single source, and who are ignorant about the measure except at the highly emotional level of the television advertising.

However, this view of voter competence seems rather narrow. Voters may not need a detailed (or "substantive") understanding of a measure in order to accurately register their preferences in the voting booth. They may be able to cast a "competent" vote (meaning a vote that reflects their underlying interests and values) by using information cues or shortcuts, such as recommendations from trusted organizations or individuals. For example, an environmentalist can cast the "right" vote (that is, a vote consistent with his or her values) on an environmental ballot proposition simply by learning whether the Sierra Club is for or against the measure, without reading or understanding anything in the voter's handbook. By way of analogy, many of us manage to take the right medications for our ailments by relying on the advice of trusted experts (our physicians) even though we know nothing about the chemical composition of the medications or the results of clinical trials. When it comes to political matters, most people have access to numerous sources of information cues—interest groups, politicians, newspapers, coworkers, family, friends, neighbors, etc.—so they should not find it difficult to decide how to vote on most issues.[4]

This is somewhat theoretical. As a matter of practice, are voters able to use cues to overcome their substantive ignorance about issues? The evidence suggests they are.[5] In one of the most convincing studies, Lupia (1994) found that substantively uninformed people could mimic the votes of substantively informed people on five complicated ballot propositions simply by knowing the endorsements of Ralph Nader and the insurance industry. Similarly, Kahn and Matsusaka (1997) and Kahn (2002) showed that aggregate voting patterns on eighteen California environmental initiatives closely reflected underlying economic interests—voters who stood to suffer an economic loss from a measure tended to oppose it. Filer and Kenny (1980) found that citizens manage to vote their interests in city/county consolidation referendums. In perhaps the most comprehensive study of information and voting in candidate elections, Peltzman (1990) found that when voting in presidential, gubernatorial, and senatorial elections, people seemed to incorporate economic information in a surprisingly sophisticated way. He concluded: "The broad picture that emerges here is of self-interested voters who correctly process relevant information. Indeed, one would be hard put to find nonpolitical markets that process information better than the voting market" (115).[6]

Even if information cues and shortcuts are less effective than the literature suggests, the implications for the initiative process are unclear. Uninformed voters will do a poor job deciding ballot propositions but they will also do a poor job selecting candidates. Does giving them a say over issues in addition to letting them choose legislators compound the problem or make it better? The answer is not clear to me and probably varies from issue to issue: some ballot propositions are simpler to evaluate than candidates while others are more difficult.

The "money" question asks whether the initiative allows rich individuals and groups to advance their agendas at the expense of the general public. Two prominent books were recently published devoted to the money question. Although the books approach the question from very different perspectives, they arrive at similar conclusions. Broder (2000) takes a journalistic approach, going inside a handful of ballot campaigns and interviewing politicians and political activists in the initiative industry. He reports how expensive it is to place a measure on the ballot and wage a campaign in a large state like California (petition costs alone exceed $1 million), and how money has become a major factor in initiative politics. Gerber (1999) takes a scholarly approach, sifting through an impressive amount of campaign spending and polling data. She systematically corroborates Broder's impression that money is important in the initiative process, but with a twist: campaign spending turns out to be much more effective in opposing a measure than in promoting one. Deep pockets provide a veto of sorts when it comes to initiatives but do not allow the purchase of favorable legislation. From the observation that money matters in the initiative process, Broder and Gerber both draw what seems like a natural conclusion: the initiative has become a tool to advance the interests of organized and wealthy special interests instead of the broad public.[7]

However, the inference—only the wealthy can afford to qualify and promote ballot propositions, therefore, the initiative process ends up helping the rich and hurting the (not particularly wealthy) majority—is not generally valid. It is easy to think of situations in which the majority is better off even if a narrow interest group monopolizes the process. To see the problem in the abstract, think about a family deciding what topping to order on a pizza (to get away from the details of state government for a moment). The default procedure is for (say) the father to choose the topping. Think of him as the legislature. His choice may be acceptable to a majority of the family members, but it might not be: he could misunderstand what the rest of the family wants, or order his personal favorite even knowing that everyone else would like something different.

Under the "initiative process," other family members are allowed to propose alternatives to the father's choice, with disagreements resolved by majority rule. If one of the kids proposes a topping that the majority prefers to the father's choice, the proposal will defeat the father's choice and the majority will end up happier than if the initiative process was unavailable. If one of the kids proposes a topping the majority considers inferior to the father's choice, it will simply be voted down. So we can see that allowing everyone in the family to make proposals generally works to the advantage of the majority. The conclusion stands even if the right to make proposals is reserved for certain family members (these members are the "narrow special interests"). The majority is still better off having an alternative to the father's proposal because superior options can be accepted and inferior options rejected.

The point: the fact that narrow interests dominate the initiative process (as Broder and Gerber seem to show) does not necessarily imply that the final outcomes are nonmajoritarian. The special interest subversion argument fails to appreciate, first, that narrow interest groups do not always have policy goals in conflict with the interests of the general public and, second, that voters are free to reject proposals they find less attractive than the legislative status quo. Indeed, the example suggests that as long as proposals are filtered through a majority-rule election, the *only* way initiatives make the majority worse off is if voters can be persuaded to approve policies contrary to their interest. It is certainly possible that voters can be misled to act against their interests, but whether that happens as a regular matter (as the subversion argument implicitly maintains) has to be demonstrated empirically, not simply assumed. The central purpose of this book is to provide evidence that reveals the extent to which voters are made worse off in practice.

Preview of the Findings

The central goal of the book is to establish whether the initiative makes policy more responsive to the will of the majority or increases the influence of narrow special interests. The investigation proceeds in two steps. First, I examine a set of fiscal policies and determine what changes are brought about by the initiative. Those policy changes are then compared with the expressed opinion of the electorate to determine if a majority of people like or dislike the changes.

The first step involves measuring how the initiative process changes policy. In theory, the initiative process can influence policy both directly, when a measure is passed and implemented, and indirectly, when the threat of an initiative induces the legislature to take a different path than it would have absent the initiative. My empirical strategy is to compare the fiscal policies of states with and without the initiative. The idea is that however the initiative works, directly or indirectly, the effect (if any) will show up in the final policies. Since tax and spending policies are influenced by a number of factors that have nothing to do with the initiative, such as income and federal aid, I employ regression analysis to isolate the effect of the initiative. Chapter 2 discusses the theory and empirical procedures underlying the analysis.

Chapter 3 contains the main evidence on fiscal effects of the initiative. I focus on the 1970–2000 period initially since the initiative was heavily used during these years (figure 1.2). Three systematic effects of the initiative emerge from the data. First, the initiative trimmed overall spending by state and local governments. Second, the initiative shifted spending away from state and toward local government, that is, it caused a decentralization of expenditure. And third, the initiative altered the manner in which funds were raised: broad-based taxes were cut and replaced with user fees and charges for services.

With these effects in mind, I then investigate who benefits from the initiative. Critics argue that special interests are the winners—they use the initiative to subvert the governmental process and secure policies that are opposed by a majority of citizens.[8] If this view is right, then a majority of citizens should have been opposed to the policy changes induced by the initiative (lower spending, decentralization, and charges instead of taxes). If, on the other hand, the initiative promotes majority rule, then we should find that a majority favored the changes.

Chapter 4 examines opinion data to see which view is correct. I study numerous opinion polls and ask whether a majority of voters approved or disapproved of the policy changes brought about by the initiative. The polls seldom pose questions exactly as we would like, but they are close enough to paint a convincing picture of public opinion. The evidence is remarkably consistent: a majority of people *supported* each of the three policy changes associated with the initiative. The view that the initiative allows narrow special interests to override the majority is inconsistent with the evidence. In fact, the most natural interpretation of the evidence is that the initiative allows the majority to defend itself against powerful groups that receive favorable treatment in the legislature.

The evidence for 1970–2000 reveals that the initiative led to policies that are usually perceived as "fiscally conservative." Does this mean that the initiative is a fundamentally conservative device, or did legislatures just happen to be more fiscally liberal than the majority of voters in the last three decades? Some prominent theories in political economy argue that governments inevitably tend to spend more than most voters would like. Chapter 5 reviews these theories and puts them to the test using data from 1902–42. If governments systematically overspend, we should see spending cuts associated with the initiative in the first half of the century, just as in the second half. This is not what we see: initiative states in the early twentieth century spent more than noninitiative states. Thus, it is inaccurate to view the initiative process as a fundamentally conservative device.

Chapters 3, 4, and 5 are the empirical core of the book. They focus exclusively on establishing several important facts. Chapters 6 and 7 begin the task of developing a theoretical framework to explain the findings. Chapter 6 ventures a new theory of direct and representative democracy, proposing that legislatures occasionally fall "out of step" with their constituents in periods when voter opinion undergoes a rapid change. When this happens, legislatures may stick with existing policies against the wishes of the voters because they fail to perceive the change in the majority's sentiments or because they favor the existing policy for their own reasons. The initiative allows voters to redirect policy more quickly than in noninitiative states, where changes require elected officials to learn about the new preferences of the majority or for stubborn incumbents to be replaced. According to this theory of "out-of-step" legislators, the gap between initiative and noninitiative states is transitory, and reflects a faster response to voter preferences in initiative states. To prove that this is the right way to understand the evidence is beyond the scope of this book. However, chapter 7 discusses the evolution of state fiscal policy throughout the twentieth century in order to build a circumstantial case in favor of the theory. While not formally testing the theory, I show that it provides a natural way to understand key episodes in the fiscal history of the states.

The main contribution of the book in my opinion is to raise serious doubts about the view that special interests benefit and the broad public suffers from the initiative. I believe this constitutes a genuine advance in our understanding of the initiative since the special interest subversion view attracts wide support. But in many ways it is a modest result. One particular view of the initiative is rejected, but the more fundamental question whether the initiative is a good or bad form of government is left open.

Chapters 8 and 9 offer some more subjective reflections on this larger question without trying to answer it definitively. If the initiative pushes policy toward what the majority wants, as the evidence suggests, we must grapple with whether majority outcomes are a good or a bad thing. Certainly, majority rule is a central principle of any democracy. However, American democracy is founded on a deep distrust of unchecked majorities. The puzzle of 1787 is the same one we face today: What form of government allows the majority to rule but protects minority rights? Since the initiative appears to be a majoritarian device, we need to know if it is prone to majority tyranny. Chapter 8 reviews the existing literature on the problem of majority tyranny, and the possibility that the initiative undermines the Constitutional foundations of American democracy. I outline the outstanding issues, review the meager empirical evidence so far available, and identify directions for future research.

In chapter 9, I step back from the specifics and consider how we think about the initiative process in general. The most common approach to the initiative process is in terms of a delegation model: legislators are the agents of the voters, and the initiative gives voters a way to override unfaithful agents. I review the logic of the delegation view and its main implications. I then offer two different but complementary approaches to the initiative process that I call the information and competition views. In the information view, the problem of democracy is collecting the knowledge and preferences of ordinary citizens and bringing them to bear on the policy process. Unlike the delegation view, the information view suggests that the initiative can be useful even if representatives are faithful agents because the initiative has a superior ability to register preferences. The competition view sees the initiative as a way to introduce competition into the lawmaking process, a process that is otherwise monopolized by the political professionals who seek to hold elective office. I review the strengths and weaknesses of competition as currently understood in the literature. Then I show how the main intuitions about competition can be applied to the initiative, and suggest that doing so leads to a number of interesting questions about the role of the process in American democracy.

A final word on the style of presentation. This is a scholarly work that pays close attention to the modern theoretical literature and adheres to the most rigorous standards of data collection and analysis. At the same time, I have endeavored to make it accessible to readers with a limited background in game theory and statistics. All of the key ideas and results are stated in plain English or displayed in figures, and the nontechnical reader should not find it difficult to follow the lines of argument. So as not to clutter the text with material that many readers will find uninteresting, all nonessential data descriptions and sources have been collected in appendix 3.

The trouble with facts is that there are so many of them.

—Samuel McChord Crothers

CHAPTER 2  A Blizzard of Data

This book examines the tax and spending policies of American states and cities over the last hundred years to determine how the initiative changes government behavior. All told, literally thousands of fiscal decisions are available for analysis, enough to paint a fairly clear picture of the initiative's consequences. Assembling these data is a time-consuming process–most of it had to be done by hand–but the real trick is figuring out how to sort through this blizzard of information. How do we find the answers to our questions in so much data?

This chapter describes the strategy used to examine the data. The approach is grounded in a body of theory developed in economics and political science. I begin by reviewing the relevant theory, and then highlight its implications for empirical analysis. After this, the empirical model is stated and various econometric issues are described in some detail.

Representatives and Initiatives: Comparing Imperfections

Since I am listed in the *Experts Directory* at USC, reporters call me from time to time to ask about initiatives. A common question is, "Do you think money influences the outcome of initiative campaigns?" The answer I give is, yes, money seems to matter. But this always seems like the wrong question to me. After all, money plays a role in the candidate elections, too. The right question is whether money plays *more* of a role in the initiative process than in the legislature.

This point applies generally: we can only evaluate the initiative by comparing it to some alternative public choice process. In practice, this means comparing the initiative to the legislative process. Too many studies, in my opinion, have focused on showing that the initiative is an imperfect process without demonstrating that the available alternatives are better. What needs to be done is consider how legislatures function, with all their imperfections, and then ask if introduction of the initiative makes things better or worse.

The modern theory of political economy provides several ways to think about how introduction of the initiative changes the policymaking process. To begin, it seems the initiative would be of little consequence in a world where all citizens were fully informed and voted, and all elected officials understood voter preferences and faithfully incorporated them in public decisions. In such a perfect world, the legislature would always do the "right thing," and the initiative would lie dormant. If the initiative has any impact then, it is because of "friction" in our real world: uninformed voters, citizens who abstain, legislators who misunderstand or ignore voter preferences, and so on. What follows is a list of key theories of how the initiative process might affect policy.

Citizens Are Not Fully Informed

One important source of political friction is that citizens are not fully informed. Few ordinary citizens follow politics closely, and even those who do are informed about only a handful of issues. There is nothing surprising about this. Since time is scarce, we all have many things to do, and an individual vote is unlikely to swing an election, most of us choose not to pay the costs (primarily in terms of time) to be well informed about politics. As Downs (1957, 259) put it,

> In general, it is irrational to be politically well informed because the low returns from data simply do not justify their cost in time and other scarce

> resources. Therefore many voters do not bother to discover their true views before voting, and most citizens are not well enough informed to influence directly the formulation of those policies that affect them.

The "rational ignorance" of voters creates an opportunity for money and interest groups to influence the policy process and possibly override majority preferences. For one thing, uninformed voters can be manipulated by advertising and other forms of political persuasion and possibly end up voting against their underlying interests. Second, uninformed voters are likely to abstain. An organized interest group that is effective at getting its members to turn out may be able to secure a majority at the polls even though its views are only shared by a minority of the citizenry. In short, when voters are not fully informed, policies unfavorable to the majority can prevail.

Perhaps the most influential development of this idea is the interest group theory associated with Stigler (1971), Peltzman (1976), and Becker (1983). According to this theory, policies are the outcome of competition between interest groups. Groups exert pressure for their favored policy by voting, but also by expending resources (time, money) to persuade others to vote. The outcome of political competition depends on which groups are better able to inform and mobilize their members. There is no guarantee that the majority rules.[1]

What would be the effect of introducing the initiative process into a world where policies are the outcome of competition between interest groups as envisioned by the interest group theory? The answer is not clear. Whatever factors (money, a dedicated group of volunteers, etc.) work to the advantage of particular interest groups in candidate elections are likely to be effective in initiative campaigns as well. Introduction of the initiative will cause a change in policy only to the extent that interest groups have different relative advantages in influencing legislatures and initiative campaigns. Groups that are particularly effective at influencing issue campaigns will thrive, while those effective in candidate elections will suffer. Whether this works to the advantage or disadvantage of the majority cannot be determined at this level of generality.

The "rational ignorance" of voters also gives elected officials some freedom to ignore the interests of their constituents. Officeholders may choose to pursue policies contrary to the interests of their constituents for ideological reasons, for reasons of conscience, or because they are corrupt. Such behavior would be severely curtailed in a world of fully informed voters; a legislator who scorned the majority would be voted out of office.

However, people seldom know how their representative voted on most issues, and it is difficult to monitor a representative's other actions, such as intervention with the bureaucracy on behalf of a constituent. The ability to ignore constituent interests is limited by the need seek reelection, but there may be enough slack to allow adoption of policies that a majority of dislikes. Introduction of the initiative when representatives "shirk" the interests of their constituents would then tend to push policy in the direction of majority rule.[2]

Representatives Are Not Fully Informed

Legislators labor with incomplete information as well. They must struggle to keep abreast of dozens of bills working their way through various committees as well as the multitudinous interests of their constituents. To be sure, they have professional staff to help and access to a tremendous amount of information: opinion polls, expert witnesses, conversations with community and business leaders, newspaper editorials, and so on, not to mention feedback from constituents at large. However, the number of people in a typical political jurisdiction is large, opinion polling is sporadic, and even when available, polls may not reveal underlying constituent preferences because people have not yet made up their minds about the issues in question. Elections provide some feedback, but they are infrequent and it is difficult to extract preferences on particular issues from election returns. The consequence of all of this is that a legislature may inadvertently approve policies that the majority dislikes, what might be called, "honest mistakes."

When the legislature makes honest mistakes, introduction of the initiative would tend to bring policy more into alignment with the will of majority. Legislative policies disfavored by the majority would be "corrected" by initiatives. However, there are some countervailing considerations. First, when legislators are not fully informed about constituent preferences, they will pay some attention to organized interest groups that claim to speak for their members. If these groups are given the power to take proposals directly to the people, legislators may give their counsel even greater weight. The legislature might even accommodate an extreme interest group in order to keep a threatened initiative off the ballot and thereby avoid the risk that voters might actually support the group's measure. Second, by taking decision-making authority from the legislature, the initiative might reduce the legislature's incentive to acquire policy-relevant information. This could degrade the quality of legislative decisions.[3]

Unbundling Logrolls

Another reason the initiative might influence policy is logrolling: the practice of trading votes to secure approval of key measures. Logrolling is common in legislatures but unimportant when it comes to ballot propositions. Initiatives unravel legislative logrolls. This may be a good or a bad thing. On the one hand, logrolls allow gains from trade: legislators can give ground on policies they consider unimportant in exchange for advancing policies that are important to them. A legislative logroll might be preferred by a majority of voters to alternative policy bundles, but the individual pieces could be defeated on an issue-by-issue vote. If the initiative undoes these "good" logrolls, the majority is made worse off. On the other hand, logrolls can be inefficient. Legislators can trade votes to deliver "pork" to their districts, providing benefits to their constituents at the cost of overall inefficiency. If the initiative undoes inefficient logrolls, the majority is better off.[4]

The possibility of issue bundling also creates a problem in candidate elections. Because candidates take positions on numerous issues, it is difficult for voters to register their preferences on specific issues in candidate elections. In most cases, voters will not agree with all of the positions taken by the candidate they support, and successful candidates will find it difficult to determine why they were chosen by the voters. It will also be difficult for voters to punish candidates who take positions they dislike. Voters may end up reelecting an incumbent they disagree with on one issue because his position on another more important issue is preferred to the challenger's position on that issue. How the initiative affects candidate bundling is not well developed theoretically, but intuition suggests that the initiative will help the majority by allowing it to keep a generally good incumbent in office while overriding him on specific issues of disagreement.[5]

To summarize: in the imperfect world where we live, there is no guarantee that representative government or initiatives will deliver policies favored by the majority. There are theoretical arguments for and against both legislatures and initiatives. Whether the initiative ends up favoring the many or the few depends on how the various frictions afflicting the two institutions compare in practice. Therefore, the initiative process can only be evaluated in comparison to representative decision-making, and only by digging through the data.

Digging for Answers

How exactly should we go about comparing the initiative and legislative processes, and what data should we use? Previous studies have looked for answers by selecting a small group of initiatives and carefully dissecting them. In contrast, this book examines thousands of cases (essentially all cases currently available for study) and looks for general patterns using modern statistical techniques. No previous study of the initiative has employed anywhere near as much data, primarily because the computational capabilities to process so much information were unavailable until about a decade ago.

The use of large samples and statistics is the emerging standard for research in the social sciences, but its virtues might not be obvious to the reader who is more familiar with the traditional (anecdotal) approaches. The main problem with focusing on a particular measure (or group of measures), even an important one like Proposition 13, is that the measure chosen might be idiosyncratic in some way that the researcher does not appreciate. The virtue of looking at a large number of cases is that the idiosyncratic factors tend to cancel out, allowing the average tendencies to be observed. It would not be difficult to find a particular initiative that benefited the majority or one that aided a narrow special interest. What we want to know is who benefits from the initiative process *on average*.

Which data hold the answers? One approach would be to collect information on ballot propositions that were approved by voters and compare those to the laws approved by legislatures. However, this approach would capture only part of the effect of the initiative, what might be called the "direct" effect. The direct effect is the actual passage of new laws. There is also an "indirect" effect: the *threat* of an initiative may induce legislatures to choose different policies than they would have if the initiative were unavailable. This indirect effect can change policy even without a measure being put before the voters.[6] By analogy, the possession of nuclear weapons influences a country's international relations even if the weapons are never used. If we tried to assess the impact of nuclear weapons only by looking at instances when they were used we would miss most of the story.

We want to estimate both the direct and indirect effects of the initiative. Or put differently, we want to know how *having the initiative available* changes policy. The solution is straightforward. Since the policies we observe are the net effect of both direct and indirect effects, we can simply compare the policies prevailing in states where the initiative is available with the policies in noninitiative states. As long we adjust for the other factors that drive the policy decision, policy differences between initiative and noninitiative states can be attributed to the initiative process itself.

The statistical procedure that I rely on is regression analysis, which can be thought of as a way to compute and compare averages holding other factors constant. For example, suppose government expenditure depends not only on whether a state has the initiative but also on personal income in the state (rich states spend more). We would like to calculate the difference between spending in initiative and noninitiative states assuming they have the same level of income, that is, "holding income constant." Regression analysis is the tool that allows this to be done.

Precise Statement of the Empirical Model

This section gives a formal statement of the main empirical model and discusses some relatively technical econometric issues. The nontechnical reader may wish to skip to the next chapter. The model used to estimate how the initiative changes policy is

$$G_{jt} = a_t + b \cdot X_{jt} + c \cdot I_{jt} + e_{jt}$$

where G is a government policy variable such as spending, X is a vector of noninitiative control variables such as income, I is a variable indicating whether or not a government had the initiative (possibly a vector characterizing the initiative's features), e is an error term, j is an index for states/cities, t is an index for years, and a, b, c are parameters to be estimated. The intercept is subscripted for time to allow for year-specific effects. If $c = 0$, then the initiative has no effect on policy.

The model should be thought of as the reduced form of some unspecified theory. For example, it could be the reduced form of a median voter model, in which the X parameters represent the median voter's preferences. Or it could represent political influence functions a la Stigler (1971), Peltzman (1976), and Becker (1983), in which case the X parameters represent the benefits and costs of the policy to the involved groups, and their organizing/influence costs. My agnostic approach about the underlying structural model entails costs in terms of efficiency but seems appropriate for the purposes here, since I am trying to establish whether the institution matters at all, and broad directions of influence. Also, since the correct structural model is unknown even in a general sense, misspecification errors from an arbitrarily imposed structure are likely to outweigh any efficiency advantages.

The goal is to compare average expenditure and tax levels in governments with and without the initiative. To the extent there are differences, I would like to attribute them to the presence/absence of the voter initiative. In order to make such an inference, any other factors that drive spending differences must be controlled. The list of possible factors is long, but it turns out that most of the variation in spending can be accounted for by a relatively short list of variables: income, population, metropolitan population, population growth over the last five years, and aid from the federal government (and year and region dummies).

The most important control variable is income. In fact, a simple regression with income and year dummies alone can account for 98 percent of the (pooled cross-sectional) variation in spending over 1957–2000. The conventional explanation is that demand for government spending increases with income. Population and urbanization are also included as controls. These variables capture variation in the benefits and costs of public spending. For example, a large population can take advantage of economies of scale in public services such as public transportation, sewers, and schools. Urban areas may demand different sorts of services, such as more police and sewers, than rural areas. The growth of population is included to control for short-run changes in demand. A state may make exceptional investments in infrastructure (such as building new roads) in response to a sudden increase in population. Federal aid is transfers from the federal government to state and local governments. Unlike the other control variables, the amount of federal aid is affected by a state government's spending decisions because most federal aid is in the form of matching funds. This creates an endogeneity problem. However, as I discuss in Matsusaka 1995a, federal aid is probably less controllable by state governments than it first seems, and in any event, even if federal aid is endogenous, its inclusion does not bias estimates of *c*.

The regressions also include two regional dummy variables, one for the South and the other for the West. The theoretical rationale for inclusion of the South dummy has never been clear, but from an empirical point of view southern spending is significantly lower than other states after controlling for the usual variables. It seems plain that there is an omitted variable specific to the southern states. I follow the preponderance of the literature by simply including a dummy to capture it. I include the dummy for western states because the initiative is particularly common in the West (figures 1.1 and 1.3). We want to be sure we are measuring an initiative effect and not a western effect. The downside is that inclusion of the West dummy runs the risk of stripping out some of the effect we are trying to measure. It turns out that the results in most regressions are essentially the same with or without the regional dummies. The few instances where they matter are noted after the results are reported.

In preliminary work, I estimated the regressions with a number of other control variables including population density, value of mineral extractions, age of population, other regional dummies, and higher order terms (for example the square of income). Inclusion of these controls does not change the sign of the key coefficients, or cause them to become statistically insignificant. I chose to present the results with the smaller set of control variables to reduce clutter in the tables.

Three states required special treatment, Alaska, Wyoming, and Illinois. Alaska and Wyoming collect significant revenues from severance taxes on oil. This causes extreme fluctuations in their finances for reasons that have nothing to do with the initiative process. For example, when oil prices were at their peak in fiscal year 1982, revenue per capita was $23,452 in Alaska and $6,314 in Wyoming; revenue per capita in the other 48 states ranged from $1,894 to $3,985 (everything expressed in year-2000 dollars). Alaska is evidently an extreme outlier, so I followed standard practice and deleted it from all regressions. Wyoming is not as extreme an outlier as Alaska, but I ended up deleting it as well because of complications arising from its initiative procedures. The state's signature requirement (15 percent) is an outlier, and it also has a strict distribution requirement, allows the legislature to block an initiative by adopting a "substantially similar" measure, and contains subject restrictions on revenue and appropriations. There is an argument for classifying it as a noninitiative state when it comes to fiscal policy, but in light of its revenue situation it seemed cleaner simply to delete it. Illinois is classified as a noninitiative state throughout because in that state the initiative can only be used to modify the organization of the state legislature; fiscal initiatives of any sort are not permitted.

With the aforementioned exception of Illinois, I classify a state as an "initiative state" if any sort of initiative (statutory or constitutional amendment, direct or indirect) is available. In principle, there is little reason to distinguish between statutory and constitutional amendment initiatives because both can be used to influence fiscal policy. It would be different if I were studying the effect of the initiative on a policy that typically resides in constitutions, such as the governor's veto power. Just to be sure, I estimated the main regressions separately for statutory and constitutional amendment initiatives (not reported), and the results were similar.

All of the financial variables (spending, taxes, income, federal aid) are expressed in per capita terms and normalized to year-2000 dollars. I also estimated the regressions with these variables expressed as a percent of income and in logarithms, with no material difference in the results.

Heteroskedasticity is an important issue when using panel data. A given state's errors are likely to be correlated across time, meaning (loosely speaking) that multiple observations of the same state do not carry as much additional information as a simple count of the observations would suggest. To address this form of heteroskedasticity, reported standard errors are adjusted for clustering of errors within states. As shown by Moulton (1986), the failure to adjust for clustering in panel data when regressors do not change over time leads to standard errors that are significantly biased downward, overstating the precision of the coefficient estimates. The popular strategy of using heteroskedasticity-consistent White standard errors does not solve the problem. See Feld and Matsusaka (forthcoming) for a review in the context of fiscal institutions, and an empirical demonstration of the importance of correcting for clustering.

I do not include state fixed effects or otherwise try to exploit the time series variation in initiative status because only one state (Mississippi) changed its initiative status during the main sample period, 1970–2000 (see figure 1.1.)

Data sources and definitions are reported in appendix 3. Almost all of the numbers come from the Census Bureau in one way or another, usually from the *Government Finances* series.

PART ONE

The Evidence

The public finances are one of the best starting points for an investigation of society, especially though not exclusively of its political life.

—Joseph Schumpeter

CHAPTER 3 

Spending and Taxes, 1970–2000

This chapter investigates how the initiative affects spending and taxes. To preview the findings, we will see that over the last three decades the initiative had three significant effects on fiscal policy. First, it cut the overall size of state and local government, as measured by revenue or expenditure. Second, the initiative shifted disbursement of funds from state to local governments, that is, it "decentralized" government spending. Third, the initiative altered the way funds are raised: it reduced the reliance on taxes in favor of user fees and charges for services. These results establish benchmarks that we can compare with opinion data later on to see if the initiative brought about policy changes supported or opposed by the majority.

The results also are interesting in their own right because they shed light on how important, if at all, the initiative is in practice. Some observers believe the initiative has a major impact on public policy. For example, the editors of *Dangerous Democracy* (Sabato et al. 2001, x), a recent collection of essays on the initiative process, assert: "Without question, ballot initiatives have had a profound influence on public policy. As a model of such influence, one need look no further than California's Proposition 13. . . . By most accounts, the effect on California's fiscal policies and public sector was monumental." Despite repeated assertions of this sort, however, there is actually very little empirical evidence that the initiative has a big (or any) effect on state policies.[1] And there are plausible reasons to doubt that it has a big impact. For one thing, the number of measures approved by the voters is small compared to the number of laws promulgated by legislatures. In 1999 and 2000, only 35 measures were adopted by initiative compared to more than 10,000 new laws enacted by legislatures. It is hard to see how a sprinkle of initiatives could stir this ocean of legislation in a significant way. And even when an initiative is approved, it may not affect policy. Successful measures are often held up or nullified by judges, and as Gerber et al. (2001) show, elected officials and bureaucrats charged with implementation often simply ignore measures they dislike. With very little hard evidence currently available on the policy effects of the initiative, one of the most basic questions about the process—how much does it matter—remains largely unanswered. Another contribution of this chapter, then, is to quantify how important, if at all, the initiative process is for fiscal policy.

The Importance of Spending and Taxes

The focus of this chapter is the spending and tax policies of state and local governments. Governments do more than just spend and tax, of course, and we could just as well search for initiative effects in other policy areas, such as business regulation or social policies. Expenditure and tax policies seem like a good place to begin because fiscal decisions are the central activities of most governments. Fiscal decisions occupy most of a legislature's time, taxes and spending are the favorite topics of initiatives (Matsusaka 1992), and budgeting is the main way that policy priorities are established. Moreover, for many citizens taxes are the most visible manifestation of government.

The numbers involved are huge, too. In 2000, government spending at all levels (federal, state, and local) totaled $2.8 trillion, equal to 36 percent of gross domestic product. Although the federal government receives the lion's share of attention, state and local governments accounted for about half of all expenditure. Figure 3.1 shows the main categories of spending by state and local governments, and the amount spent in each category by

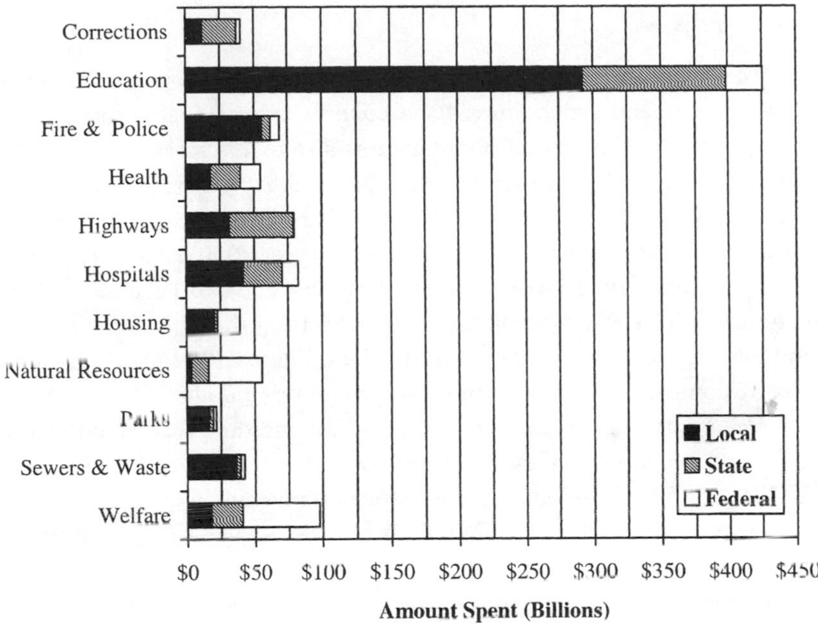

Figure 3.1 Who Spends the Money: State, Local, and Federal Expenditure

federal, state, and local governments. Easily the biggest chunk of state and local spending goes for education. Hospitals and highways are a distant second, followed by fire and police, then corrections, health, and welfare. State and local governments are the primary providers of public education, hospitals, roads, police and fire protection, corrections, sewers, and parks, all of which have direct and daily impacts on many citizens. When we look at the tax and spending behavior of state and local governments, we are looking at a significant part of the economy.[2]

First Effect: How the Initiative Changes the Size of Government

The first question is: How did the initiative change the size of government, as measured by total spending or revenue? I focus here on the *combined* spending (or revenue) of state and local government. Conceptually, it makes sense to look for the effect of statewide initiatives on combined state and local spending because initiatives can be and are targeted at the behavior of both state and local governments. For example, California's Proposition 13 was primarily a restriction on *local* property taxes.

Basic Findings

Table 3.1 presents the main regressions showing how the initiative affects revenue and expenditure. Each column reports coefficients from a single regression. The unit of observation is a state in a given year over the period 1970–2000. The dependent variable is either general revenue from own sources ("revenue") or direct general expenditure ("expenditure"), as indicated at the top of the column, expressed in year 2000 dollars per capita. The key explanatory variable is a dummy variable equal to 1 if a state allows the initiative. The R^2s are typically 0.99, suggesting that the variables do a good job accounting for variation in the data. The coefficients on the non-initiative control variables present no surprises—each dollar of state income results in about 11 cents more revenue and expenditure, federal aid stimulates spending, and so on—so I will pass over them without comment.

Consider first the effect of the initiative on revenue in column (1). The coefficient on the initiative dummy indicates that states with the initiative

Table 3.1 Regressions of State and Local Revenue and Expenditure on Initiative and Control Variables, 1970–2000

Variables	Revenue (1)	Expenditure (2)	Revenue (3)	Expenditure (4)
Dummy = 1 if initiative state	−133.38*	−147.26**	−253.97	−320.26*
	(76.32)	(70.86)	(183.56)	(182.66)
Signature requirement × initiative dummy	—	—	18.87	27.13
			(23.05)	(22.71)
Income	0.11***	0.11***	0.12***	0.11***
	(0.01)	(0.01)	(0.01)	(0.02)
Federal aid	1.17***	2.08***	1.20***	2.12***
	(0.29)	(0.32)	(0.30)	(0.31)
Population, logarithm	48.12	39.60	49.88	42.12
	(73.75)	(71.42)	(73.39)	(69.99)
Metropolitan population, %	0.55	1.87	0.43	1.70
	(2.21)	(1.97)	(2.31)	(2.10)
Growth of population, previous 5 years, %	4.25	10.54*	1.89	7.16
	(5.90)	(6.10)	(6.19)	(6.13)
Dummy = 1 if southern state	−214.56**	−212.35**	−206.00**	−200.04*
	(99.27)	(101.31)	(98.75)	(100.10)
Dummy = 1 if western state	182.89*	167.29*	183.08*	167.56*
	(91.25)	(88.53)	(91.57)	(87.28)
R^2	0.992	0.994	0.992	0.994

Note: Each column is a regression with 1,488 observations. The main entries are coefficient estimates; standard errors adjusted for within-state clustering are in parentheses. Revenue and expenditure are combined totals for state and local government. Revenue, expenditure, income, and federal aid are expressed in year-2000 dollars per capita. The sample includes all states except Alaska and Wyoming and covers the years 1970–2000. Each regression included year dummies whose coefficients are not reported. Significance levels are indicated as follows: * = 10%, ** = 5%, *** = 1%.

raised $133.38 per capita less revenue than states without the initiative. The estimate is statistically significant at better than the 10 percent level using standard errors adjusted for clustering within states. To put the estimate in perspective, the numbers imply that a family of four paid $534 less in taxes and fees if they lived in an initiative state than if they lived in a noninitiative state. Another way to look at it is in terms of average revenue. Revenue during the sample period averaged $3,186 per capita, meaning the initiative reduced revenue by about 4 percent. The initiative clearly matters, but does not put the government on a major diet.

Regression (2) estimates the effect of the initiative on spending. It can be seen that expenditure was $147.26 per capita lower in initiative states than noninitiative states. The estimated effect is significant at better than the 5 percent level. Voters appear to have used the initiative to chip away at both revenue and spending. The estimate works out to about a 4 percent reduction compared to the average per capita expenditure of $3,891 during the sample period. Here again we see that the initiative matters, but is not the primary driver of fiscal policy.

It is sometimes argued that voters cannot be trusted to vote on tax and spending measures because they are short sighted. Given the opportunity, the argument goes, voters will approve tax cuts and at the same time increase spending, forcing the government to borrow until it runs out of credit. Regressions (1) and (2) show that is not what happens: the initiative drives down both taxes and spending. How much of this is due to voter foresight and how much to institutional safeguards such as balanced budget requirements is not clear from these results, but the notion that voter control of budgeting decisions will lead to a fiscal breakdown is clearly incorrect.[3]

Regressions (1) and (2) adopt a specification that assumes the initiative has the same effect in every state. These results give the "average" effect of the initiative for the various forms it takes in practice. However, since the form of the initiative varies across states, we expect its effect to differ across states. One important difference from state to state is in the difficulty of qualifying a measure for the ballot. In practice, the difficulty depends on several factors, such as the number of signatures required, the amount of time allowed to collect them, and whether they must be distributed across the state in some way. Perhaps most important is the number of signatures, which ranges from 2 percent to 15 percent of the electorate.[4] As it becomes more difficult to put a measure on the ballot, we expect the use and impact of the initiative to decline. To give an example, Wyoming has the highest signature requirement of all states, 15 percent. Although the initiative was adopted in Wyoming in 1968, it took a quarter century—until 1992—for the first measure to qualify for the ballot. During the same time period, North Dakota, with a 2 percent signature requirement (and roughly the same size population) voted on 31 measures. It seems reasonable to expect that the initiative would have less of tax-cutting effect in Wyoming than North Dakota.

Regressions (3) and (4) allow the initiative's effect to depend on the signature requirement by adding an explanatory variable equal to the signature percentage for initiative states and zero for noninitiative states. In principle, this specification allows better estimates of the initiative's effect, and serves as a check on the interpretation of the results. If we really are picking up an initiative effect (rather than something spurious), the size of the effect should diminish as the signature requirement rises, holding population constant (as the regression does).

Consistent with the view that the regressions are actually picking up an initiative effect, the coefficients on the signature requirement variable are positive in both the revenue and expenditure regressions. The full effect of the initiative is difficult to see from the estimates reported in table 3.1 since it depends on two coefficients. To make things more transparent, figure 3.2 reports the effect of the initiative for a given signature requirement, calculated using the coefficients from columns (3) and (4) of table 3.1.[5] For example, the first bar from the left indicates that a state with a 2 percent signature requirement raised $216 per capita less than an otherwise equivalent noninitiative state. I report signature percentages from 2 percent to 10 percent because almost all of the observations lie in that range.

Figure 3.2 shows that the initiative had a negative effect on revenue and expenditure for all reported signature requirements. The estimated effects are statistically different from zero for signature requirements from 4 percent to 6 percent for revenue, and for 2 percent to 7 percent for expenditure. In the states where the process is used the most, California, Colorado, North Dakota, and Oregon, the signature requirement ranges from 2 to 6 percent. An initiative state in the middle of this range, with a 4 percent signature requirement, raised $179 per capita less and spent $212 per capita less than an otherwise equivalent noninitiative state, which translate into 5 to 6 percent reductions in average revenue and expenditure. The initiative cuts the size of government, but even with frequent use, not all the way to the bone.[6]

I have estimated these regressions with literally hundreds of other specifications. The main result—that revenue and spending are lower in initiative states—is highly robust. In particular, the results are robust to expressing the key variables as a fraction of income (instead of per capita) or logarithmically. They are robust to deletion of the South dummy or the West dummy. The

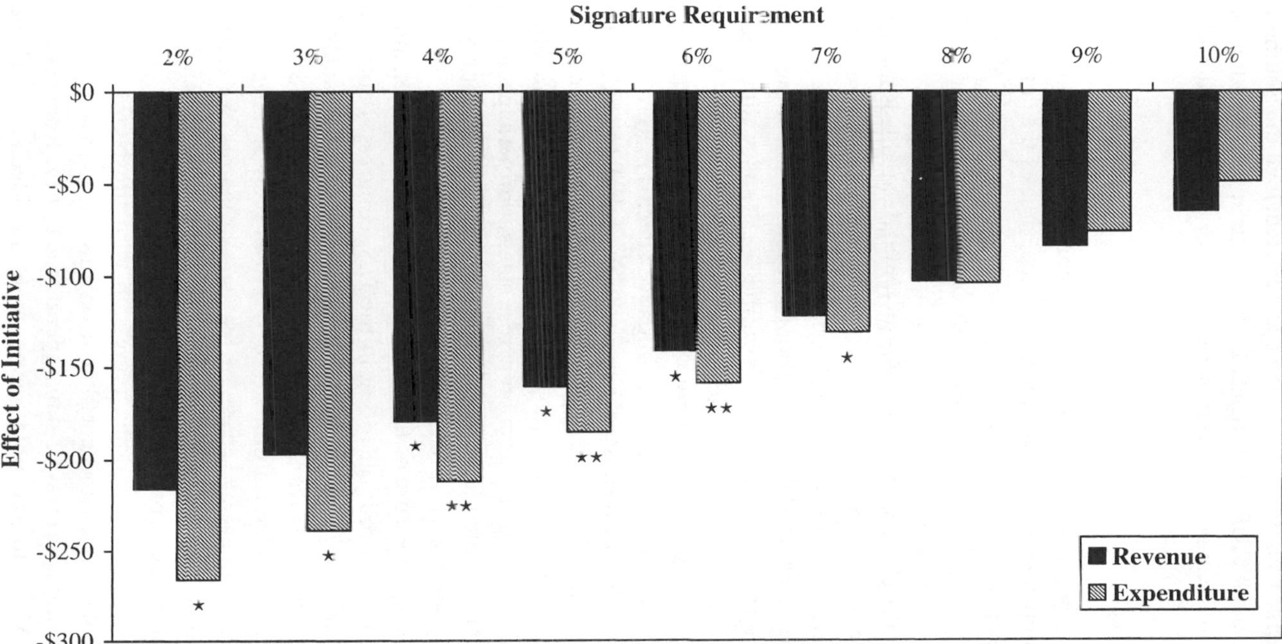

Figure 3.2 Effect of the Initiative on Revenue and Expenditure by Signature Requirement.

Note: This chart indicates the difference between revenue/expenditure in initiative and noninitiative states depending on the signature requirement. For example, the first bar shows that revenue was $216 per capita lower in an initiative state with a 2 percent signature requirement than in an otherwise identical noninitiative state. Estimates are computed from regressions (3) and (4) of table 3.1, and expressed in year-2000 dollars. Significance levels are reported beneath the bars as follows: * = 10%, ** = 5%.

main patterns emerge if all the Western states are deleted, if all the Southern states are deleted, and if California is deleted. The results appear if additional control variables are included such as mineral wealth or population density.

Initiative or Ideology?

Initiative states spend and tax less than noninitiative states (at least since 1970), but how do we know the initiative is the *cause* of the cutbacks? Perhaps some other factor leads states to adopt the initiative and also to reduce the size of government. This "spurious correlation" problem boils down to a question of whether a key variable has been omitted from the regressions. The most plausible candidate for an omitted variable is the ideology of a state's electorate. Suppose that residents of initiative states happen to be more fiscally conservative than residents of noninitiative states. Their conservatism might lead them to adopt the initiative and at the same time restrain spending. If this were the case, the fiscal policy differences between initiative and noninitiative states would actually be caused by the underlying ideology of the electorate, not the availability of the initiative.

As it turns out, the possibility that the initiative effect is merely a proxy for ideology can probably be dismissed. I show this in several ways. The first and most direct approach is to include measures of citizen ideology directly in the spending regressions. The demographic variables, such as income, capture some of the ideological variation across states, but perhaps not all of it. Table 3.2 reports expenditure regressions that include three proxies for voter ideology (unreported revenue regressions look the same).

The first proxy is a measure of the ideology of a state's U.S. senators. In an exhaustive study of roll call voting in the U.S. congress, Poole and Rosenthal (1991) assigned a score to each member based on an analysis of all of his or her roll call votes. These "NOMINATE" scores place each senator on a spectrum that runs from −1 (liberal) to +1 (conservative). The proxy I use is simply the average score for the state's senators. We expect that as voters become more conservative, the voting records of their U.S. senators will become more conservative.[7]

Column (1) reports the spending regression with the NOMINATE variable included. The estimated coefficient on this ideology variable is negative as expected if conservative states spend less, but far from statistical significance. More to the point, even with the ideology variable included the initiative coefficient is still negative, almost the same magnitude as before, and statistically significant.

Table 3.2 Expenditure Regressions Controlling for "Ideology"

	Expenditure			
	(1)	(2)	(3)	(4)
Dummy = 1 if initiative state	−152.87**	−142.29*	−153.94	−159.32
	(70.68)	(70.89)	(96.04)	(99.48)
Income	0.10***	0.11***	0.11***	0.11***
	(0.02)	(0.01)	(0.02)	(0.02)
Federal aid	2.03***	2.06***	2.25***	2.18***
	(0.36)	(0.34)	(0.39)	(0.40)
Population, logarithm	40.38	41.19	151.05*	156.64*
	(72.65)	(71.81)	(85.05)	(84.04)
Metropolitan population, %	1.67	1.55	−2.89	−3.77
	(1.91)	(1.95)	(2.98)	(2.93)
Growth of population, previous 5 years, %	11.71*	11.28*	9.55	11.03
	(5.75)	(6.06)	(8.63)	(8.97)
Dummy = 1 if southern state	−206.51*	−211.42**	−242.22**	−202.89*
	(103.03)	(101.91)	(117.14)	(121.99)
Dummy = 1 if western state	175.38*	164.13*	185.91	197.76
	(90.58)	(86.62)	(141.14)	(138.00)
Ideology 1: NOMINATE for U.S. senators, average	−97.69	—	—	20.91
	(120.60)			(148.67)
Ideology 2: "Citizen Ideology" from Berry et al. 1998	—	0.81	—	3.08
		(1.21)		(2.74)
Ideology 3: "Liberal/ Conservative" thermometer from NES, median*	—	—	6.21	7.18*
			(3.96)	(4.23)
R^2	0.994	0.994	0.994	0.994
N	1,488	1,440	472	472

Note: Each column is a regression. The main entries are coefficient estimates; standard errors adjusted for within-state clustering are in parentheses. The dependent variable is combined state and local direct general expenditure per capita. Expenditure, income, and federal aid are expressed in year-2000 dollars per capita. The sample includes all states except Alaska and Wyoming and covers 1970–2000. Each regression included year dummies whose coefficients are not reported. Significance levels are indicated as follows: * = 10%, ** = 5%, *** = 1%.

The NOMINATE variable is a good proxy for citizen ideology if senators vote according to constituent interests. It seems possible, though, that some representatives may emphasize the interests of their supporters more than the electorate as a whole. If this happens, the NOMINATE variable will indicate the ideology of their supporters, not the state as a whole. The second ideology variable, developed by Berry et al. (1998), addresses this possibility by taking into account both the voting record of elected officials and the positions of their election challengers. The ideology variable was constructed by calculating the ideological position of each incumbent congressman using ratings by Americans for Democratic

Action (ADA) and the AFL-CIO Committee on Political Education (COPE), two liberal interest groups. Positions of challengers (who did not vote and hence were not rated by ADA and COPE) were imputed using the average score for members of their party in the state. The incumbent and challenger scores were then averaged based on election vote shares and aggregated across all districts to yield a state measure. The final variable takes on values between 0 and 100, with 100 representing the most liberal position. Berry et al. call this variable "citizen ideology," but it is more accurate to think of it as a measure of *candidate* ideology.

Column (2) reports the spending regression with the "citizen ideology" variable included. The sign on the ideology variable is positive—suggesting that liberal states spend more, all else equal—but statistically insignificant. The important result, however, is that a significant negative initiative effect continues to appear.[8]

The NOMINATE and "citizen ideology" variables are indirect measures of state ideology—citizen preferences are inferred from the voting behavior of their elected representatives. The third variable measures voter ideology directly using opinion data from the National Election Studies (NES). NES surveys are given to a sample of voters prior to each election. Among other things, respondents are asked two "thermometer" questions about their perception of liberals and conservatives. Based on these responses, each person is assigned a number between 0 and 97, where 0 is the most liberal and 97 the most conservative. I use the median value of each state for the ideology variable. The underlying questions are not asked in every year or for every state, so the sample size falls by about three-quarters.[9]

Column (3) reports the spending regression that includes this variable. The ideology variable is positive but statistically insignificant. Its inclusion has no material effect on the initiative coefficient. The significance level falls because there are many fewer observations.

Just for good measure, column (4) reports a spending regression that includes all three ideology variables at the same time. Nothing new turns up. Two of the three ideology variables continue to fall short of statistical significance (the NES variable is significant at the 10 percent level), and the initiative effect continues to appear. The limited explanatory value of the three ideology variables suggests that the demographic variables already are capturing most of the relevant variation in state ideology.

So far, we have seen that inclusion of three different ideology variables does not make the initiative effect go away. A different approach is to directly compare the ideology of initiative and noninitiative states. Figure 3.3 and table 3.3 report six different comparisons. The first three are simply

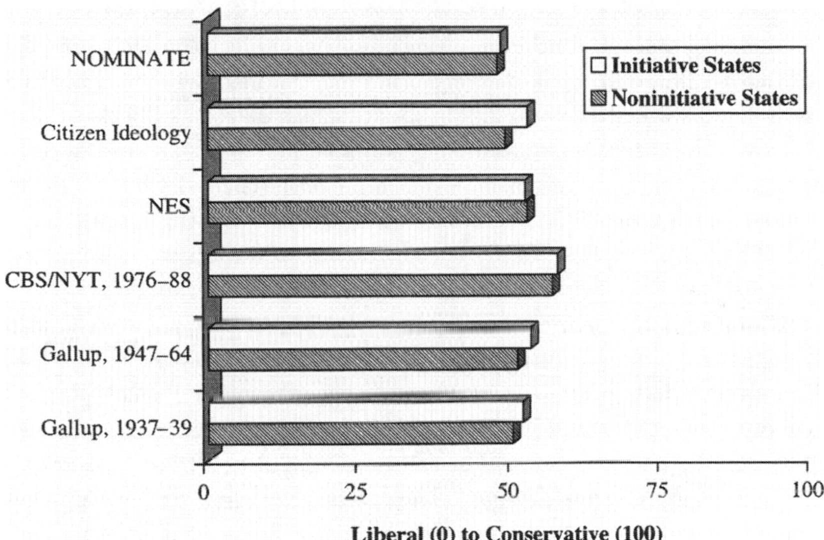

Figure 3.3 Average "Ideology" of Initiative and Noninitiative States.
Note: All ideology measures are normalized so that 0 is the most liberal and 100 is the most conservative. NOMINATE is the average DW-NOMINATE score for the state's U.S. senators, based on roll call votes. Citizen Ideology is the index constructed by Berry et al. (1998). NES is the median self-reported ideology of respondents to the National Election Surveys. The polls are index numbers computed by Erikson, Wright, and McIver (1993).

Table 3.3 "Ideology" of Initiative and Noninitiative States

Ideology measure	Initiative states	Noninitiative states	*t*-statistic
(1) NOMINATE of U.S. senators, average	−0.037	−0.051	0.64
(liberal = −1, conservative = +1)	N = 324	N = 444	
(2) "Citizen Ideology" from Berry et al. 1998	47.4	51.2	3.11***
(conservative = 0, liberal = 100)	N = 607	N = 833	
(3) "Liberal-Conservative" index from NES,	50.6	50.9	1.01
median	N = 189	N = 283	
(liberal = 0, conservative = 97)			
(4) *CBS News/New York Times* polls, 1976–1988	−15.3	−13.4	0.87
(conservative = −100, liberal = 100)	N = 21	N = 26	
(5) Gallup polls, 1947–1964	−6.1	−1.7	1.31
(conservative = −100, liberal = 100)	N = 20	N = 26	
(6) Gallup polls, 1937–1939	−3.3	−0.1	0.96
(conservative = −100, liberal = 100)	N = 20	N = 26	

Note: The main entry in each cell is the mean value of the ideology measure. *N* is the number of observations. The *t*-statistic is for the hypothesis that the means are the same. The extreme values for "liberal" and "conservative" are indicated in parentheses after each measure is described. Alaska and Wyoming are omitted from all calculations, Nevada is omitted from all polling data, and Hawaii is omitted from the Gallup poll data. Initiative status is defined as of 2000. Significance levels are indicated as follows: * = 10%, ** = 5%, *** = 1%.

the mean NOMINATE, "citizen ideology," and NES scores, respectively. The next is based on CBS News/*New York Times* polls from 1976–88. The last two are based on Gallup polls from 1937–39 and 1947–64. The three opinion polls asked respondents to identify themselves as liberal or conservative. The responses were then aggregated for each state and normalized to yield a number from −100 to +100, where higher numbers correspond to more liberal respondents. Table 3.3 reports the raw statistics. Figure 3.3 simplifies things by converting each measure to a uniform scale ranging from 0 (most liberal) to 100 (most conservative).

If we focus on the first four measures that most closely correspond to the 1970–2000 sample period, we see that initiative states were more conservative than noninitiative states according to the NOMINATE, "citizen ideology," and CBS/NYT measures, and more liberal according the NES measure. The only difference that can be distinguished from zero at conventional levels of statistical significance is the one using "citizen ideology." Going back before the sample period, we see that initiative states were more conservative according to the Gallup polls, but again the differences are not statistically significant. Statistical significance seems almost beside the point here, though. A glance at figure 3.3 suggests that whatever ideological differences might exist or might have existed are quantitatively trivial (except, perhaps, when the "citizen ideology" variable is used). It is hard to avoid the conclusion that the citizens of initiative and noninitiative states are not now (and were not going back to 1937) much different in ideology.

It is also worth pointing out that the initiative in most cases was adopted over fifty years before the start of the sample period. As Erikson, Wright, and McIver (1993) show, there is little correlation in state ideology over such long periods of time. Even if the initiative was adopted by conservatives, there is no reason to think that the adopting states were still conservative in the sample period. Moreover, fiscal conservatives were generally opposed to adoption of the initiative. The initiative was promoted by Populists and Progressives, and the historical evidence suggests that they wanted new government programs, not spending cuts.[10] Indeed, as will be shown in chapter 5, the initiative had the effect of *boosting* spending in the early part of the century. A final observation, developed at greater length in chapters 6 and 7, is that the effect of the initiative varies over time even in the postwar period, and in some periods there is no difference is spending between initiative and noninitiative states. If the initiative effects in tables 3.1 and 3.2 were really caused by some unobserved ideology of the electorate, we would not expect to see initiative effects appear and disappear over time (unless ideology is much more transient than commonly believed).

In short, there is little reason to believe that the estimated initiative effects are spuriously caused by unmeasured citizen ideology. Absent another plausible omitted variable that could have caused initiative states to spend less than noninitiative states, it seems fair to attribute the spending difference to the initiative itself.[11]

Summary: The Initiative Cuts the Size of Government

This section documents that the initiative reduced the combined size of state and local government (measured by revenue or expenditure) by about 4 percent over the period 1970–2000. The results are robust to alternative estimation procedures, and are not the spurious consequence of an omitted citizen ideology variable. The initiative appears to bring about a modest reduction in spending. It does not trigger monumental cuts or lead to systematic deficits.

Second Effect: How the Initiative Changes the Centralization of Spending

In the previous section, we saw that the initiative led to cuts in the overall size of state and local government during the period 1970–2000. This section investigates how those cuts were achieved: did they come from state government, local government, or both? The answer will provide a second benchmark that we can compare with opinion data in order to determine if the majority supports or opposes the changes brought about by the initiative.

The evidence is also of independent interest because the division of spending between state and local governments affects the degree of government centralization. Spending is centralized if the state government makes the preponderance of expenditure decisions, and decentralized if local governments make most decisions. It is well documented that government centralization of revenue and expenditure increased throughout the twentieth century (Wallis 1995). Whether this was a good or a bad thing is a matter of dispute. Central governments may be the most efficient providers of services with benefits or costs that spill over across jurisdictions (national defense is a prime example at the federal level). Local governments, on the other hand, are probably better at tailoring policies to local conditions. Local governments are also subject to competition from other local governments (called Tiebout competition): people can shop among local governments and settle in the jurisdiction of the one that provides a desirable mix of spending and taxes. Competition puts pressure on local governments to adopt efficient public policies, but it could also result in a "race to the bottom" (or top) as local governments sacrifice their environment to attract businesses (see Fischel 2001 for a discussion and evaluation).

The dispute over centralization is especially vivid when it comes to education, the largest single category of state and local expenditure (figure 3.1). Some argue that spending decisions should be left primarily to local governments, who have better information about the benefits and costs of spending in their communities. Others argue that local governments are unable to police themselves, and involvement by state government is needed to protect the interests of children (particularly when it comes to standards: testing, curriculum, and teacher certification). Others favor state involvement in order to transfer resources from rich to poor districts.

Although the trend toward increasing centralization is known, and the main arguments for and against it are clear, we understand relatively little about the politics of centralization. A particularly interesting question is whether the growth of centralization has been a response to (or in opposition to) voter demands.[12] By measuring the effect of the initiative on centralization, and assessing whether it serves the many or the few, we will arrive at an answer of sorts.

Basic Findings

To understand how the initiative affects state versus local spending, I decompose expenditure into the amount disbursed by the state government and the amount disbursed by local governments, and estimate the effect of the initiative on each. The spending measures indicate which level of government ultimately spent the money, not where the money was raised. That is, money raised by the state and then transferred to a local government shows up as a local expenditure. Since state grants often come with strings attached, my measure of state spending probably understates the importance of state government in spending decisions.[13]

The results are reported in table 3.4. The layout is the same as before: each column is a regression, the main entries are coefficient estimates, and the standard errors adjusted for clustering are in parentheses. The dependent variable is indicated at the top of each column. The usual control variables are included as well as the NOMINATE ideology variable (nothing important changes if the ideology variable is deleted).

In regression (1), the dependent variable is state (only) expenditure per capita. The estimate indicates that state spending was $215.24 per

Table 3.4 Separate Regressions for State Expenditure and Local Expenditure

	State expenditure (1)	Local expenditure (2)	Centralization (3)
Dummy = 1 if initiative state	–215.24**	62.36	–3.32
	(103.29)	(113.97)	(2.14)
Income	0.04***	0.07***	–0.00
	(0.01)	(0.02)	(0.00)
Federal aid	1.27***	0.76	0.01**
	(0.15)	(0.47)	(0.00)
Population, logarithm	–317.20***	357.57***	–7.14***
	(68.23)	(95.57)	(1.44)
Metropolitan population, %	5.93***	–4.25*	0.10***
	(2.09)	(2.26)	(0.01)
Growth of population previous 5 years, %	–9.88	21.59*	–0.28***
	(9.29)	(11.15)	(0.19)
Dummy = 1 if southern state	107.87	–314.38**	3.68
	(109.87)	(150.92)	(2.67)
Dummy = 1 if western state	166.94	8.44	0.74
	(219.25)	(191.81)	(3.89)
Ideology 1: NOMINATE for U.S. senators, average	–197.87*	100.19	–3.17
	(102.49)	(156.06)	(2.24)
R^2	0.978	0.974	0.984

Note: Each column is a regression with 1,488 observations. The main entries are coefficient estimates; standard errors adjusted for within-state clustering are in parentheses. The dependent variable is either state direct general expenditure (DGE), local DGE, or "centralization"—state DGE as a percent of combined state and local DGE—as indicated at the top of each column. Revenue, expenditure, income, and federal aid are expressed in year-2000 dollars per capita. The sample includes all states except Alaska and Wyoming and covers the years 1970–2000. Each regression included year dummies whose coefficients are not reported. Significance levels are indicated as follows: * = 10%, ** = 5%, and *** = 1%.

capita less in initiative states than noninitiative states, all else equal. The coefficient is different from zero at better than the 5 percent level. State spending averaged $1,790 per capita over the sample, so the initiative triggered about a 12 percent reduction. The effect of the initiative on state spending is more dramatic than we saw for combined state and local spending, suggesting the process may be more important for the composition of spending than its level.

Regression (2) is the same as (1) except that the dependent variable is local expenditure per capita. The unit of observation here is the sum of all spending by local governments within a state (not individual cities, counties, etc.), and the initiative variable shows whether a state-level initiative was available (not whether a local initiative was available). The coefficient on the initiative dummy variable is $62.36, implying that local spending was about 3 percent *higher* in initiative than noninitiative states, based on a sample average of $2,101. However, there is enough imprecision in the estimate that we cannot rule out the possibility that local spending was the same in initiative and noninitiative states.

Regressions (1) and (2) reveal that the overall spending reduction triggered by the initiative was accomplished by drastically cutting state spending while holding constant or even increasing local spending. As a result, the initiative ended up decentralizing overall expenditure. Regression (3) makes this point more directly. The dependent variable is the percent of combined state and local expenditure disbursed by state government, what Wallis (1995) calls the "centralization index." The coefficient on the initiative variable indicates that initiative states were 3.32 percent less centralized than noninitiative states, although the estimate is not quite distinguishable from zero at conventional levels of significance. For reference, the mean centralization index for the sample is 46 percent.

As with most regressions reported in this book, I checked the results by estimating the models with literally hundreds of alternative specifications. The finding that the initiative cuts state spending is highly robust. The positive effect on local spending is not. The initiative coefficient in the local spending regression is particularly sensitive to whether or not the regional dummies are included, and becomes about zero when Hawaii (where the state runs the public schools) is excluded. In any event, the key result—the initiative reduces the centralization of spending—does not depend on the treatment of Hawaii or the regional dummies.

How would an initiative bring about decentralization? There are probably few if any measures that legislate directly on the division of spending between state and local governments. However, measures that provide funds for local governments are not that hard to find. For example, California's Proposition 98 in 1988 required the state to provide specified minimum levels of spending for schools districts. This money is raised by the state, but ends up being spent by local governments.

Evidence from Cities

One way to get a clearer picture of how the initiative affects local government is to take a closer look at municipal spending.[14] The regressions that follow estimate how the initiative changed tax and spending policy in a sample of several thousand cities, towns, and villages. The first purpose of these estimates is to provide another perspective on how *state* initiatives affect the size of *local* government. By taking cities as the unit of observation, we can also assess how *local* initiatives affect the size of local government.

It is useful to disentangle the effects of state and local initiatives because we know that cities in initiative states are more likely to have the initiative themselves (figure 1.3). We would like to know to what extent the estimates in table 3.4 compound the effects of state and local initiatives.

Data on local governments are difficult to collect and assemble. The regressions that follow make use of three data sources. The first are Form of Government Surveys conducted by the International City/County Manager Association (ICMA) in 1981, 1986, 1991, and 1996. These surveys ask each city a series of questions about their government, including whether or not the initiative process is available. Unfortunately, the questions change over time, making the 1980s information incompatible with the 1990s information.[15] In addition, the city officials who fill out the surveys sometimes make mistakes. Nevertheless, the ICMA surveys are the best available data source on city initiative status and, if used properly, can be informative. City financial data are available from the census for 1982, 1987, 1992, and 1997. I matched the two data sources assuming that each city's initiative status was the same one year after the ICMA survey, and appended census demographic information. In the end, there are two panels, one covering 1982 and 1987 with about 5,500 observations, and the other covering 1992 and 1997 with about 8,100 observations.

Table 3.5 reports revenue and spending regressions for the two samples. These regressions are of the same form as the state-level regressions except that the unit of observation is a city and the control variables are slightly different. The controls pertain to a city now; for example, income represents income per capita in the city. The main difference in control variables is that intergovernmental aid is disaggregated by source: federal, state, and other local governments (although nothing important hinges on this.) The South and West dummies are still included, although the case for doing so is rather weak and they are generally insignificant. The results are the same if the region dummies are excluded.[16]

The first two regressions are for the 1980s, and the last two regressions are for the 1990s. Two initiative dummy variables are included, one indicating whether the city had the initiative, and another whether the state had the initiative. Both coefficients are positive and statistically different from zero for both revenue and expenditure in both decades. For example, the estimates in column (4) for the 1990s imply that an initiative city spent $57.63 per capita more than a noninitiative city, and that a city in an initiative state spent $127.11 per capita more (in 1992 and 1997). Average municipal spending in the two sample years was $986 per capita, implying that city spending was boosted 6 percent by the local initiative and 13 percent by the state initiative.

Table 3.5 City Revenue and Expenditure Regressions, 1982–1997

	1982 and 1987		1992 and 1997	
	Revenue (1)	Expenditure (2)	Revenue (3)	Expenditure (4)
Dummy = 1 if city has initiative	33.02***	27.04**	68.25***	57.63***
	(10.32)	(10.82)	(11.29)	(14.69)
Dummy = 1 if city is in state with statewide initiative	40.72***	21.88*	125.59***	127.11***
	(12.90)	(13.20)	(11.92)	(15.44)
Income	0.01***	0.01***	0.02***	0.01***
	(0.00)	(0.00)	(0.00)	(0.00)
Federal aid	0.44***	1.25***	0.99***	2.20***
	(0.07)	(0.09)	(0.14)	(0.19)
State aid	0.69***	1.71***	0.84***	1.82***
	(0.05)	(0.05)	(0.03)	(0.05)
Local aid	−0.13	0.79***	−0.06	1.56***
	(0.14)	(0.15)	(0.10)	(0.15)
Population, logarithm	64.90***	63.12***	36.72***	25.92***
	(4.84)	(5.30)	(4.78)	(6.27)
Dummy = 1 if southern city	16.19	1.57	59.00***	147.86***
	(12.13)	(13.10)	(11.22)	(16.28)
Dummy = 1 if western city	−28.30*	−13.66	−28.62**	−15.90
	(15.11)	(16.10)	(16.71)	(20.24)
R^2	0.771	0.834	0.763	0.783
N	5,493	5,505	8,077	8,078

Note: Each column is a regression in which the unit of observation is a city. The main entries are coefficient estimates; standard errors—adjusted for within-city clustering in (1) and (2)—are in parentheses. The dependent variable and sample years are indicated at the top of each column. Financial variables are expressed in year-2000 dollars per capita. Observations with financial variables in the top and bottom percentile were deleted, as were cities in Alaska and Wyoming. Each regression included two year dummies whose coefficients are not reported. Significance levels are indicated as follows: * = 10%, ** = 5%, *** = 1%.

For the 1980s, with mean spending of $687, the percentages were 5 percent for the local initiative and 3 percent for the state initiative.

Two things are worth noting about these results. First, the local initiative *increases* local spending, the reverse of what the state initiative does to state spending. Based on the state initiative results, one might be tempted to view the initiative as fundamentally a tax-cutting device. That conclusion would seem to be premature. It is not the case for cities and, as will be seen in chapter 5, it was not even the case for state initiatives in the first half of the twentieth century.

Second, the large positive coefficients on state initiatives reinforce the findings from earlier in the chapter that state initiatives result in decentralization of expenditure from state to local governments. We saw earlier that state spending was clearly reduced by state initiatives, but the effect on local spending was hard to distinguish from noise. Here we see that state initiatives clearly boosted city spending, a big component of local spending. Thus, these regressions corroborate the basic message that state initiatives result in decentralization.

Summary: The Initiative Shifts Spending from State to Local Government

The main finding of this section is that states with the initiative ended up with more decentralized spending over the period 1970–2000. The initiative cut state spending by about 12 percent, and apparently stimulated local spending (although the evidence on the size of this effect is somewhat mixed). The estimates indicate that state spending accounted for all of the reduction in combined state and local spending brought about by the initiative, and suggest that the initiative might have a larger effect on the division of spending than on its level.

Third Effect: How the Initiative Changes the Way Money Is Raised

So far we have seen that the initiative altered the size of government and the way money was spent. This section investigates how the initiative changed the way money was raised. The results provide a third policy effect of the initiative that can be compared to public opinion.

Governments raise funds in a number of ways. Table 3.6 lists the major revenue sources for state and local governments in 1997, and the fraction of revenue that each provided. Most revenue is collected in the form of

Table 3.6 Revenue Sources of State and Local Governments, 1997

Source	Amount ($ billions)	Percent of total
General revenue from own sources	1,044.6	100.0
Taxes	728.6	69.7
Sales taxes	261.7	25.1
Property taxes	218.8	20.9
Individual income taxes	159.1	15.2
Corporate income taxes	33.8	3.2
Motor vehicle taxes	14.0	1.3
Other taxes	41.1	3.9
Charges for Services	190.5	18.2
Education charges	52.7	5.0
Hospital charges	49.6	4.7
Sewerage	22.0	2.1
Other charges	66.2	6.3
Miscellaneous	125.5	12.0
Interest	61.6	5.9
Other miscellaneous	63.8	6.1

taxes, primarily sales, property, and income taxes. A significant chunk of money is also raised from user fees and charges for services ("charges" for short), primarily tuition fees to attend public schools, colleges, and universities, and charges for hospital services and sewerage. The analysis to follow focuses on these two broad categories of revenue: taxes and charges (the third category is miscellaneous revenue and interest income, which I do not examine). The conceptual difference between taxes and charges is that a person's tax bill does not depend on how many government services he uses, while his charges are directly related to his use of government services. States have a fair amount of flexibility when deciding whether to finance public spending with taxes or charges. For example, the education of a student in a public university can be funded with fees paid by the student (tuition) or with taxes paid by the population at large.

The balance of taxes and charges is important because it affects economic efficiency and the amount of wealth redistribution. Economic efficiency generally requires the price of a service to be set equal to its marginal cost of provision. Efficiency considerations then point to heavy reliance on charges (the "price" of government services). When taxes are used to subsidize and provide a service at below marginal cost, consumption of the service will be excessive (from the viewpoint of economic efficiency) and there will be distortions in the markets where the taxes are assessed. If there are externalities associated with public spending (for example, a person who has a flu shot will not transmit the disease to others), it might be efficient to set the charge below marginal cost even though distortionary taxes will be needed to provide the subsidy.

The mix between taxes and charges also affects the amount of redistribution in society. Taxes allow wealth to be transferred from taxpayers to the recipients of services, while charges restrict the amount of redistribution. For example, if college students are charged 100 percent of the cost of their education, there is no redistribution. On the other hand, if tuition is free and the costs of provision are paid by general tax revenue, wealth is transferred from taxpayers to students. We know from casual observation that changes in the level of tuition at state universities are highly contentious.

In short, the mix of taxes and charges in a government's finances is important because it affects economic efficiency and the amount of redistribution. The evidence in this section sheds light on what determines the ratio in practice, and allows us to assess whether the initiative pushes the mix in a direction favored by the public.

Basic Findings

Table 3.7 reports the main results in the usual format (each column is a regression, standard errors are beneath coefficient estimates, etc.). The dependent variable is indicated at the top of the column. The standard control variables are employed as well as the NOMINATE ideology variable.

Consider first how the initiative affected tax revenue. Column (1) shows that initiative states raised $110.00 per capita less from taxes than noninitiative states, all else equal. The coefficient is significantly different from zero at better than the 5 percent level. In percentage terms, the initiative is associated with about a 5 percent reduction in tax revenue compared to the average of $2,280 per capita. Recall from earlier in this chapter that the initiative cut *total* revenue by about $133 per capita (table 3.1, column 1). It appears that taxes bore the brunt of the revenue cutbacks.

Table 3.7 Regressions for State and Local Taxes and Charges

	Taxes (1)	Charges (2)	Taxes/ Revenue (%) (3)
Dummy = 1 if initiative state	–110.00**	1.62	–0.90
	(48.34)	(38.51)	(0.98)
Income	0.10***	0.00	0.00***
	(0.01)	(0.01)	(0.00)
Federal aid	0.90***	0.06	0.00
	(0.28)	(0.10)	(0.00)
Population, logarithm	80.79	–8.21	–0.69
	(49.58)	(34.25)	(0.81)
Metropolitan population, %	–0.06	0.35	–0.01
	(1.10)	(1.60)	(0.04)
Growth of population previous 5 years, %	3.09	0.90	0.03
	(4.27)	(3.48)	(0.10)
Dummy = 1 if southern state	–228.55***	71.21	–4.29***
	(71.79)	(48.16)	(1.32)
Dummy = 1 if western state	59.57	48.74	–0.79
	(74.25)	(54.57)	(1.41)
Ideology 1: NOMINATE for U.S. senators, average	–86.03	8.41	–1.33
	(88.46)	(42.81)	(0.98)
R^2	0.992	0.960	0.998
N	1,488	1,104	1,104

Note: Each column is a regression. The main entries are coefficient estimates; standard errors adjusted for within-state clustering are in parentheses. The dependent variable is indicated at the top of each column. Taxes, charges, income, and federal aid are expressed in year-2000 dollars per capita. The sample includes all states except Alaska and Wyoming and covers 1970–2000 (column 1) or 1978–2000 (columns 2 and 3). Each regression included year dummies whose coefficients are not reported. Significance levels are indicated as follows: * = 10%, ** = 5%, and *** = 1%.

The regression in column (2) corroborates this impression. Here the dependent variable is charges per capita.[17] The coefficient on the initiative dummy is trivially small, and statistically insignificant. We might have expected the revenue cuts triggered by the initiative to be apportioned to taxes and charges more or less proportionately, but that does not appear to be the case.

The regression in column (3) provides another perspective on this. The dependent variable in this regression is the percentage of revenue that comes from taxes divided by the sum of tax and charge revenue. This is a measure of the importance of tax revenue relative to charge revenue. As can be seen, the initiative led to a .9 percent reduction in the percentage of revenue coming from taxes. The estimate cannot be differentiated from zero at conventional levels of significance, however, and the effect is modest compared to the sample average of about 81 percent.

As usual, I also estimated these regressions a number of other ways to check robustness. Among other things, I included/excluded ideology variables, ran the regressions without the western states and without the southern states, used log-of-the-odds specifications for regression (3), and checked for influential state observations. The negative effect of the initiative on taxes is highly robust, as is the small and insignificant effect on charges. The effect of the initiative on the taxes/revenue ratio is always negative, but the magnitude of the effect is much larger and achieves statistical significance in some specifications (for example, when southern states are deleted). The broad picture that emerges is that the initiative cuts taxes, absolutely and as a proportion of revenue.

Evidence from Cities

To gain additional insight into how the initiative affects public financing, table 3.8 reports estimates of the effect of the initiative in cities. Here the unit of observation is a city rather than a state, but the format and approach are otherwise the same as in table 3.7. The reported regressions use only data from 1982 and 1987 since I was unable to find robust results for the 1992 and 1997 samples.[18] Recall from table 3.5 that the initiative drove up revenue in cities. Was the extra revenue raised from taxes or charges?

The regression in column (1) estimates the effect of the initiative on taxes and column (2) reports the effect on charges. The first thing to note is that availability of a city initiative had a modest and insignificant effect on taxes but a large and statistically significant effect on charges. The

Table 3.8 City Taxes and Charges Regressions

	Taxes (1)	Charges (2)	Taxes/ Revenue (%) (3)
Dummy = 1 if city has initiative	−0.55	16.95***	−1.86***
	(4.95)	(5.01)	(0.56)
Dummy = 1 if city is in state with statewide initiative	28.23***	12.36*	−0.44
	(5.95)	(6.65)	(0.70)
Income	0.01***	−0.00***	0.00***
	(0.01)	(0.00)	(0.00)
Federal aid	0.15***	0.14***	−0.02***
	(0.03)	(0.03)	(0.00)
State aid	0.43***	0.12***	−0.00
	(0.03)	(0.02)	(0.00)
Local aid	−0.14**	−0.09*	−0.00
	(0.07)	(0.05)	(0.01)
Population, logarithm	37.79***	8.47***	0.81***
	(2.71)	(2.52)	(0.28)
Dummy = 1 if southern city	23.89***	−5.62	1.50**
	(5.73)	(5.70)	(0.69)
Dummy = 1 if western city	−8.10	−7.76	−0.92
	(8.02)	(7.33)	(0.79)
R^2	0.809	0.419	0.949
N	5,505	5,534	5,433

Note: Each column is a regression in which the unit of observation is a city. The main entries are coefficient estimates; standard errors adjusted for within-city clustering are in parentheses. The dependent variable is indicated at the top of each column. Financial variables are expressed in year 2000 dollars per capita. The sample covers 1982 and 1987. Observations with financial variables in the top and bottom percentile were deleted, as were cities in Alaska and Wyoming. Each regression included two year dummies whose coefficients are not reported. Significance levels are indicated as follows: * = 10%, ** = 5%, and *** = 1%.

estimate for charges, $16.95 per capita, translates into an increase of roughly 14 percent compared to the mean of $122. Local initiatives, like state initiatives, appear to have shifted the revenue mix away from taxes and toward charges. The regression in column (3), which has the taxes/revenue ratio as the dependent variable, makes this point more directly. It indicates that city initiatives cut the fraction of revenue raised from taxes by 1.86 percent, a value different from zero at high levels of statistical significance.

The regressions also include a variable indicating whether a city was located in a state with a statewide initiative. The presence of a state-level initiative drove up both taxes and charges in cities. This is presumably the decentralizing effect of state initiatives noted earlier in this chapter. The regression in column (3) suggests that cities relied more on charges than taxes to raise the additional revenue, but the estimate is not statistically significant.

Summary: The Initiative Shifts Revenue from Taxes to Charges

The main finding of this section is that the initiative shifted the financing mix of state and local governments away from taxes and into user fees and charges for services. At the state level the initiative led to about a 5 percent reduction in taxes and no change in charges. At the city level, the initiative led to about 14 percent more charges and no change in taxes. The revenue structure of initiative states and cities therefore ended up less reliant on taxes and more reliant on charges, with fewer possibilities for redistribution of wealth.

Conclusion: Three Policy Changes

The central question of this book is whether the initiative serves the many or a special interest few. This chapter lays the groundwork for answering the question. The chapter documents three policy changes brought about by the initiative: (1) the initiative reduces total government spending, (2) the initiative shifts spending from state to local governments, and (3) the initiative shifts the sources of revenue from taxes to user fees and charges for services. The next chapter examines an array of public opinion data over the last three decades to determine if the majority was in favor of these three changes or, as the special interest subversion view maintains, if the changes were brought about contrary to the will of the majority.

All that we can ask of a law, in a democracy, . . . is that it shall be reasonably acceptable to that vague thing which we call public opinion.

—Charles Beard

CHAPTER 4 

For the Many or the Few

This chapter takes up the central question of the book: Does the initiative benefit the many or the few? The previous chapter documented several ways the initiative changed tax and spending policies in the states over the last three decades: it cut spending, decentralized expenditure from state to local governments, and led to less reliance on taxes and more on charges for services. Did the public want these changes to occur? Or were the changes forced upon the public by narrow special interests who used the initiative to manipulate the policy process for private gain?

These questions are at the heart of the debate over the initiative. The Progressives believed the initiative would allow citizens to approve popular policies that were suppressed in the legislature by special interests. Critics of the initiative turn the argument on its head and argue that special interests use the initiative to thwart the will of the voters. Which argument is correct is an empirical question.

The existing evidence is meager and mostly indirect.[1] To recap the discussion in chapter 1, attempts to answer the question have revolved around two facts. The first is that money matters in initiative campaigns. It is expensive to collect signatures and qualify a petition for the ballot, and it is expensive to advertise and run a campaign. Numerous studies have shown that by spending enough money, a group can usually defeat a ballot proposition (the best evidence is in Gerber 1999). Critics conclude that the initiative allows wealthy interests to subvert the popular will. However, the fact that money is influential in initiative politics misses the point. After all, money buys access in legislatures, too. The relevant question (for which I have seen no evidence) is whether money is more influential in the initiative or legislative process. It is entirely possible that money matters less in the initiative than legislative process, and if so, the initiative may help level the playing field even if it remains tilted toward wealthy, organized interests.

The second fact is that voters appear to have a limited understanding of the details of most ballot propositions. Critics argue that because ordinary citizens are uninformed about the substance of measures, they are vulnerable to manipulation by organized interests that can control the flow of information. However, recent research suggests that citizens might not need detailed information; they may be able to vote their interests by relying on information cues or shortcuts such as endorsements from trusted organizations or individuals (Lupia and McCubbins 1998). But the issue of voter competence has more to do with the advisability of democracy in general than with the relative merits of the initiative and legislative processes. Ignorant voters will make mistakes when electing their representatives, too. The question is whether mistakes are more common in initiative or candidate elections.

In short, the evidence at hand is inconclusive. While the initiative has been shown to be an imperfect process (like the legislative process), virtually no evidence has been produced that tells us whether the initiative leads to policies favorable to special interests or the general public.

This chapter presents such evidence. My approach is very simple. I focus on the three dimensions of fiscal policy studied in chapter 3: (1) total spending/revenue, (2) expenditure centralization, and (3) taxes versus charges. Figure 4.1 summarizes the information documented in chapter 3 concerning the specific changes brought about by the initiative in each of these policy dimensions. With these empirical regularities in mind, I collected polling data in which citizens registered their preferences on each policy dimension. This chapter compares the expressed preferences of the

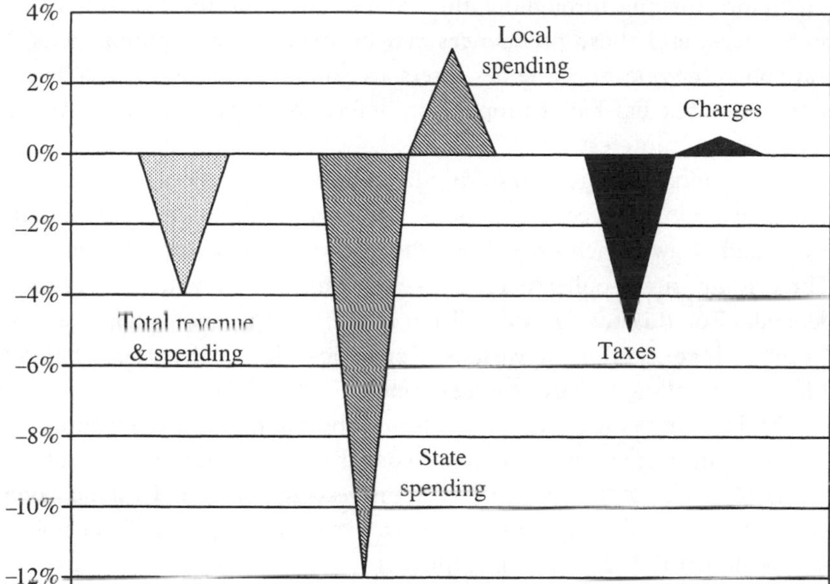

Figure 4.1 Summary of How the Initiative Changed Fiscal Policy, 1970–2000.
Note: This figure summarizes the findings from chapter 3. For example, the first triangle shows that the initiative cut total revenue and spending by about 4 percent.

public to the policy changes brought about by the initiative and asks: Was the majority in favor of the changes or opposed to the changes? If the majority supported the changes, we can say that the initiative served the interests of the many; if the majority opposed the changes, it would seem the initiative served the interests of the few.

Some limitations of my approach are worth noting before considering the evidence. The most significant is that opinion surveys seldom pose questions exactly as we would like. I will call attention to this problem throughout. In my view, the limitation is outweighed by the consistency of the responses across different polls, but the reader should nevertheless keep this limitation in mind.

Another issue is whether the answers given to pollsters are the actual preferences of voters. It is fairly clear that ordinary citizens are generally uninformed about policy, and their views about specific pieces of legislation may not necessarily reflect their true preferences. This is why we wonder if ballot elections truly reflect the public's interests. But it does not seem a stretch to imagine that citizens do know their preferences in a general sense, at the broad level of the survey questions I employ, such as whether they would like government spending increased or decreased.[2]

I therefore assume throughout that people do know their broad policy preferences, and those preferences can be captured by opinion polls. I leave open the question whether voters are sophisticated enough to determine if a particular ballot proposition before them will actually advance or hinder their interests.

The general strategy is to study a large amount of data of various types and from various sources and periods—none of which are decisive on their own—and draw conclusions from the preponderance of the evidence. There is no silver bullet here, no key parameter on which everything depends. For this reason, we will not end up with conclusions that are "true" with conventional measures of statistical significance, but I believe a fairly compelling picture emerges even so.

Finally, a note on the use of the term "special interest" is appropriate. Although this term is common in everyday discourse, it is not well defined. As many have noted, we are all special interests to a degree. I will be using the term in the following sense: Suppose a majority of people favor policy X over policy Y. If policy X is implemented, I will say that the outcome reflects the majority interest. If policy Y is selected, I will say that it reflects a special interest. When I refer to a "special interest," then, I simply mean the interest of less than a majority of the population. I believe this is a sensible definition of "special interest," and captures the essence of what the term means in practice. But my primary motivation in using the term is to avoid a cumbersome repetition of the phrase "interest of the numerical minority." *It is very important to note that I am not claiming that the policy favored by a majority is necessarily a "better" policy than the one favored by a minority.* That is a deeper issue.[3] My goal here is simply to test whether the initiative pushes policy toward or away from what the majority wants.

Data Sources

I rely on several sources for opinion data. One important set of surveys were conducted under the auspices of the Advisory Commission on Intergovernmental Relations (ACIR), a bipartisan federal commission created in 1959 and closed in 1996. The purpose of the commission was to study and make recommendations to improve the federal government's relations with state and local governments. From 1972 to 1995, the ACIR commissioned a set of surveys to measure attitudes toward federal, state, and local governments and their policies. The actual polling of 1,000+ men and women was conducted by the Opinion Research Corporation of Princeton (1972–82) and the Gallup Organization (1983–95).

The second source of opinion data is the American National Election Studies (NES), collected by the Survey Research Center/Center for Political Studies at the University of Michigan. The surveys have been conducted biennially since 1948, usually prior to federal elections, but sometimes afterward. Respondents are asked a huge battery of questions to measure how they feel about issues and candidates. Survey sizes range from 1,181 in 1960 to 2,705 in 1972.

I also use *Los Angeles Times*/ABC News (LAT/ABC) polls, the *April 2003 Internet Survey* conducted by the USC/Caltech Center for the Study of Law and Politics, and a scattering of other sources. These are described in the text when referenced. More precise information on the data sources appears in appendix 3.

Who Wants Smaller Government?

Consider first total revenue and spending. We saw in chapter 3 that the initiative triggered a cut in the size of state and local governments. Was this because special interests used the initiative to hijack the policy process and impose their anti-spending views on a pro-spending majority? Or did the initiative allow an anti-spending majority to restrain pro-spending interests in the legislature?

To answer these questions, we must determine if the majority was in favor of or opposed to spending/revenue cuts during the sample period. Two reasonably good surveys cover the sample period. The ACIR provides fairly clean evidence for 1975–86. Respondents were asked:

> Considering all government services on the one hand and taxes on the other, which of the following statements comes closer to your view?
> 1. Decrease services and taxes.
> 2. Keep services and taxes about where they are.
> 3. Increase services and taxes.
> 4. No opinion.

I like this question because it forces respondents to take into account the link between spending and taxes. Responses to surveys that ask only about spending or only about taxes are harder to interpret, and sometimes contradictory. People tend to respond positively to questions about spending and negatively to questions about taxes.

Figure 4.2 reports the percentage who gave each response in each sample year. The most popular response in every year was to keep services and

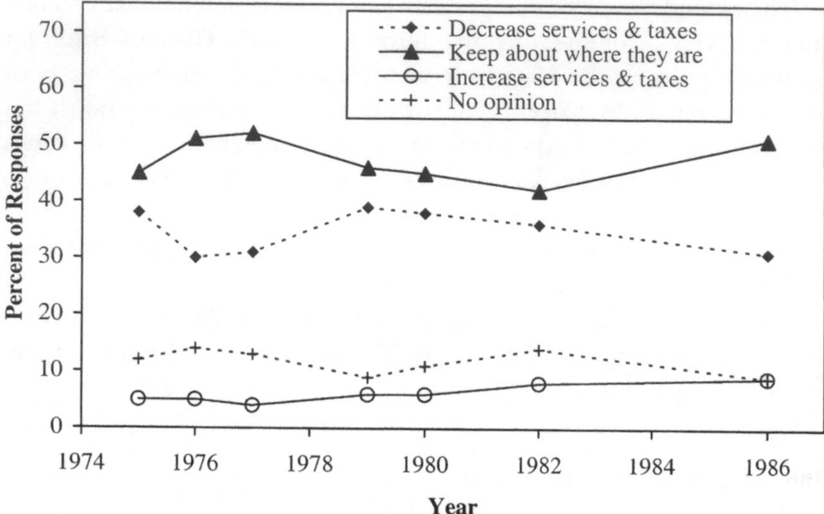

Figure 4.2 Views about Government Services and Taxes, ACIR Surveys.
Survey question: "Considering all government services on the one hand and taxes on the other, which of the following comes closest to your view?"

taxes "about where they are," with the number giving this answer ranging from 42 percent to 52 percent. The second most popular response, not too far behind, was to decrease spending and taxes, with numbers ranging from 30 percent to 39 percent. The least popular response, even below "No opinion" and always in single digits, was to increase spending and taxes.

These numbers, taken at face value, can accommodate two views, depending on how we interpret the "keep services and taxes about where they are" response. At one extreme, if we think all people who said they wanted to keep things "*about* where they are" really wanted to keep things "*exactly* where they are," then there was not a majority in favor of spending cuts or spending increases. The majority (or plurality) view was to maintain the status quo.

However, an argument can be made that a majority of people favored *modest* cuts in spending, perhaps on the order of the 5 percent cuts that actually occurred. Presumably, among the people who wanted to keep spending and taxes "about where they are" were some who would have liked to see modest increases in spending and others who would have liked to see modest cuts. If we suppose, as an approximation, that there were equal numbers of both types of people, then a majority of 56 to 62 percent existed in favor of modest spending cuts (calculated by adding together the number of respondents who explicitly expressed a desire for less spending and the imputed number of people who wanted modest cuts). In this case (and under most reasonable assumptions about the distribution of preferences), a majority of people were in favor of the spending and revenue cuts brought about by the initiative.[4]

This conclusion is reinforced by evidence from *Los Angeles Times*/ABC News polls from 1984–2000. Respondents were asked:

> Would you say you favor smaller government with fewer services, or larger government with many services?

A difference between this question and the ACIR question is that those in favor of modest changes were forced to indicate whether they wanted cuts or increases. A downside is that the question does not allow those people who supported the status quo to express that opinion. Another deficiency of the question, from my perspective, is that it only asks about spending and not taxes. Respondents tend to express more favorable opinions about government when it comes to spending and less favorable views when it comes to taxes. Therefore, I would expect the question to be biased in a pro-spending direction.

Figure 4.3 reports the percentage of respondents giving each answer in the LAT/ABC surveys. The figure shows that those who wanted fewer

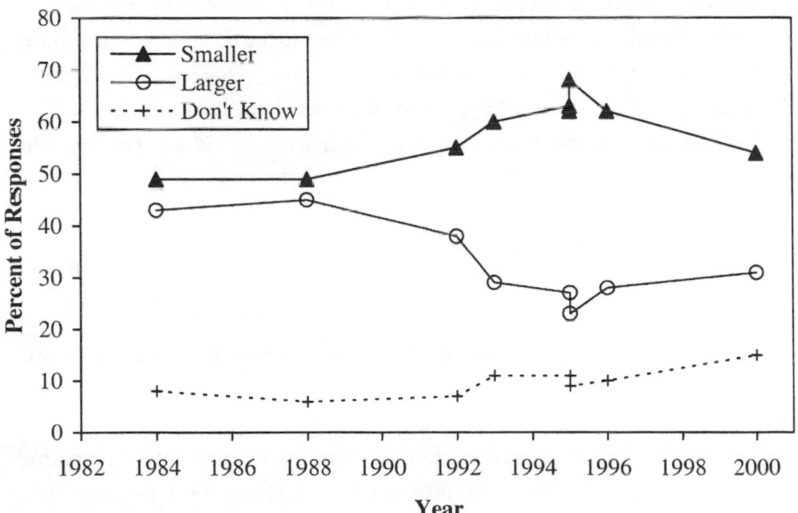

Figure 4.3 Views about Government Services, LAT/ABC Surveys.
Survey question: "Would you say you favor smaller government with fewer services, or larger government with many services?"

government services outnumbered those who wanted more services throughout the sample period. If those without opinions are ignored, we see absolute majorities in favor of spending cuts in all years.

Taken together, figures 4.2 and 4.3 strongly suggest that a majority of people were in favor of spending reductions during our sample period. There is perhaps an argument that a majority favored the status quo, but it feels somewhat forced to me.[5] There is nothing at all in the figures suggesting that a majority favored spending increases. The evidence, then, is that voters wanted less spending throughout the sample period. The initiative, which did cut spending, was therefore pushing policy in the direction favored by the majority. This evidence is inconsistent with the special interest subversion hypothesis.

One concern with these surveys is they only reveal the preference of the *national* majority. The surveys do not reveal if a majority in the *initiative states* favored spending cuts. We saw in chapter 3 (particularly figure 3.3) that citizens of initiative and noninitiative states are quite similar ideologically, but more direct evidence would be helpful. The ACIR data unfortunately are not available for disaggregation, but a similar survey by the NES can be used instead.

The NES asked the following question:

> Some people think the government should provide fewer services, even in areas such as health and education, in order to reduce spending. Other people feel that it is important for the government to provide many more services even if it means an increase in spending. Where would you place yourself on this scale, or haven't you thought about this?
>
> 1. Government should provide many fewer services: reduce spending a lot.
> 2.
> 3.
> 4.
> 5.
> 6.
> 7. Government should provide many more services: increase spending a lot.

Compared to the ACIR question, this question is loaded toward producing a pro-spending response. Health and education, two popular programs, are identified as targets of spending cuts rather than an unpopular program such as welfare, and tax cuts are nowhere mentioned as a benefit of lower spending. As a result, responses to this question tend to indicate a greater demand for spending (although the average is only 4.1) than the ACIR and LAT/ABC surveys, and others that ask more balanced questions.[6] Although the wording induces an upward bias in favor of spending, there is no reason to believe the biases will be different for initiative and noninitiative states. Thus, we can use the survey to assess whether residents of initiative and noninitiative states had significantly different views.

Figure 4.4 shows the percentage of people who gave each response in initiative and noninitiative states. The dots are connected to give a visual sense of the distributions. The main thing to note is that respondents in initiative and noninitiative states had fairly similar opinions on spending. This suggests that the aggregated numbers from the ACIR and LAT/ABC surveys are probably good proxies for opinion in both types of states. Two other patterns are perhaps worth noting in passing. First, the largest difference between initiative and noninitiative states is the number of people who indicated they do not have an opinion about spending: there were 3.6 percent more "don't know" responses in the noninitiative states. It seems possible—although we can only speculate here—that the initiative causes citizens to become more informed. The need to make real tax and spending decisions in the voting booth may lead people to think through their own positions more thoroughly (see Benz and Stutzer forthcoming). The

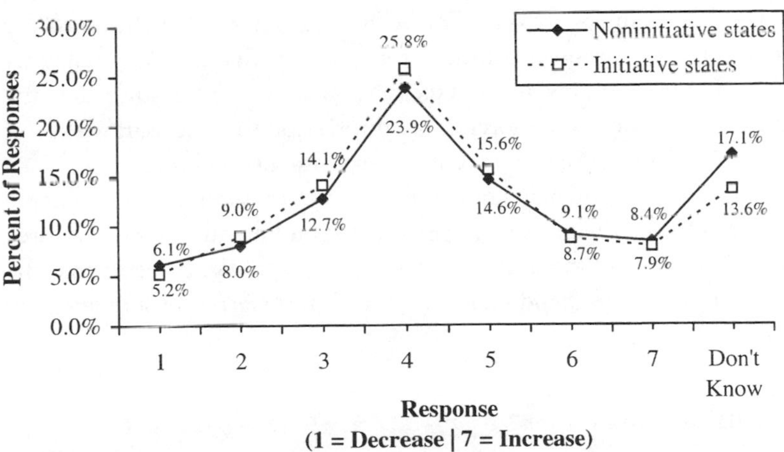

Figure 4.4 Distribution of Opinions on Spending, NES.
Survey question: "Some people feel the government should provide fewer services, even in areas such as health and education, in order to reduce spending. Other people feel that it is important for the government to provide many more services even if it means an increase in spending. Where would you place yourself on this scale?"

second largest difference is in the percent of people who responded with "4"—roughly speaking, these are the people who think spending is just right. We see that 1.9 percent more people gave this response in initiative states than noninitiative states. Similarly, the combined percentage answering 3, 4, and 5 (people who think spending is about right) is 4.3 percent higher in initiative than noninitiative states. This could be taken as evidence that the initiative gets the right spending policy for more voters, but again, some caution in drawing conclusions is warranted from the loaded wording of the question.[7]

Another concern with these survey questions is their failure to distinguish between federal, state, and local spending. Attitudes toward spending at different levels of government are likely to be correlated, but it would be nice to have something more concrete to go on. Fortunately, evidence of a different kind appears in a study by Peltzman (1992), and it corroborates the conclusions from the surveys.

In his study, Peltzman examined the relation between votes received by state governors when they stood for reelection and growth of state spending during their term of office (over 1950–88). A substantial literature in economics and political science documents that voters tend to reward and punish officials for economic performance during their term. Peltzman measured how voters responded to government spending growth in addition to economic performance. He found a significant negative reaction to state spending growth: each +1 percent change in state spending during the governor's term cost .25 percent of the vote when he or she stood for reelection. The important point for our purposes is that the marginal voter considered *state* spending to be excessive. It is also interesting that the magnitudes are modest, reinforcing the impression that the marginal voter wanted only a modest retrenchment of government spending.[8]

To sum up, the evidence consistently shows that a majority of people wanted (modest) reductions in government spending during the last three decades. The effect of the initiative was to cut spending. It seems that the initiative nudged state spending in the direction preferred by a majority of citizens.

Who Wants Decentralization?

Consider next the decentralizing effect of the initiative: initiative states spent less at the state level and more at the local level than noninitiative states. Here we investigate if decentralization conformed or was contrary to the wishes of the majority. The opinion data on this question are at best indirect. The surveys do not ask people whether they wanted to change the mix between state and local spending. Nevertheless, the available polls, if analyzed carefully, provide a good indication what the answer would be.

The longest running survey that speaks to our question was compiled by the ACIR. Respondents were asked the following question:

> From which level of government do you feel you get the most for your money?
> 1. Federal
> 2. State
> 3. Local
> 4. Don't know.

The answers give a broad sense how people assessed the three levels of government during the sample period. Figure 4.5 plots the percentage of people giving each response for surveys conducted between 1970 and 2000. The numbers bounce around over time, but in every year more people selected local government than state government as providing the most value for their money. The ACIR also asked variations of the question: "Which level of government do you think spends your tax dollars most wisely?" (1989, 1991) and "Which level of government do you think responds best to your needs?" (1989). In all cases, local government

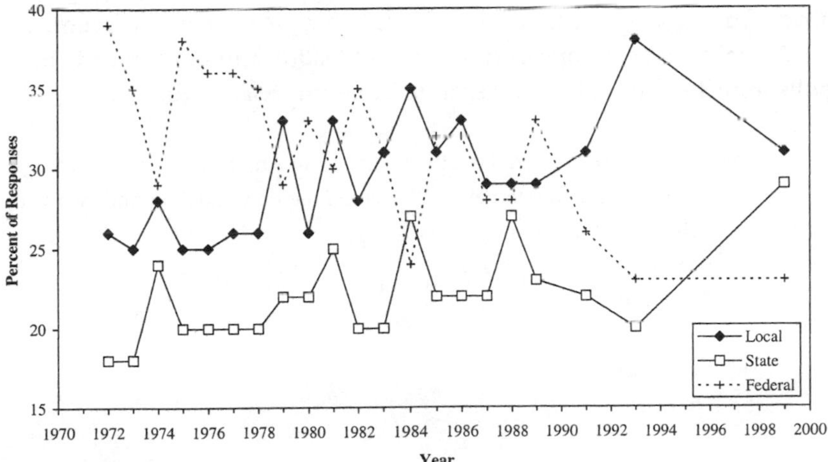

Figure 4.5 Views about Government Spending, ACIR Surveys.
Survey question: "From which level of government do you feel you get the most for your money?"

received the most responses, followed by state government, and then the federal government.

Although figure 4.5 suggests that the majority looked more favorably on local than state government, it does not provide enough information to be conclusive. The problem is that we do not know the relative ranking of state and local governments among those people who ranked federal spending as the most valuable. If, for example, every person who chose federal spending as the most valuable happened to rank state spending ahead of local spending, the majority would have preferred state to local government.

The ACIR asked a different question in 1988 that allows us to get around this problem:

> In your opinion, how often does the federal/state/local government perform its duties efficiently and at the best possible cost?
> 1. Almost all of the time
> 2. Most of the time
> 3. Some of the time
> 4. Hardly ever
> 5. Don't know.

Here each person expressed an opinion about each level of government. Figure 4.6 reports the percentage of people who gave each response. As can be seen, more people considered local government efficient "almost always" or "most of the time" than felt the same about state government.[9]

A similar pattern appears in a series of Gallup and of Hart and Teeter polls from 1975 to 1998 that ask a different but related question:

> I am going to read you a list of institutions in American society (state government/local government). Please tell me how much confidence you, yourself, have in each one.
> 1. A great deal
> 2. Quite a lot
> 3. Some
> 4. Very little or none
> 5. Don't know.

Figure 4.7 compares the responses for state and local governments. Again, more people expressed "a great deal" or "quite a lot" of confidence in local than state government. Based on figures 4.6 and 4.7, it seems likely that

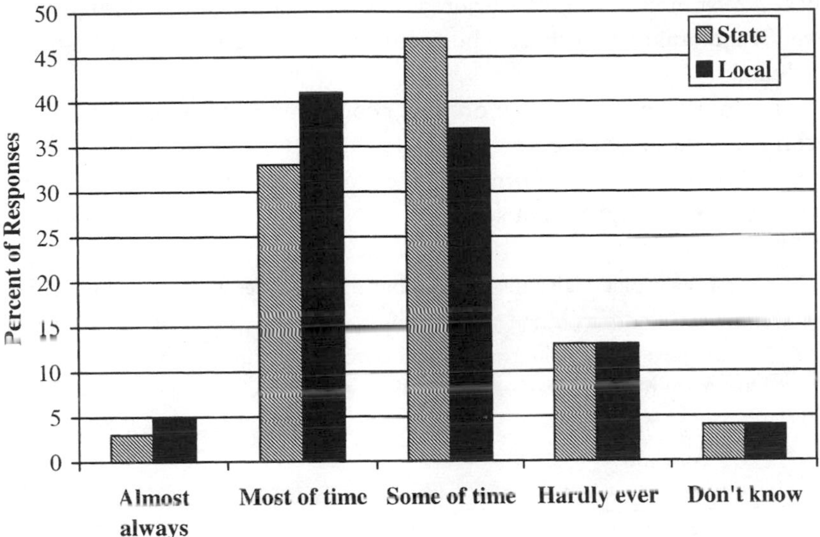

Figure 4.6 "How Often Does Government Perform Its Duties Efficiently and at the Best Cost Possible?"

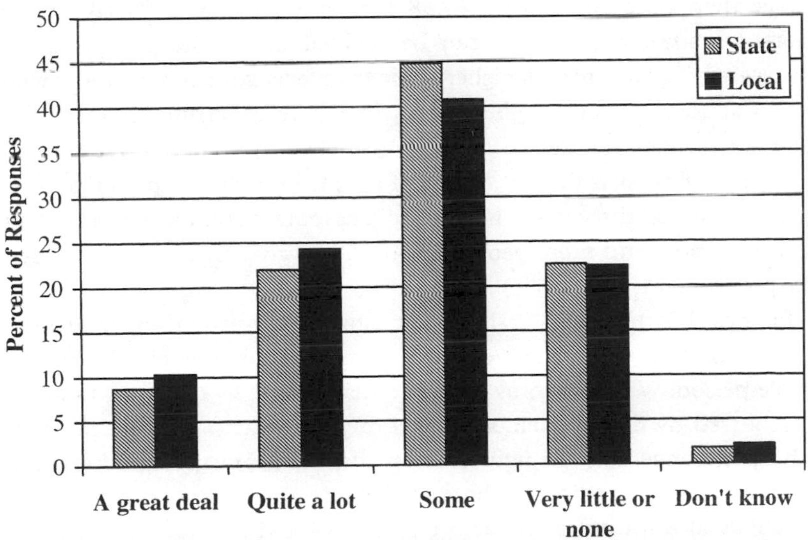

Figure 4.7 "How Much Confidence Do You Have in State/Local Government?"

local governments would be favored over state governments in figure 4.5 even if the rankings of those who listed the federal government first were included.

The most direct evidence on how people compare state to local government comes from NES surveys in 1974, 1976, and 1980. Respondents were asked to rate the performance of federal, state, and local governments separately on an eight-point scale:[10]

> As I read, please give me the number that best describes how good a job you feel that part of the government is doing for the country as a whole (state governments in general/local governments in general).
>
> 0. Very poor job
> 1.
> 2. Poor job
> 3.
> 4. Fair job
> 5.
> 6. Good job
> 7.
> 8. Very good job
> 9. Don't know/No opinion/Haven't thought about it.

As with the ACIR survey, local government received a higher grade on average than state government (4.38 compared to 4.31). Based on the reported grades, respondents can be divided into three groups: those who gave state government a higher grade than local government, those who gave local government a higher grade than state government, and those who graded them the same.

Figure 4.8 reports the percentage of people in each group. The pattern is the same for all three years: most people gave state and local government the same grade, and more people favored local government than favored state government.[11]

Figures 4.5 through 4.8 show that citizens consistently viewed local government as more efficient/effective than state government during the sample period. While it seems plausible that people would want funds to be disbursed by the most efficient level of government, we can only infer such a preference from the figures. In an effort to get even more direct evidence, I placed a question on the *April 2002 Internet Survey* conducted by the USC/Caltech Center for the Study of Law and Politics that explicitly

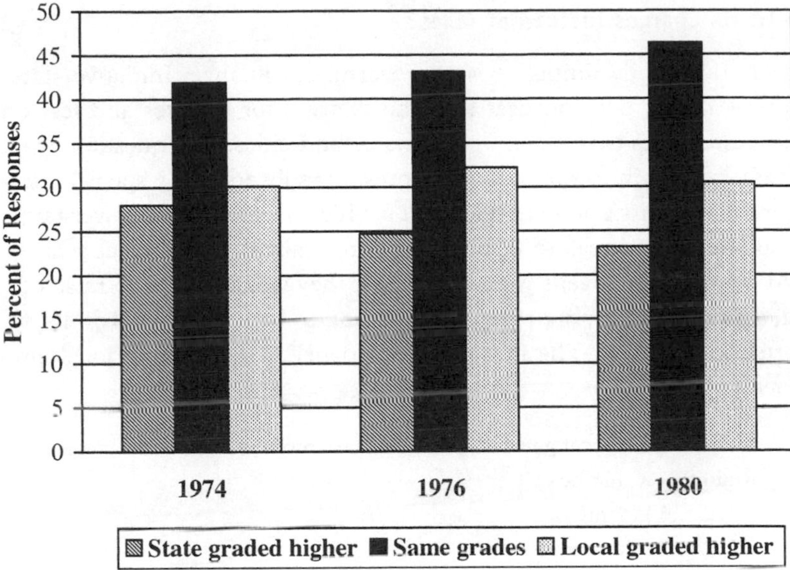

Figure 4.8 Comparison of State and Local Grades for "Government Performance," NES.

asked if people would like to shift spending from state to local government, or from local to state government, or keep it the same. Because the survey was completed over the internet, the sample is unlikely to be representative of the general population. The nature and extent of the biases are not yet known, but the responses to a question about the overall size of government suggests the respondents are more conservative than the general population.[12] Since state spending offers greater scope for redistribution, sample respondents may be more inclined toward decentralization than the population at large. Be that as it may, the survey at least provides concrete information on the views of a subset of the population. The most popular response, selected by 30 percent, was to shift spending from state to local government. Almost as many people, 29 percent, wanted to keep spending about the same. Only 14 percent want to shift local spending to the state.

To summarize, the initiative shifted the disbursement of funds from state to local governments over the last thirty years. Every piece of opinion data we have seen suggests that the majority of voters approved of a shift in that direction. Again, it seems the initiative brought about a policy change that was supported by the majority.

Who Wants Charges Instead of Taxes?

A third effect of the initiative is on government finance. Initiative states and cities relied more on user fees and charges for services and less on broad-based taxes than noninitiative states and cities. The question again is whether this shift toward charges represents subversion by special interests or the majority's actual preference for higher charges and lower taxes. Opinion data that speak to this question are available from select years of the ACIR survey. Citizens were asked how they would prefer to raise revenue, assuming that more revenue was going to be raised. The results are reported in table 4.1. The first question (panel A) focused on local government:

> Suppose your local government must raise more revenue. The better way to do this would be . . .
> 1. Local income tax
> 2. Local sales tax

Table 4.1 Views about How to Raise Local and State Revenue

A. "Suppose your local government must raise more revenue. The better way to do this would be . . ." (1981, 1986, 1987)

	1981	1986	1987
Local income tax	7%	9	9
Local sales tax	21	26	20
Local property tax	5	7	9
Charges for specific services	55	49	33
Other/don't know	12	9	29

B. "If your state government decided to raise a small amount of additional revenue to help meet costs and improve services, which one of these would you prefer?" (1987)

Cigarette and liquor taxes	54%
Gasoline and diesel fuel taxes	4
State income taxes	6
State sales tax	8
User fees or charges	13
Other/don't know	7

C. "If there is a need to raise additional revenues to improve public works services, which one of these would you prefer?" (1988)

User fees or charges for specific services	35%
Special taxes dedicated to funding specific services	37
General purpose taxes	12
Other/don't know	16

Note: The question in Panel A was slightly different in 1987 than in 1981 and 1986; see Appendix 3.

3. Local property tax
4. Charges for specific services
5. Don't know/no answer.

The responses were similar for all three years that the question was asked. Charges were favored by the greatest number of people, and commanded an absolute majority of those who expressed a preference in 1981 and 1986. In 1987, the number of people who preferred a tax of some sort (income, property, sales) exceeded the number who preferred charges, 38 percent to 33 percent. The decline in popularity of the "charges" answer may be due to a change in question wording. In 1987, the question enumerated specific charges: "things like the use of local parks and swimming pools, parking, library use, garbage pick-up, or ambulance service." The unusually large number of "other/don't know" responses in 1987 was due to 17 percent of respondents who rejected the premise of the question and volunteered that taxes should not be raised at all. Taken together, the responses suggest that most people would have opted for charges instead of taxes if forced to choose.[13]

The second question (panel B) asked about state revenue.

> If your state government decided to raise a small amount of additional revenue to help meet costs and improve services, which one of these would you prefer?
>
> 1. An increase in cigarette and liquor taxes
> 2. An increase in the general state sales tax
> 3. An increase in gasoline and diesel fuel taxes
> 4. An increase in state income tax rates, or an income tax if your state does not now have one
> 5. An increase in user fees or charges for things like the use of state parks, automobile registration, boating licenses, or toll roads
> 6. Don't know.

Among the options, the runaway favorite was cigarette and liquor taxes, supported by 54 percent of respondents. These are neither broad-based taxes nor a user fees, although some people may have viewed them as akin to a user fee since they can be avoided with modest changes in behavior (unlike sales and income taxes). Leaving aside cigarette and liquor taxes, we see that user fees and charges were the most popular revenue source.

The third question (panel C) did not distinguish between levels of government and simply addressed the need to raise additional revenue.

> If there is a need to raise additional revenue to improve public works services, which one of these would you prefer?
> 1. User fees or charges for specific services
> 2. Special taxes dedicated to funding specific services
> 3. General purpose taxes
> 4. Other
> 5. Don't know.

General purpose taxes were the least popular way to raise revenue. More than three times as many people preferred user fees or charges. The most popular response, selected by 37 percent of respondents, was "special taxes dedicated to funding special services." In practice, this probably meant something like gasoline, cigarette, or liquor taxes, but whether respondents understood the question this way is unclear. Running a close second was "user fees or charges for specific services," selected by 35 percent of respondents.

I placed a related question on the *April 2002 Internet Survey* that simply asked if people would like to see more, less, or the same reliance on taxes versus charges. The potential (conservative) bias of the internet survey discussed above should be kept in mind. The most popular response, selected by 37 percent, was to keep the mix of taxes and charges about the same. A close second with 33 percent was to reduce taxes and rely more on charges. Only 8 percent wanted to rely more on taxes and less on charges.

To summarize, the survey evidence shows that most people preferred user fees and charges to broad-based taxes for both state and local government. We saw in chapter 3 that the initiative shifted the revenue mix in exactly this direction at both the state and local level. Again, the initiative pushed policy in the direction favored by the majority.

Conclusion

Fiscal policy from 1970 to 2000 differed between initiative and noninitiative states in three systematic ways: initiatives states (1) spent/taxed less, (2) decentralized expenditure from state to local governments, and (3) raised less money from taxes and more from charges for services.

This chapter reviewed a great deal of opinion data to assess what voters thought about these policies. The data were collected from a variety of sources, spanned several decades, and solicited opinions using a number of different questions. Yet, remarkably, they all tell essentially the same story: a majority of people preferred the policies brought about by the initiative. None of the polls individually is conclusive, at least to me, but I find their cumulative effect rather convincing. It is hard to escape the conclusion that the initiative promoted the interests of the many and not the few.

Some thoughtful observers, such as Broder (2000), have argued that the initiative allows wealthy individuals and groups to bring about policies contrary to the public interest. Their argument is based on the observation that the initiative process is expensive to use, and appears to be dominated by rich individuals and groups. The evidence here, however, shows that even if wealthy interests are prominent players in initiative politics, their efforts ultimately redound to the benefit of the majority. There is no mystery how this could happen. Without the initiative, voters are forced to accept the policy choices of the legislature. With the initiative, voters are given choices. If the alternative on an initiative is worse than the legislature's policy, the initiative can be rejected and no harm is done. If the alternative is better, the voters can accept the initiative and are better off. In short, even if there is unequal access when it comes to proposing initiatives, the ability of voters to filter out the bad proposals and keep the good ones allows the process to work to the advantage of the majority.

To be clear, the evidence here shows that the initiative serves the many and not the few when it comes to fiscal policy. None of this precludes the possibility that the initiative allows special interests to subvert policy in some other dimension, such as regulation or social policy.[14] However, to say that something is possible does not mean it is true or even likely to be true. Since all of the evidence to date is inconsistent with the subversion hypothesis, the burden of proof would seem to be upon those who argue for the special interest view. Until such evidence is produced, at least the subversion hypothesis should no longer be peddled as embodying either knowledge or wisdom.[15]

Finally, I want to emphasize that the evidence is value neutral; it does not tell us whether the initiative process is a good or bad form of government. The evidence simply shows that the initiative promotes the will of the majority. To be sure, majority rule is a core principle of democracy, but it is not the only one. For example, we also care about protecting the rights of minorities from the tyranny of the majority. To make a judgment about the desirability of the initiative requires a weighing of all its consequences, not just whether it promotes or hinders majority rule. Chapters 8 and 9 discuss some of these other consequences in depth.

CHAPTER 5 Conservative or Liberal

The initiative, from the evidence so far, is a fiscal conservative's dream. During the period 1970–2000, it cut the overall size of government measured by revenue or expenditure. It removed spending authority from the hands of distant state governments and gave it to local governments, which probably curbed intrastate redistribution. And it switched revenue out of broad-based taxes and into user fees, forcing those who benefit from government services to pay for them. It is tempting to view the initiative as an inherently conservative device.

This chapter reports evidence suggesting that such a view is probably incorrect. The initiative's conservative influence during 1970–2000 is better seen as a response to idiosyncratic features of the political environment. We saw a hint of this in the municipal data, where city initiatives actually led to more spending in the 1980s and 1990s. This chapter investigates how the initiative affected state and local fiscal policy in the early twentieth century, specifically 1902–42. The data are sparse and sometimes coarse, but good enough to generate reliable estimates. It turns out that the initiative *increased* the size of government—again, as measured by revenue or spending—in the early part of the century. Since the initiative sometimes pushes policy in a liberal ("progressive" in the language of the early twentieth century) direction and other times in a conservative direction, it does not seem to be ideologically biased.[1] A more natural view is that it simply promotes the interest of the majority, whatever that may be.

This conclusion should provide some grist for policymakers and activists who see the initiative as a cause or cure for fiscal policies they dislike. For better or worse, the initiative is not a sure path to limited government.

The evidence also touches on a more theoretical issue concerning the nature of representative government. The flip side of "the initiative brought about fiscally conservative policies" is "the legislature brought about fiscally liberal policies." Since the liberal tendency of legislatures in the last thirty years seems contrary to the wishes of the majority, what does this tell us about how representative government works? I will take up this question more directly in the next chapter, but some preliminary conclusions emerge from the results in this chapter. In particular, the fact that citizens sometimes want more spending than their representatives deliver, as in the early twentieth century, weighs against the popular "leviathan" theory that representative government inevitably grows larger than citizens wish.

The Initiative Drove Up Spending 1902–42

The main obstacle to estimating the effect of the initiative before World War II is the paucity of fiscal data, particularly for local governments. Aggregate numbers are not too difficult to find, but information on individual states and localities is hard to come by. Fortunately, Richard Sylla, John Legler, and John Wallis recently assembled a unique data set from the original documents of the U.S. Census. There are some inconsistencies in the information collected by the Census Bureau, but the primary sources are good enough to allow construction of comparable numbers for each state and its local governments in 1902, 1913, 1932, and 1942. Demographic information for the control variables is available from the Census. With information available for 48 states each year (Alaska and Hawaii were not states at the time), the basic sample has 192 observations.

I approach the data as I have throughout the book, by estimating revenue and expenditure regressions that compare initiative and noninitiative states. The regressions include the same control variables as in chapter 3 (so far as the data allow) to maintain comparability with the postwar results.

Table 5.1 reports the main findings. As usual, each column reports a single regression with standard errors (adjusted for within-state clustering) in parentheses. The dependent variable is indicated at the top of the column, and represents the combined total for all governments (state and local) in the state. Financial numbers are expressed in year-2000 dollars per capita. Each regression contains four year-dummies whose coefficients are not reported.

In column (1), we see that initiative states raised $43.54 per capita more than noninitiative states. Column (2) shows that initiative states outspent noninitiative states by $36.38 per capita. Both affects come close but fail to achieve statistical significance at the 10 percent level. The initiative effect works out to an increase of 8 percent for revenue and 6 percent for expenditure, compared to sample averages. In contrast to the evidence

Table 5.1 Regressions of State and Local Revenue and Spending on Initiative and Control Variables, 1902–42

Variables	Revenue (1)	Expenditure (2)	Revenue (3)	Expenditure (4)
Dummy = 1 if initiative state	43.54	36.38	120.20	101.91
	(27.90)	(26.25)	(76.93)	(71.75)
Signature requirement × initiative dummy	—	—	−8.03	−4.25
			(10.20)	(9.17)
Income	0.06***	0.06***	0.05***	0.05***
	(0.01)	(0.01)	(0.01)	(0.01)
Federal aid	0.91***	1.82***	0.88***	1.68***
	(0.13)	(0.13)	(0.14)	(0.15)
Population, logarithm	29.28*	33.17**	1.30	6.38
	(14.98)	(15.93)	(19.49)	(23.06)
Urban population, %	1.38	1.66**	3.15**	3.42**
	(0.87)	(0.82)	(1.38)	(1.56)
Growth of population, previous 5 years, %	−0.82	−0.13	0.92	0.96
	(0.79)	(0.73)	(0.80)	(0.95)
Dummy = 1 if southern state	−68.51*	−51.61	−16.66	−18.78
	(35.28)	(33.87)	(50.06)	(46.45)
Dummy = 1 if western state	46.51	35.93	40.54	50.88
	(29.75)	(24.24)	(34.95)	(33.48)
R^2	0.979	0.982	0.984	0.988

Note: Each column is a regression with 192 observations covering the years 1902, 1913, 1932, and 1942, and all 48 states in the Union at the time. Standard errors adjusted for within-state clustering are in parentheses beneath the coefficient estimates. Revenue and expenditure are combined totals for state and local government. Revenue, expenditure, income, and federal aid are expressed in year-2000 dollars per capita. All regressions included four year dummies whose coefficients are not reported. Significance levels are indicated as follows: * = 10%, ** = 5%, *** = 1%.

from 1970–2000, it appears the initiative drove up spending in the first part of the twentieth century.

One reason for the imprecision of the estimates in columns (1) and (2) is that all initiative states are treated alike. In columns (3) and (4), initiative states are differentiated according to the signature requirement to qualify a measure for the ballot. If initiative states taxed and spent more because of the initiative, the difference between initiative and noninitiative states should drop off as the signature requirement rises. Consistent with this interpretation, the coefficients on the signature requirement variable are negative and the coefficients on the initiative dummy remain positive.

The net effect of the initiative depends on both the initiative dummy and signature requirement coefficients, and on the signature requirement itself, and cannot be seen from regressions (3) and (4). To make the net effect more transparent, figure 5.1 reports the effect of the initiative by signature requirement using the estimates from regressions (3) and (4). For example, the first bar on the left indicates that an initiative state with a 2 percent signature requirement raised $104 per capita more than an otherwise equal noninitiative state. Significance levels are indicated with asterisks above the bars. As can be seen, the initiative increased revenue and expenditure for all signature requirements in the sample. For a state with a 4 percent signature requirement, the initiative drove up revenue by $88 per capita, roughly 16 percent of the average, and drove up spending by $85 per capita, roughly 14 percent of the average. The initiative effect is different from zero at conventional levels of significance for signature requirements from 2 percent to 8 percent when it comes to revenue, and from 3 percent to 9 percent when it comes to expenditure.

The general pattern here—more spending and taxing in initiative states—is robust to a number of alternative specifications. For example, the results still appear when the NOMINATE ideology variable is added, when the West dummy is deleted, and when state fixed effects are included. The results also survive inclusion of additional control variables, such as the percentage of the population that is male, the percentage that is older than 65, and the percentage immigrant. See Matsusaka (2000) for a battery of robustness tests.

Leviathan Is Not Enough

Initiative states spent more than noninitiative states before World War II, and spent less afterwards. The data speak clearly, but what do they mean? What are they telling us about American government? One thing, I

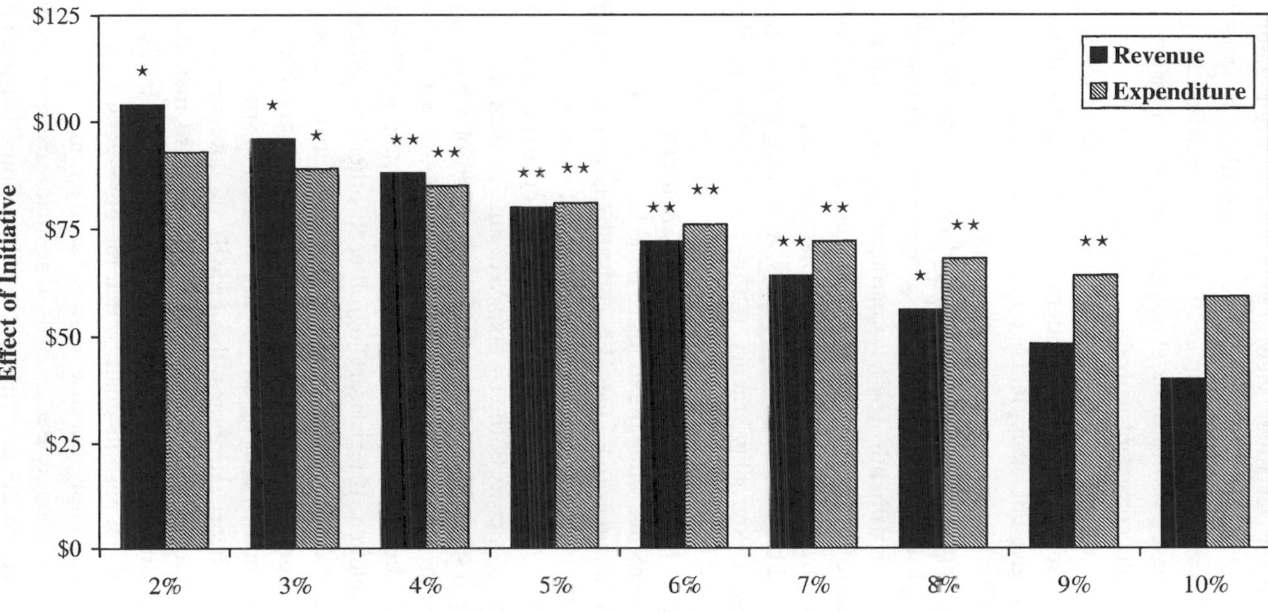

Figure 5.1 Effect of the Initiative on Revenue and Expenditure by Signature Requirement, 1902–42

Note: This chart indicates the difference between revenue/expenditure in initiative and noninitiative states depending on the signature requirement. For example, the first bar shows that revenue was $104 per capita higher in an initiative state with a 2 percent signature requirement than in an otherwise identical noninitiative state. Estimates are computed from regressions (3) and (4) of table 5.1, and expressed in year-2000 dollars. Significance levels are reported above the bars as follows: * = 10%, ** = 5%.

believe, is that the popular "leviathan" view of government is not enough to explain fiscal behavior. Here I briefly outline the leviathan view, and explain why it provides an incomplete explanation of the evidence. In the next chapter I will suggest a way to think about government—a theory, if you will—that is generally consistent with the evidence.

The leviathan view was developed largely to explain the explosive growth of government spending in the twentieth century. The broad pattern is well known: to give one example, government revenue at all levels was 7 percent of GNP at the start of the century, and close to 40 percent at the century's end. Explanations for the growth of government fall into two groups, broadly speaking: either it was a response to citizen demands, or it was in spite of citizen demands. The leviathan view belongs to the second group. According to the leviathan view, government takes on a life of its own, expanding regardless of the wishes of its masters, the people.[2]

Overspending could happen for several reasons. According to the "fiscal commons" or "fiscal externality" theory, the root problem is that the benefits of spending are often concentrated while the costs are dispersed across the population.[3] For example, the primary beneficiaries of a city park are the nearby residents, while the funds to build and maintain it are provided by taxpayers at large. To budget efficiently, officials should weigh the benefits against the costs of each project. However, since legislators represent narrowly defined geographic constituencies, they may be unconcerned with the portion of costs borne by taxpayers outside their district. If local taxpayers are responsible for a low enough fraction of a project's costs, their representative may support a spending program with total costs in excess of benefits. The tax base in effect is a "common pool" that ends up being overexploited. If legislators logroll each other's programs, the collective outcome can be a large number of wasteful spending programs. In such an environment, the initiative would enable voters to eliminate the inefficient programs, causing an overall reduction in spending.

Another leviathan theory attributes the growth of government to bureaucracies.[4] The premise here is that bureaucrats seek to maximize their agency's budget. Bureaucrats want a larger budget because it allows their agency to better accomplish its goals, which the bureaucrat believes are important, or more simply because a larger budget increases the bureaucrat's prestige and power. Because most agencies are monopoly suppliers of their services to the government, they have some bargaining power that may allow extraction of rents from elected officials in the form of an inefficiently large budget. The initiative could allow voters to cap agency budgets at an efficient level, leading to a decline in total spending.

Despite their differences in details, leviathan theories (and others that imply systematically excessive government spending) have in common the implication that the initiative reduces government spending. The leviathan view therefore seems to provide a way to understand the 1970–2000 evidence: in all states government tended to expand more than the majority wanted, but in initiative states the majority was able to curb the growth. The problem with the leviathan explanation is that if government inevitably grows too large, we should not observe the initiative increasing spending in some periods; we should see the initiative cutting expenditure whenever and wherever the process is available. However, as we have seen in this chapter, the initiative did drive up state and local spending in the early twentieth century, and as we saw in chapter 3, the initiative also drove up spending in cities in the 1980s and 1990s. The leviathan theory seems to be missing something.

Conclusion

Since 1970, the initiative has prodded states toward fiscally conservative policies: lower spending, lower taxes, less centralization of spending authority, and greater reliance on user fees. This chapter evaluates whether the initiative is inherently a conservative institution. It is not: evidence from the early part of the twentieth century shows that the initiative *increased* government expenditure at the time by about 6 percent, pushing fiscal policy in a liberal ("progressive") direction. The initiative does not appear to have an ideological bias. Rather, it seems to be biased toward the majority, whether conservative or liberal.

In this chapter I also began the task of identifying a framework, or theory, that could help us understand the somewhat paradoxical evidence. As a first step, I suggested that the class of leviathan theories are not enough to explain the evidence, at least as they are currently formulated. These theories posit that governments systematically expand beyond the wishes of the electorate. If true, the initiative should always reduce the size of the government, which is not the case.

Even so, I would not dismiss the leviathan view entirely. It still seems possible that voters disliked the growth of certain government programs and in certain periods. Indeed, the next chapter sketches an explanation of the evidence with exactly this flavor.

PART TWO 

Explaining the Facts

CHAPTER 6 

When Legislators Get Out of Step

So far the book has concentrated on questions with fairly direct answers: How does the initiative change fiscal policy? And do the changes favor the many or the few? Several facts emerged from the data: the initiative was used to increase spending in the early twentieth century; it was used to cut spending in the last three decades of the century; and the initiative brought about fiscal policies favored by the majority, not a special interest minority. The facts provide more-or-less direct answers to the initial questions, but they also raise other questions: *Why* did initiative states spend more than noninitiative states in the early twentieth century? *Why* did they spend less at the end of the century? To answer these questions, we need to understand how legislatures make decisions. Since the initiative appears to push policy toward what the majority wants, we need to know why legislatures sometimes choose policies that the majority does not want.

The divergence in fiscal policies of initiative and noninitiative states at the beginning and end of the century also appeared intermittently *within* these periods. Figure 6.1 provides an illustration by plotting the difference in spending between initiative and noninitiative states year-by-year, from 1957 to 2000 (the chart shows, for example, that initiative states spent $87 per capita less than noninitiative states in 1957, all else being equal). The figure captures the tendency of initiative states to spend less than noninitiative states throughout the period (as chapter 3 describes in more detail), but also reveals that the difference rose and fell over time. The antispending effect of the initiative was particularly large in two periods, the early 1970s and the 1990s. The gap between initiative and noninitiative states closed in the mid-1980s to the point that we cannot claim statistically that a difference even existed from 1983 to 1988. Since initiative states seem to reflect the majority's preferences, figure 6.1 suggests that policies in noninitiative states drifted out of alignment with voter preferences for a while in the 1970s and 1990s. The dynamic nature of behavior—the possibility that legislatures might get out of step with voters for several years but then find their way back—has not received a great deal of attention in the scholarly literature.

The goal of this chapter is to weave together some of the theory that does exist to provide a framework for understanding why initiative and noninitiative states periodically choose different spending levels. I suggest that representative government is subject to certain frictions that cause representatives to get out of step with their constituents. When they do get out of step, legislatures choose policies that a majority of their constituents dislike. In initiative states, policies are brought back into alignment with constituent preferences quickly. In noninitiative states, the adjustment process is slower, working through the machinery of periodic candidate elections. In chapter 7, I show how the theory provides a way to understand the divergence of fiscal policies in initiative and noninitiative states during the twentieth century. In particular, I suggest why initiative states spent *more* than noninitiative states early in the century and *less* late in the century, particularly the 1970s and 1990s.

Throughout this chapter, I assume that certain facts have been established—initiative and noninitiative states periodically select different fiscal policies and those in the initiative states are closer to what the majority wants—and attempt to assemble a theory that is consistent with them, what is essentially an exercise in inductive theorizing. The "facts" that are the input to this exercise are not as simple or obvious as this chapter sometimes suggests, something I have tried to make clear in the rest of the

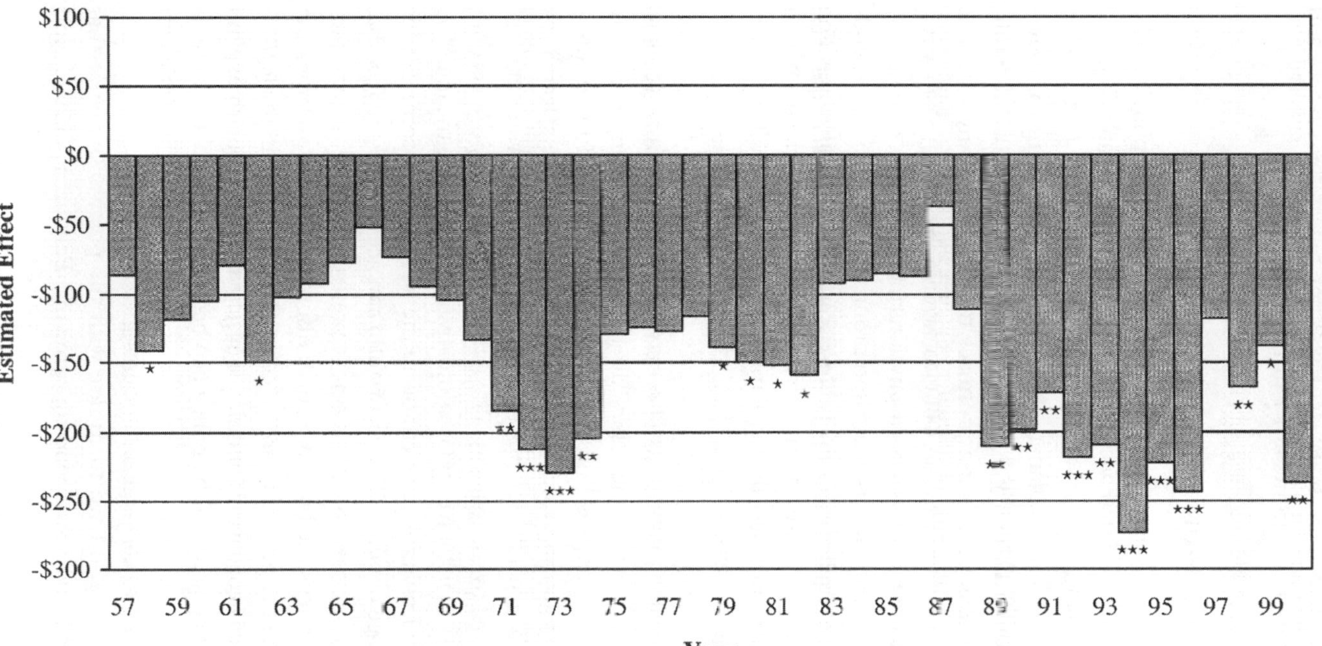

Figure 6.1 Estimated Effect of the Initiative on Expenditure Year-by-Year, 1957–2000.

Note: This figure shows the difference in per capita spending between initiative and noninitiative states for each year. For example, the first bar shows that initiative states spent $86 per capita less than noninitiative states in 1957. The estimates are from a regression of per capita spending on the usual controls and year-specific initiative dummies. All states are included except Alaska and Wyoming. Estimates are expressed in year-2000 dollars. Significance levels are indicated with asterisks below the bars: * = 10%, ** = 5%, *** = 1%.

book. For ease of exposition, however, I will not repeat the caveats and detailed counterarguments from earlier in the book.

Frictions in the Representation Process

The two most prominent theories of how governments select policies—the median voter theory associated with Downs (1957) and the interest group theory associated with Stigler (1971), Peltzman (1976), and Becker (1983)—do not offer easy explanations for the facts we want to understand. The median voter theory is driven by competition between candidates. Candidates make campaign promises to attract as many voters as possible, eventually converging on policies favored by the median voter (that is, policies a majority prefers to any alternative). Once elected, the winner faithfully implements his campaign promises, and taxes and spending end up perfectly aligned with the preferences of the median voter. The problem is that in such a world, initiative and noninitiative states would end up with the same policies (the median voter's favorite), contrary to the facts we are trying to explain.[1]

In the interest group theory, policies are the outcome of competition between interest groups. Politicians choose policies to maximize votes as in the median voter theory, but they do not count all people equally because some groups (typically smaller groups with concentrated interests) are better at delivering votes than others. As a result, the selected tax and spending levels generally are not optimal for the median voter and are unlikely to be favored by the majority. The interest group theory can account for different policies in initiative and noninitiative states because the initiative changes the rules of political competition to the advantage of some groups and the disadvantage of others. The theory also can account for the fact that initiative states come closer to the majority's preferences if we assume that the initiative strengthens the hand of broad, disorganized groups, providing a counterbalance to the power of narrow, concentrated groups in the legislature. However, the theory would require significant fleshing out to explain why the size and magnitude of the policy gap between initiative and noninitiative states changes over time. And the interest group theory gives little reason to expect policies to converge, as it seems they do.

Both theories are also hard to square with the postwar evidence that voters punish officials for spending growth. Peltzman (1992) and Niskanen (1973) document that elected officials who presided over rapid expenditure growth tended to lose votes when they stood for reelection. Peltzman (1992, 328) notes: "None of these models [median voter or interest group] imply any political penalty for the excess size of the public sector. Political agents deliver that result because it maximizes their vote."[2]

Conscience and Shirking

Why then would some states end up with policies that a majority of citizens dislike? One possibility is that politicians deliberately ignore the wishes of the electorate. A legislator might "vote his conscience" instead of following the majority view in the belief that he knows better than his constituents. Such behavior has long been considered a legitimate prerogative (or even a responsibility) of elected officials.[3] Indeed, the Founders believed that a legislator's freedom to follow his or her own counsel was one of the virtues of representative government (*Federalist* no. 63):

> There are particular moments in public affairs, when the people stimulated by some irregular passion, or some illicit advantage, or misled by the artful misrepresentations of interested men, may call for measures which they themselves will afterwards be the most ready to lament and condemn. In these critical moments, how salutary will be the interference of some temperate and respectable body of citizens, in order to check the misguided career, and to suspend the blow meditated by the people against themselves, until reason, justice and truth, can regain their authority over the public mind?

"Your representative owes you, not his industry only, but his judgment," said Edmund Burke in his speech to the electors of Bristol, "and he betrays you, instead of serving you, if he sacrifices it to your opinion."

Modern observers take a more skeptical view of such behavior. Representatives typically are seen as agents of the voters, with a duty to follow the wishes of their constituents. Willful neglect of constituent preferences is considered "shirking." According to this view, legislators might choose policies that the majority dislikes in order to advance their personal policy objectives ("ideologies") or to curry favor with campaign contributors.[4]

It is natural to ask why elections don't entirely prevent shirking.[5] After all, representatives who want to stay in office will try to please their constituents, and those who flagrantly ignore the wishes of the electorate will eventually be voted out of office. We can point to at least three distinct problems.

First, elected officials may have interests qua elected officials that are distinct from those of ordinary citizens. "If we wish to face facts squarely, we must recognize that, in modern democracies . . . politics will unavoidably be a career. This in turn spells recognition of a distinct professional interest in the individual politician and of a distinct group interest in the political profession as such" (Schumpeter 1950, 285). There are certain issues in which politicians will have shared values, and replacing one with another is unlikely to result in a change in policy. An example is term limits. Politicians are generally hostile to term limits even in the face of overwhelming popularity among the electorate. The fact that term limits were placed on legislators in 23 of 24 initiative states and only 3 of 26 noninitiative states testifies to the inability of candidate elections to bring about policies that are opposed by professional politicians en bloc.

Even so, issues where politicians have distinct interests from the majority of their constituents are probably the exception rather than the rule. A more important reason why elections work imperfectly is that voters have incomplete information about what government does. It would be hard enough for an ordinary citizen to know much about the activities of any particular officeholder, but the citizen is called upon to monitor not one but a multiplicity of representatives. In any given four-year period, I am asked to vote for candidates for about two dozen offices: three federal (president, senator, congressman), eight statewide (governor, lieutenant governor, attorney general, secretary of state, treasurer, controller, insurance commissioner, superintendent of public instruction), two state legislators, a board of equalization member, a county commissioner, a county sheriff, a city mayor, a city councilman, school board members, as well as numerous judicial positions. Voters do have cues to cut through the information overload, but these can never be perfect. Inevitably, voters are going to make some mistakes at the polls, and not every unfaithful agent will be rooted out.

A third reason why elections might not solve agency problems is that candidates represent "bundles" of issues. If a race between two candidates hinged on a single issue, the voter's task would be fairly simple: choose the candidate closest to his or her position. In practice, though, candidates take positions on a large number of issues. The voter seldom has the choice of a candidate with identical policy views along every dimension. Instead, the voter has to weigh the various issues and choose the candidate who is closest "on average" or on a few key issues. For many voters, this boils down to a choice between the lesser of two evils. As a result, legislators might be in tune with their constituents on high profile issues, but act against their interests on less visible or less important issues.[6]

Honest Mistakes

Legislators might approve a policy the majority dislikes because they misunderstand the electorate's preferences, what might be called an "honest mistake." Information is so costly that it seldom pays to collect enough of it to be absolutely certain what policy the majority wants. Faced with limited information, even representatives who try to act as faithful agents of the voters are bound to make mistakes from time to time.[7]

This is not to say that legislators know nothing about constituent preferences. In fact, they often have a great deal of information about how voters view the policy options. One source of information is opinion surveys. Opinion surveys are increasingly sophisticated and common. However, we should not exaggerate the information they provide. Despite their proliferation in the last few decades, survey data are generally available for only a small set of high profile issues. Even when they exist, survey data do not always speak clearly since subtle variations in question wording and context can affect responses. And for some issues, respondents might not have well-formed opinions; their responses might simply parrot back conventional wisdom. As Lupia and McCubbins (1998) point out, voters are likely to use information cues and shortcuts to make decisions instead of developing substantive knowledge on an issue. If citizens rely on the advice of informed "cue providers," their underlying preferences will be unmeasurable until the cue is available, which might not happen until shortly before an election. This is one reason why early polls on ballot propositions are notoriously unreliable (Matsusaka and McCarty 2001).

Another important source of information about constituent preferences is election returns. When two candidates take opposing positions on a prominent issue, voter preferences are clearly signaled at the ballot box. Even so, election returns rarely speak clearly about specific issues. Candidates usually take positions on a large number of issues, making it unclear which issue(s) determined the election outcome. Voters may not base their decisions on issue positions; they may care more about a candidate's personal characteristics or a constituent service he or she provided in the past. Both candidates may take the same position on an issue, in which case election returns provide no information about voter preferences on that issue. On top of all this, elections are periodic, typically two to four years apart. Election returns thus provide a noisy signal of preferences so that even a well-intentioned representative might require several elections to understand what the people really want.

Gerrymandering: When Majority Rule Leads to Minority Rule

One other cause of nonmajority policies is worth noting. It stems from the fact that legislators in the United States are elected from geographic districts. District lines can be drawn so as to give a particular group a disproportionate share of the seats in the legislature, what is usually called "gerrymandering." For example, in California, a Democratic gerrymander gave the party control of about two-thirds of the seats in the legislature in the 1980s even though it attracted only about half of the votes. Buchanan and Tullock (1962) showed theoretically that a clever gerrymander can give control of the government to a group as small as a quarter of the population even when the "one person, one vote" rule applies. When districts can contain unequal numbers of people, as was the case in the United States until the late 1960s, even smaller minorities can rule. The important point is that a numerical minority can control the government even if the majority rules in each district.[8]

How Legislatures Get Out of Step

We have now identified frictions in electoral institutions that might cause legislatures to choose policies the majority dislikes. What remains is to flesh out how these frictions can lead to periodic divergences between the policies of initiative and noninitiative states.

Divergences are triggered by changes in the preferences of ordinary citizens. Preferences can shift for a number of reasons. First, a change in the aggregate economic environment can alter the electorate's views about the desirability of government programs. For example, voters might be more willing to support welfare spending in the midst of recession than during an economic boom (they might reason that during a recession people are unemployed because of bad luck while in a boom most of the unemployed are just lazy). A change in an individual's personal economic situation might shift the private benefits and costs of government programs. For example, evidence suggests that as people grow richer, they become more willing to pay for environmental amenities such as clean air and water (Kahn and Matsusaka 1997). People with children and homeowners might be more willing to support expenditures for public schools (Fischel 2001). Similarly, support for state spending on sewers, parks, and city streets is likely to grow as the population becomes more urban and less rural.

Preferences can also change as people learn about the consequences of policies. Voters may support a program initially, then several years later discover that it has unanticipated costs and want to repeal it. This might account for evolution in popular attitudes toward welfare spending in the last thirty years, where the program's perverse effect on incentives may not have been appreciated at the beginning.[9]

The Rise and Fall of Policy Divergences

We can now describe how divergences in the policies of initiative and noninitiative states might emerge and disappear. Consider first a world of "shirking" legislators, or legislators who vote their consciences. Suppose initially that in all states representatives and voters share the same views. Then tax and spending policies will be the same in all states, and will reflect the majority's preferences. Now suppose that constituents start to change their minds about what they want (leaving aside why this happens). To make it concrete, suppose voters become more fiscally conservative. Legislators in both initiative and noninitiative states believe that the liberal fiscal policies they have been pursuing are the right policies (even if the majority disagrees), and they continue along the same path as before. In the short run, incumbency advantages provide some protection at the polls from conservative challengers. In initiative states, however, voters would begin to overrule their representatives and make the cuts themselves. A divergence in policy between initiative and noninitiative states would emerge.

To see how divergences appear in a world where legislators make "honest mistakes," suppose again that initially all legislators understand and implement the preferred fiscal policies of their constituents. Initiative and noninitiative states would then have the same policies, namely those preferred by the majority. Now suppose that citizens begin to want tax cuts but legislators fail to perceive the new mood of the electorate. In noninitiative states, tax and spending continues at the same level as before. In initiative states, however, policy begins to adjust toward the new preferences: successful ballot measures bring about changes directly, and initiative elections bring about changes indirectly by informing legislators of the changing popular mood toward taxes. Again, a gap emerges between initiative and noninitiative states.

Whether caused by shirking or honest mistakes, policy divergences will not persist forever. Candidates whose views are more attuned to the electorate will gradually replace incumbent "shirkers" through retirement or elections. "Faithful" representatives will stop making honest mistakes as election returns and opinion surveys communicate the electorate's new views. As legislatures get back in step with voters, taxes and spending will begin to decline in noninitiative states. Once legislatures have become informed about the new fiscally conservative views of the electorate and, if necessary, have been reconstituted to reflect those views, fiscal policies in initiative and noninitiative states will converge. Policies will reach an equilibrium again, at least until another shift occurs in voter preferences.

Conclusion

This chapter started with a few facts—periodic divergences between the policies of initiative and noninitiative states and the tendency of policies in initiative states to more accurately reflect the majority view—and outlined a theory to explain those facts. The main idea is that representatives can get out of step with their constituents because of frictions in the representation process. When representatives get out of step, they tend to choose policies that the majority does not support. In initiative states, voters use the initiative to bring policies back into line with their preferences relatively quickly. But in noninitiative states, policy corrections can only be brought about by changing the behavior of representatives, either by replacing them or informing them of the public's new views, which is a somewhat slower process. Because political institutions respond to preference changes more slowly when the initiative process is not available, policies can be different in initiative and noninitiative states for short periods of time. There are not enough frictions to sustain a divergence in the long run, however (where the data suggest the long run is now about five years), so the differences tend to disappear over time. In a sense, the theory here blends together two perspectives that are often presented as conflicting views of American politics. It captures the insights and intuitions from a large literature showing that legislators do not always follow their constituents' interests. And it also incorporates a compelling body of evidence that voting markets are fairly efficient and politicians are fairly responsive to constituent interests over the long run.[10] The next chapter turns to the specifics of the twentieth century, and shows how the theory can help understand the divergences between initiative and noninitiative states that show up in the data.

CHAPTER 7

Key Episodes in the Twentieth Century

This chapter provides a history of key episodes in the twentieth century. I use the theory developed in the previous chapter to sketch a picture of how the initiative changed the evolution of state and local fiscal policy during these important periods. My goals are fairly modest. First, I want to offer the reader a way to interpret the many facts that have accumulated throughout the book, since it is natural to wonder how everything fits together. Second, I want to suggest that the historical evidence is easy to understand in terms of a theory in which the initiative serves the majority and the legislature sometimes gets out of step—and therefore to reinforce the central message of the book. I do not attempt to "test" this explanation formally, and I do not believe it is the only possible way to read the evidence. The qualitative evidence is intended to complement the more quantitative statistical analysis reported earlier, give a feel for how the initiative really worked, and suggest directions for future research.

Why the Initiative Drove Up Spending in the Early Twentieth Century

The first fact to be explained is that initiative states spent more than noninitiative states in the first decades of the twentieth century (chapter 5). "When one recognizes, first, that Progressivism was the dominant ideology of economic and political elites on the eve of World War I and, second, that Progressivism was fundamentally at odds with the dominant ideology of ruling elites in the late nineteenth century, it is evident that an ideological turnabout must have taken place around the beginning of the twentieth century" (Higgs 1987, 113). I first describe why preferences shifted in favor of higher spending early in the twentieth century. Then I suggest why legislatures were slow to respond to the changing preferences, providing an opening for initiatives to drive up spending.

Why Preferences Changed: The Rise of Cities

The Industrial Revolution is the dominant feature of U.S. economic history from the Civil War to the Great War. During this period the country went through a sweeping transformation from a primarily agrarian economy into an industrial economy based on manufacturing, transportation, and trade. The causes and consequences of the Industrial Revolution are the subject of an extensive literature that need not concern us here.[1] What is important for our purposes is the immense shift in population from rural to urban areas that it engendered.

Figure 7.1 shows the basic pattern. At the outset of the Civil War, over 80 percent of the population lived in rural areas. This fraction steadily declined over the next seventy years as people moved to the cities, in many cases to work in the new industrial enterprises. By 1930, less than 45 percent of the population lived in the country, a dramatic and unprecedented change.[2]

City dwellers wanted different government services than people living in the countryside, especially when it came to services provided by state and local governments. For one thing, externality problems were more severe. In the densely populated cities, communicable diseases spread more easily than in farmlands, and unsanitary conditions made things even worse. Tuberculosis, typhoid, and diphtheria were major health problems. People in cities wanted greater expenditures on water purification, sewage treatment, garbage collection, and swamp drainage.[3]

City dwellers also demanded greater expenditure on "public goods"—services that once purchased benefit additional people at virtually no additional cost, such as parks, roads, and public transportation systems.

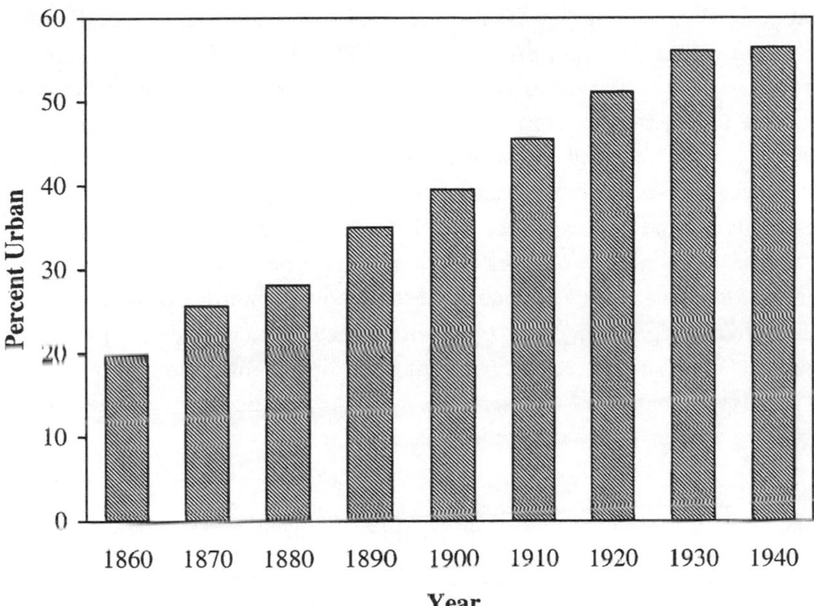

Figure 7.1 Urban Population in the United States, 1860–1940.

With so many people living close together, each dollar spent on a public good provided a high "social" return. Fire and police protection also have significant public good aspects and were highly valued by urban residents.

Education spending was another source of disagreement between the cities and countryside. City dwellers had a higher demand for education; their children could attend school at low cost and their benefits from formal education were large. One reason the cost of attending school was lower in the cities was that city children had a narrower set of employment opportunities (and these were foreclosed by child labor laws as the century progressed) while children in the countryside could work productively on the farm. Rural schools also tended to be smaller and less efficient, and the travel costs to reach them were higher than in the cities. On the benefit side, the value of a formal education was higher for people who contemplated working in the new industrial firms than those who planned to work on the family farm. As Becker (1981, 110) notes, "the early stages of economic development raise rates of return on investments in the education of *urban* children."[4] The general skills taught in schools were of little value to a child destined to work on the farm: "Practically all farming skills were transmitted on the farm, often within the family" (Higgs 1971, 36). The relatively low demand for formal education in the countryside is attested by the fact that even when schooling was available, most farm children attended school only for three or four months of the year. Why city residents favored *public* instead of private provision of education is not obvious (perhaps an element of redistribution from country to city was involved?), but it seems clear that they did. A glance at election returns from California initiatives reveals that pro-education initiatives were more popular in the urban counties of Alameda, Los Angeles, and San Francisco than in the rural counties.

Finally, the nature of work in cities gave urban residents a different demand for government services. Most obviously, manufacturing workers were interested in unemployment insurance (although such programs need not entail increased government spending if the funds are provided by employers), and old age pensions were more important to the manufacturing worker on a salary than a family farmer.

How the Government Got out of Step: Rural Gerrymandering

Recall that the fact to be explained is why initiative states spent more than noninitiative states in the early twentieth century. The reason I suggest is that legislatures were slow to respond to the spending demands of the new urban majority. In initiative states, voters were able to take matters into their own hands. As they drove up spending, the policies of initiative and noninitiative states began to diverge. To explain why initiative states spent more, then, we need to understand why legislatures did not respond to the demand for services from the growing urban population. Why did it take initiatives to bring them about?

The main reason urban interests were frustrated by state legislatures is because seats were apportioned in a way that gave control to rural voters. Until the U.S. Supreme Court developed the "one person, one vote" rule in the 1960s, few states regularly adjusted their district lines to take into account population changes. Legislative seats often were assigned using district lines that had been in place for a long time. The key one person, one vote decisions, for example, concerned apportionment in Tennessee and Alabama.[5] At the time of the Court's decisions, neither state had changed its district lines in over sixty years, despite significant population growth and migration to the cities. In addition, most states apportioned their legislatures using some version of the "Federal Plan," which assigned seats in the upper house on the basis of population *and area,* deliberately over-representing rural voters (as in the U.S. Senate). As people moved from the countryside to the cities, rural voters were left with a disproportionately large number of seats while urban voters were packed into a relatively small number of seats. Thus, rural interests often ended up in control of state legislatures instead of the new urban majority. In this way, the government fell out of step with the majority of people, creating an opportunity for the initiative to play a role. "Under [the] representative form of government the counties hold the balance of power," said Mary Lee in a 1912 speech: "Under direct legislation the city will control. The farmers have always been dead weight about the necks of the laboring men. We will get the initiative and referendum and will then give them a taste of the same kind of legislation they have been giving us."[6]

Boiled down to its essence, the explanation for why initiative states spent more than noninitiative states in the early decades of the twentieth century is this: The population shifted from the country to the city, and urban voters had a higher demand for government services than rural voters. However, since district lines were drawn to favor people in the countryside, rural interests remained in control of the state legislatures. In initiative states, urban voters were able to use their numerical majority to push through their spending programs, but they were stifled in the noninitiative states. Hence, a divergence appeared.[7]

A Look at the Initiatives

The subject matter of actual initiatives fits this explanation well. If the initiative drove up spending because it allowed city dwellers to approve programs that were blocked by rural-dominated legislatures, we should be able to find examples of actual initiatives from the time that were targeted to urban voters.[8] Such initiatives are easy to find. To give a few examples: In 1936, Colorado voters approved public assistance to indigent tuberculosis sufferers. In 1938, Oregon voters approved a water purification and pollution prevention measure. Initiatives to raise taxes to pay for policemen's and firemen's pensions were put before the voters of Missouri and Arkansas (in 1928 and 1940, respectively; the first measure failing).

A particularly large number of initiatives proposed increases in spending on education, highways, and aid for the elderly, sick, and blind. Rather than list specific examples, table 7.1 gives a sense of the intense interest in these issues by reporting the number of measures of each type by decade for each state.[9] As can be seen, these "urban issues" attracted initiative activity across a wide array of states throughout the period. Eleven states considered a total of 38 pro-education initiatives, measures that raised taxes and appropriated funds for schools, set minimal levels of state aid for school districts, and made education compulsory. Only five initiatives (not listed in the table)

Table 7.1 Initiatives Increasing Education, Highways, and Welfare Expenditure, 1910–49

Decade	Number of Initiatives by State																Total
	AZ	AR	CA	CO	ID	MA	MI	MO	MT	NE	NV	ND	OH	OK	OR	WA	
								Education									
1910s	—	2	—	—	—	—	—	2	—	—	—	—	—	1	4	—	9
1920s	—	1	2	1	—	—	2	—	2	—	—	—	—	1	1	2	12
1930s	—	1	1	1	—	—	1	1	—	—	—	—	—	—	—	—	5
1940s	—	—	2	—	—	—	—	—	1	1	—	3	—	2	3	—	12
								Highways									
1910s	1	—	—	4	—	—	—	2	—	—	—	—	—	—	4	—	11
1920s	3	—	3	4	—	—	—	2	1	—	—	1	—	—	1	—	15
1930s	2	—	1	—	—	—	—	1	—	—	—	1	—	—	—	—	5
1940s	3	—	—	—	—	—	—	1	—	1	—	2	1	—	—	—	8
								Welfare (Primarily Aid for Elderly, Sick, and Blind)									
1910s	1	—	—	3	—	—	—	—	—	—	—	—	—	—	—	—	4
1920s	—	—	—	—	—	—	—	—	—	—	—	—	1	—	—	—	1
1930s	—	—	2	2	—	—	—	2	—	—	1	2	2	4	2	1	18
1940s	1	—	3	3	1	2	—	—	—	—	1	2	—	1	3	4	21

Note: Education initiatives include measures increasing taxes and appropriating funds for schools, setting minimal levels of state aid, and making education compulsory. Highways initiatives include measures approving bond issues for roads, appropriating funds for specific road projects, increasing gas taxes, and dedicating funds for road projects. Welfare initiatives include measures increasing aid to the elderly, retired, sick, and blind.

attempted to reduce or cap education expenditure. Nine states considered a total of 39 highways measures, most of which authorized bond issues, appropriated funds for road or tunnel construction, or raised vehicle and gas taxes for road maintenance and construction.[10] Twelve states voted on 44 pro-welfare measures. The most popular such measures provided aid for the elderly. Others provided aid for the blind and sick. I could find only one initiative that attempted to eliminate a welfare program.

Of course, there were also initiatives addressed to rural issues, such as water systems and crop insurance programs. I have not broken them out separately, but they were much less common than the initiatives appealing to urban voters. In fact, the only subject that rivaled these "city issues" was alcohol prohibition.

My explanation for why legislatures fell out of step is based on the malapportionment of state legislatures in favor of rural interests. Consistent with this view, in many states citizens tried to use initiatives to push through redistricting plans (table 7.2). Most of these proposals attempted to transfer legislative seats from rural to urban areas. The proposals took a variety of forms, from straightforward redistricting on the basis of population, to proportional representation in Oregon, to elimination of the upper chamber in Arizona, Missouri, Nebraska, and Oregon (remember that the upper chambers were generally apportioned on the basis of area as well as population, so tended to be the most favorable to rural interests). All told, twenty-three initiatives on this subject came before the voters in ten states.

The conflict between urban and rural voters for representation also played out at the federal level. Urban/rural conflicts led to the failure of the U.S. Congress to reapportion itself at all after the 1920 Census, in effect, sticking with the 1911 districts for twenty years. By 1930, the over-representation of rural interests was remarkable: for example, New York had a rural district with a population of 90,671 and an urban district with a population of 799,407 (Eagles 1990).

Table 7.2 Initiatives Affecting Apportionment of Legislature

	Number of Initiatives by State										
Decade	AZ	CA	CO	MI	MO	NE	OH	OK	OR	WA	Total
1910s	3	—	2	—	—	—	1	1	4	—	11
1920s	—	2	1	1	—	—	—	—	—	—	4
1930s	1	—	1	2	—	1	—	—	—	1	6
1940s	—	1	—	—	1	—	—	—	—	—	2

Note: This table indicates the number of initiatives by state and decade that proposed to change the apportionment (where the district lines are drawn) of the state legislature. The measures proposed new apportionment plans, new apportionment procedures, and elimination of one house of the legislature.

It is also interesting to note the parallels with Great Britain around the turn of the century. Great Britain went through its industrial revolution with the attendant rural-urban migration earlier than the United States. Like the United States, legislative seats were not reallocated to adjust for the growing urban population. As a result, rural interests came to control the government, particularly the hereditary House of Lords. And like the United States, the government was slow to respond to the demand for new programs by the urban majority, causing political turmoil. The battle between urban and rural interests culminated in the Parliament Act of 1911, which stripped the rural-based House of Lords of its veto power over ordinary legislation. Around the same time, the government began approving new social programs favored by urban voters, such as the Education Act of 1902 (making secondary education an obligation of the state), the Old Age Pensions Bill in 1908, the Labour Exchange Bill in 1909, and the National Insurance Act in 1911 (disability insurance). The sluggish response of the established parties to the demographic shift led to the rise of the new city-based Labour Party and the eventual dissolution of the venerable Liberal Party.[11]

Why the Initiative Cut Spending in the Later Twentieth Century

For the postwar period, there are actually three facts to explain: less spending by initiative states than noninitiative states in the 1970s, approximate convergence in the mid-1980s, and then less spending by initiative states again in the 1990s (figure 6.1). The explanation I offer is that popular opinion unexpectedly shifted to the right in the 1970s and 1990s, and legislators were slow to pick up the change and adjust fiscal policy. That is, I suggest that "honest mistakes" can account for part of the initiative effect.

The California Tax Revolt

It is useful to begin with a close look at the California tax revolt in the 1970s.[12] The California case is interesting because of its national prominence—most readers know at the least the outline of the story—and it illustrates rather clearly the electorate's preference change and the role of the initiative in bringing about policy adjustment.

As background, figure 7.2 summarizes state and local expenditure in California from 1957 to 2000. The figure reports real spending per capita, but it would look almost the same if spending was expressed as a percentage

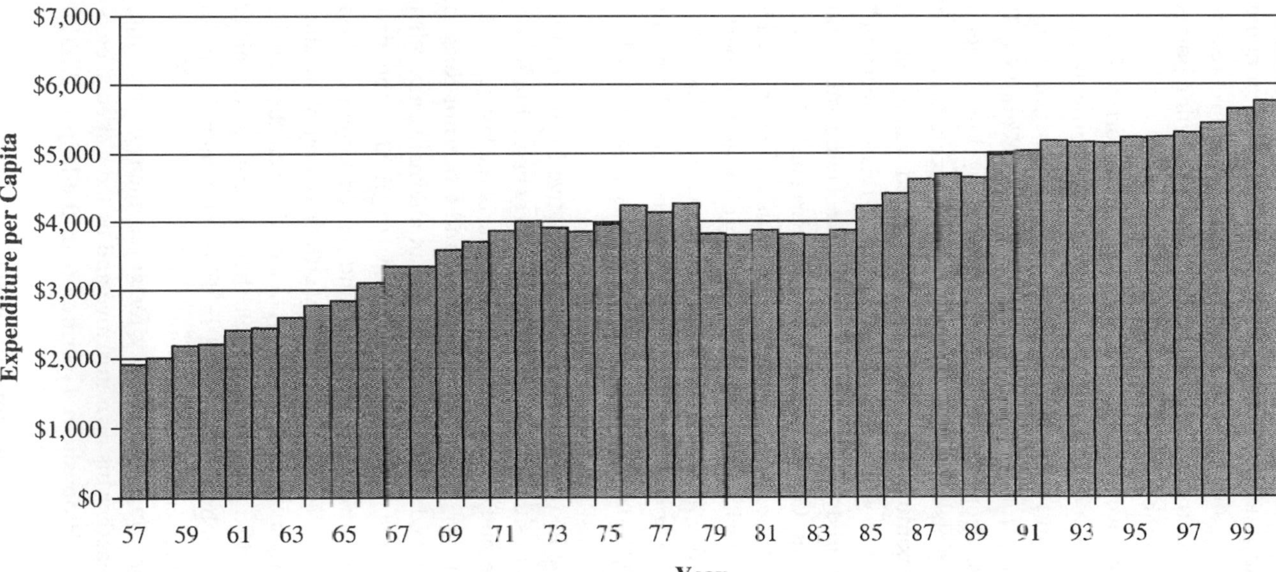

Figure 7.2 State and Local Expenditure in California, 1957–2000.
Note: Expenditure is combined spending of state and local governments, expressed in year-2000 dollars per capita.

of income or if revenue was reported instead of expenditure. Spending grew without interruption from 1957 (actually, even earlier) to the early 1970s. Then it jumped around for a bit in the early 1970s before plunging at the end of the decade. California's spending pattern is fairly representative of the rest of the country: the same broad trends and turning points appear in the aggregate numbers.

What follows is a narrative history of the tax revolt in California. There was evidently something of a consensus in favor of spending growth until the late 1960s, when tax and expenditure cutting initiatives began to appear. In 1968, the first tax-cutting initiative since the end of World War II came before the voters. Proposition 9 was sponsored by Los Angeles County Assessor Philip Watson. It offered voters the chance to cut their property taxes to a maximum of 1 percent of assessed value, and it restricted the use of property tax revenue to "property-related services." The initiative was opposed by leaders of the state Democratic and Republic parties, including GOP Governor Ronald Reagan. To stave off the initiative, Reagan and the Democrat-controlled legislature approved a competing measure, Proposition 1A, that offered more modest property tax relief (it exempted the first $750 in a home's assessed value from taxes). On election day, voters rejected Watson's initiative (only 32 percent voted in favor) and approved Proposition 1A. Spending continued to grow.

In 1972, Watson qualified another tax-cutting initiative for the ballot. Like its predecessor, Proposition 14 set limits on property taxes, but it also increased sales, corporate, and sin taxes to make up some of the lost revenue. Again leaders of both parties opposed the initiative, and Governor Reagan and the Democrat-controlled legislature approved an alternative tax relief program that increased the exemption on homes to include the first $1,750 in assessed value, increased sales taxes, and placed some limits on local taxes. On election day, Watson's second try attracted a bit more support, 34 percent, but was still overwhelmingly rejected. Even though the initiative failed, elected officials must have felt that something was afoot because spending growth abruptly stopped in 1973 and then began to decline (in per capita terms and also as a percent of income).

Perhaps sensing a growing constituency for government downsizing, Governor Reagan put together his own initiative and called a special election to decide it in 1973. Proposition 1, written with the help of Milton Friedman, limited property taxes like the Watson initiatives, but also cut the income tax and restricted the growth of state government to the growth rate of personal income. Leaders of the Democratic Party and public employee unions led the opposition to the measure. The Reagan initiative attracted 46 percent of the votes on election day, an improvement over the Watson initiatives, but not enough to become law.

Reagan left office at the end of 1974 and was replaced by Democrat Jerry Brown. Democrats maintained majorities in the state senate and assembly, giving the party control of both branches of the government for the first time since 1966. Spending surged in 1975–77 to an all-time high.

Then came Proposition 13 in 1978. This measure was sponsored by two citizen activists, Howard Jarvis and Paul Gann. It capped property tax rates at 1 percent of assessed value and limited assessment increases. In many respects, the initiative was not that different from Watson's 1968 initiative. Proposition 13 was opposed by Brown, the state's Democratic leaders, most of the prominent Republicans in the state (including George Deukmejian, Ken Maddy, and Pete Wilson, then candidates for statewide offices), the public employee unions, the AFL-CIO, chambers of commerce, and the major businesses in the state including Bank of America, Crown Zellerbach, and Southern California Edison. The legislature again attempted to stave off the initiative threat by approving a property tax cut roughly half the size of the one promised by Proposition 13, and placing a measure on the ballot (Proposition 8) that would amend the constitution to allow the tax cut. Proposition 13 passed with an astounding 65 percent in favor. The government's counter-proposal was rejected with 53 percent against.

Proposition 13 was approved in the June primary election. With an eye on the general election in November, the state's elected officials turned on a dime and became tax-cutting enthusiasts, most notably Governor Brown who declared himself a "born-again tax cutter." Rather than fighting the measures in court, as is so often the case nowadays, the governor and legislature set about to implement the will of the voters. For example, the governor ordered a hiring freeze and took a tough bargaining position with public employee unions. Also, in short order the legislature approved a $1 billion income tax cut, partially indexed income tax rates to inflation, and increased income tax credits. The cumulative effect shows up clearly in figure 7.2. Spending plunged in 1979 and stayed flat for six years.

Next came Proposition 9 in 1979. This initiative, sponsored by Paul Gann, limited the growth of government to the growth rate of population and income. It also required government surpluses to be rebated to taxpayers, and required the state to reimburse local governments for the cost of state mandates. Proposition 9 attracted only token opposition and was approved by 74 percent of the voters on election day.

Proposition 9 turned out to be the high-water mark of the tax revolt. A Jarvis-sponsored measure to cut income taxes (another Proposition 9) was rejected in 1980 although voters approved his initiative that fully indexed income tax rates to inflation (Proposition 7) in 1982. And a "Save 13" initiative in 1982 that attempted to close some loopholes in Proposition 13 was rejected in 1984.

Several features of the California tax revolt are worth highlighting. First, it is evident that citizen preferences shifted to the right in the 1970s, and the shift was rapid and substantial. This can be seen clearly in the steadily increasing approval rates for initiatives that proposed tax and expenditure limits (figure 7.3). Second, it appears that elected officials did not perceive how conservative the electorate was becoming until the votes were counted for Proposition 13. The fact that leaders of both parties, even bona fide conservatives such as Ronald Reagan and George Deukmejian, opposed some of the measures is one kind of evidence. To be sure, many officeholders may have had a personal preference for more spending, but the abrupt about-face of Governor Brown and the legislature following the passage of Proposition 13 shows how responsive they could be to public opinion when the public spoke clearly. It is not hard to see why elected officials failed to perceive the popular mood shift until Proposition 13 hit them over the head. After all, spending had been on a more or less continual upward trend since the Great Depression, and the voters had rejected all of the tax cutting initiatives that came before them

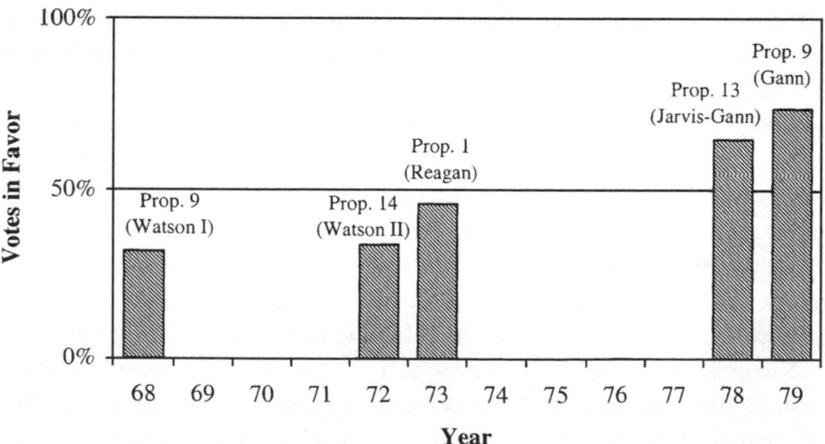

Figure 7.3 Growth of Support for California Tax-Cutting Initiatives.
Note: This figure reports the percentage of votes in favor of each of the five tax and expenditure limitation initiatives during the California "tax revolt." The initiative's primary sponsor is indicated in parentheses.

as late as 1973, even one sponsored by an extremely popular incumbent governor.

This history of California is also interesting because it points to a significant role for the initiative. It is, of course, impossible to know what would have happened in California if the initiative was unavailable. Still, it seems safe to say that without Watson's initiatives in 1968 and 1972, the legislature might have delayed taking the initial steps that slowed the growth of spending. And it is hard to believe that spending would have been cut anywhere near the amount it was without the clear signal sent by Proposition 13.

The 1970s, 1980s, and 1990s

Consider now the picture depicted in figure 6.1. Roughly speaking, there are three periods to explain, the 1970s, 1980s, and 1990s. In the 1970s, initiative states spent considerably less than noninitiative states. In the mid-1980s, spending was roughly equal (remember, the differences there are not statistically significant). And in the 1990s, initiative states again spent significantly less than noninitiative states. The explanation I want to entertain is that representatives made "honest mistakes": public opinion shifted in a conservative direction in the 1970s, taking elected officials by surprise; by 1980, the rightward shift in the electorate was well understood and legislatures accommodated the new preferences; and then public opinion unexpectedly shifted to the right again in the 1990s. I do not have incontrovertible proof for this interpretation, but I think a pretty good case can be made in its favor.

The first part of the story concerns public opinion. Literally thousands of opinion surveys were taken over the last several decades, but no single survey was repeated enough to give a consistent long-term perspective of the public's sentiments about spending. However, Stimson (1999) developed a clever method to extract the common ideological component from these diverse surveys and construct a consistent index of public opinion that spans our entire time period. Stimson's strategy was to treat the aggregate response of each survey question (such as the percentage of respondents indicating support for more spending) as having a common year-specific "mood" component and an idiosyncratic component related to the particular issue addressed, question wording, and so on. Roughly speaking, he standardized the mean and variance of each series across time and then averaged all questions from each year to cancel out the idiosyncratic terms, leaving the mood component for each year. Stimson's index is based on almost 150 separate questions and over 2,000 question-years. One could quibble with

Stimson's approach on a number of grounds, but it is the most convincing long-term index of public ideology available, and one of the best known.

Figure 7.4 plots the "liberalness" of public opinion year-by-year from 1957 to 2000 (the units of the public opinion index are meaningless).[13] The movement in public opinion as reflected in opinion polls fits the story reasonably well. Stimson (1999, 68) notes that the data up to 1962 are somewhat unreliable due to limitations in the underlying surveys, so I will not dwell on those years. From 1963 to 1968, opinion was fairly stable, but in 1969 it began to turn conservative. The conservative tide ran through the entire 1970s, cresting at the end of the decade. A liberal resurgence followed, reaching a peak in 1991. In 1992–94 the public shifted back to the right where it stayed for the rest of the decade (other than the anomalous liberal bounce in 1995).[14] In short, the opinion polls suggest that the electorate's views shifted to the right in the 1970s, moved back to the left in the 1980s, and then turned right again in the 1990s.

Of course, as economists are keen to point out, opinion surveys capture what people say, not what they do. What the voters did, though, points in the same direction. We already saw above the steady growth in popularity of tax-cutting measures in California in the 1970s. This pattern was repeated across the country (albeit less decisively), and, by the late 1970s, tax and expenditure limitations were being adopted across the nation at all levels of government. In 1978–80 alone, forty-three states approved tax relief or tax limitation measures (Sears and Citrin 1985).

Voters also acted in a decidedly conservative direction when choosing their representatives. In 1980, the crest of the conservative wave according to opinion surveys, the country elected Ronald Reagan president by a landslide. Reagan was the first bona fide conservative to hold the office in the second half of the century, and the loser, Jimmy Carter, was the first (elected) incumbent to be denied a second term by the voters since Herbert Hoover in 1932. Perhaps even more remarkable, the voters handed control of the U.S. Senate to the Republicans for the first time since 1954 by throwing twelve Democratic incumbents out of office. We also know from Peltzman's (1992) study of election returns that voters were consistently penalizing incumbent presidents, senators, and governors for spending growth during their terms of office.

The 1990s are less clear, with few high-profile tax-cutting measures coming before the voters. The liberal resurgence peaked at the beginning of the decade, coinciding with the defeat of President George Bush in 1992. Although a Democratic president held office for most of the decade, the signal political event of the period was the 1994 congressional

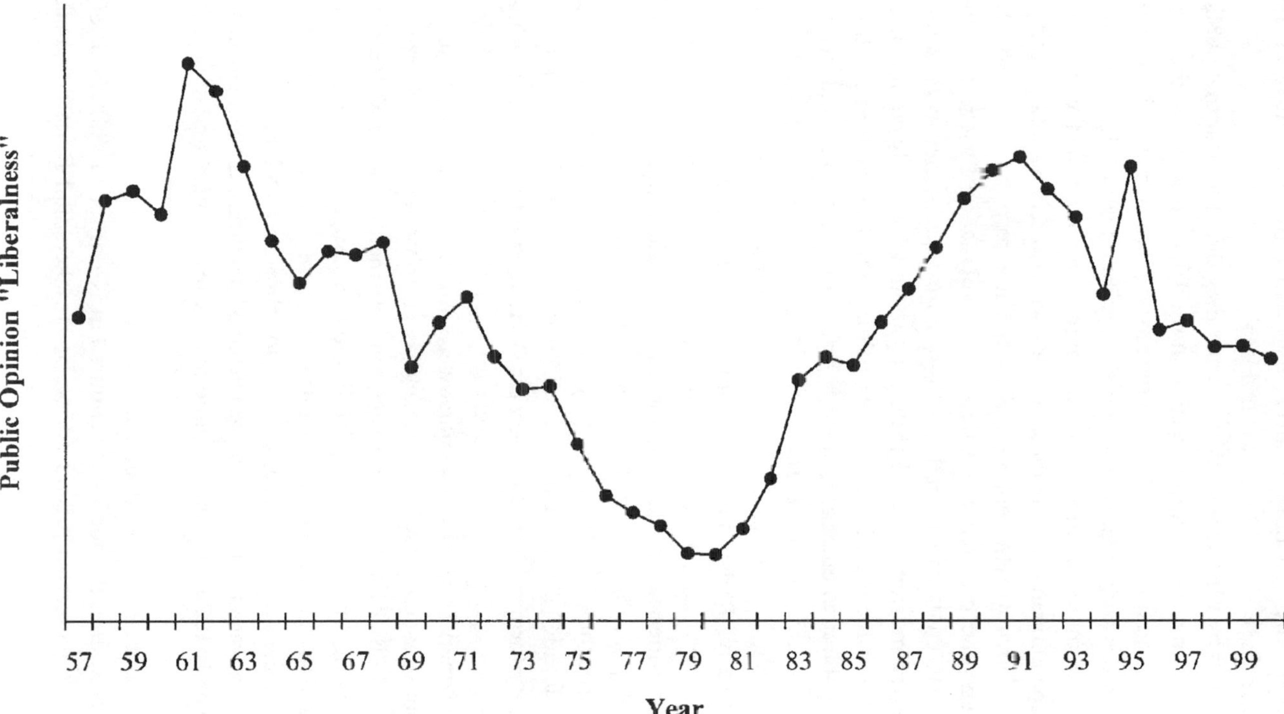

Figure 7.4 Public Opinion "Liberalness," 1957–2000.
Note: Public Opinion "Liberalness" is the measure of "policy mood" constructed by Stimson (1999). Its units are meaningless.

elections: voters gave the Republicans a majority in the House of Representatives for the first time in forty years and returned control of the Senate to the GOP (it had been lost in 1986).

Judged both by what voters said and what they did, it is clear that public opinion shifted in a conservative direction in the 1970s and 1990s, the periods when the largest initiative effects appeared. It is worth noting in passing that this provides additional support for the central thesis of the book, that the initiative promotes the interests of the many rather than the few. The initiative cut spending in precisely those periods when voters wanted it cut.

It is less obvious why representatives did not respond more expeditiously when voter preferences changed. The explanation I suggest, tentatively, is that elected officials made an "honest mistake"—they were simply unaware of the magnitude of the shift in opinion. I feel fairly confident of this explanation for the 1970s. For one thing, expert opinion at the time was divided about whether a rightward shift in public opinion was occurring. It can be difficult to see trends in a collection of disparate polls. In fact, most public opinion scholars rejected the notion of a rightward drift even in the early 1980s: "The first major analyses of the [1980] election appeared in 1981, and, almost without exception, they rejected the contention that American public opinion had become more conservative" (Mayer 1992, 2). On top of this, even though voters were souring on spending throughout the 1970s, they did not seem to demand action until late in the decade (if California is at all representative). Election returns also provide information on the electorate's view, and it is true that politicians were paying a price at the polls for spending during most of this period (Peltzman 1992). But elections were intermittent and voter sentiment about financial issues may have been obscured by Watergate, Vietnam, and other nonfinancial issues. As Peltzman (1992, 360) puts it, "there is enough noise in the [election return] data for the required Bayesian updating to have taken a while."

Although the state of opinion was muddy through much of the 1970s, some learning was taking place. State and local spending growth began to slow in the early 1970s and almost came to a standstill by the end of decade (that is, spending in most states looked similar to California, figure 7.2).

The electorate's rightward shift became crystal clear to politicians (if not academics) after the votes were counted in November 1980. The 1980 elections were a great surprise. London bookmakers had Ronald Reagan losing until about ten days before his landslide victory, and the GOP takeover of the U.S. Senate was even more unexpected (Roberts 1990). The disappearance of the initiative effect in the 1980s, in my view, came about because elected officials had learned by then of the electorate's fiscal conservatism and made the appropriate spending adjustments. For instance, at the federal level, even the Democrat-controlled House of Representatives agreed to the Reagan tax cuts in 1981. With legislatures serving the majority, there was no winning coalition for tax-cutting initiatives. For example, voters rejected two of the three tax-cutting measures Howard Jarvis placed on the California ballot in the 1980s.

I suspect that the initiative gap in the 1990s was also an "honest mistake" by elected officials, but I am not as confident of this explanation as I am about the 1970s. It is clear that the public turned conservative in the 1990s after a decade of drifting to the left, but there is no easy explanation for the right turn, no singular event that would serve as a flag to a well-intentioned representative. Indeed, to the extent the electorate was sending signals, one of the most visible was the outcome of the 1992 elections, when the presidency and both houses of the Congress were entrusted to the Democrats for the first time since 1980. President Bill Clinton, not unreasonably, interpreted this as evidence of a leftward shift in public opinion, and spent his first two years in office trying to pass a fairly liberal national health care plan. His apparent surprise at the lack of support for the plan is one indication that politicians were unaware of the rightward drift in public opinion. Another indication is the near universal shock among political observers at the GOP victory in 1994. For example, prices on the Iowa Stock Market, an online exchange that allows people to trade based on their expectations of who will win elections, implied a 95 percent probability of a Democratic victory until the day before the election.

The reason I am somewhat hesitant about the honest mistakes explanation for the 1990s is that the evidence of a conservative shift in public opinion was widely available by 1994 (although perhaps 1995 muddied the waters?) At the federal level, President Clinton soon became something of a fiscal conservative, declaring, "the era of big government is over." Why didn't state legislatures respond in the same way, and cut spending on their own? Why didn't the initiative effect vanish by the mid-1990s? It did decline in the second half of the decade, suggesting that politicians made some adjustments, but a significant difference remained between initiative and noninitiative states. Perhaps some version of the "shirking" story deserves consideration. It may be that government officials chose to maintain high spending levels (and, as it turns out, high spending growth) in the face of popular disapproval because they believed it was in the public interest, and popular opinion was wrong. Unfortunately, without more data and a bit of historical perspective, we can do little more at this point than list possibilities.

Conclusion

This chapter provides an interpretation of several key episodes in the fiscal history of the twentieth century. The purpose is to flesh out the picture of how the initiative affects government policy, and to provide a framework to understand the facts accumulated throughout this book, some of which appear contradictory at first glance.

The interpretation is based on the idea that popular preferences for government spending evolve over time, and politicians are often slow to adjust public policy to accommodate the new preferences. I suggest that initiative states spent more than noninitiative states in the early twentieth century because the population became more urban, urban voters wanted more spending, but legislatures were controlled by rural interests because district lines were not adjusted to account for population movements. Initiatives were used then to override the legislature and drive up spending. In the later part of the twentieth century, initiative states spent less than noninitiative states. I suggest that voters became more conservative, but representatives made an "honest mistake"—it took them a while to see the shifting popular mood. In the meantime, voters used initiatives to begin cutting taxes and spending.

PART THREE

Open Questions

It may well happen that the public voice pronounced by the representatives of the people, will be more consonant to the public good, than if pronounced by the people themselves convened for the purpose. On the other hand, . . . men of factious tempers, or local prejudices, or of sinister designs, may by intrigue, by corruption or by other means, first obtain the suffrages, and then betray the interests of the people.

—James Madison, *Federalist* no. 10

CHAPTER 8 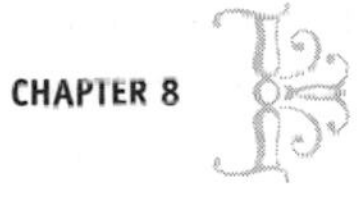

Majority Tyranny and the Constitution

The initiative process is a controversial part of American government, and has been for more than a century, yet the terms of debate have hardly changed. Opponents argue (as they did one hundred years ago) that the initiative allows narrow interests to subvert the political process, while defenders maintain (as they did one hundred years ago) that it allows the majority to counteract special interest subversion of the legislature. The main purpose of this book is to sort through the huge amount of data available after one hundred years of initiative lawmaking, and make an objective, factual assessment of whether the initiative brings about policies favored by the many or the few. I focus on fiscal policy, perhaps the most important function of government, and certainly the one that attracts the most attention, and utilize a century of data for all fifty states and almost five thousand cities. These are the main findings:

1. Over the last three decades, the initiative significantly changed state and local policy (chapter 3):
   a. It cut expenditure and taxes.
   b. It decentralized spending from state to local governments.
   c. It shifted financing away from taxes and into user fees and charges for services.
2. Opinion surveys show that a majority of people favored the changes brought about by the initiative (chapter 4).
3. In the early part of the twentieth century, the initiative increased state and local spending, and there is some reason to believe that a majority favored these spending increases (chapter 5).
4. The initiative had the biggest impact in periods where legislatures were slow to respond to changes in public opinion (chapters 6 and 7).

The natural interpretation of these facts is that the initiative pushed policy in the direction favored by a majority of people. Not a single piece of evidence links the initiative to nonmajority policies as the special interest subversion hypothesis would predict. There are, of course, a number of caveats that must be kept in mind with this and any other empirical work, and I have tried to note them in the preceding chapters. Yet the fact that a comprehensive examination of fiscal policies from the beginning to the end of the twentieth century reveals not a shred of evidence for the special interest subversion view makes as compelling a rejection of a hypothesis as we ever get in empirical research. This is the main message of the book: based on the facts, the initiative serves the many and not the few.

Beyond this conclusion, the interpretation of the evidence is fairly open. In particular, I do not think the evidence in itself tells us whether the initiative is a good or bad thing for American government. An overall assessment of the initiative requires understanding not only whether it serves the many or the few, but also how it affects the rights of minorities, how it impacts the Constitutional structure of American democracy, how it affects the responsiveness of legislators to constituent interests, how it affects the innovativeness of public policy, and a host of other issues.

I want to conclude the book by discussing some of the more important issues that have been skipped over so far. This and the next chapter identify what I see as the key unresolved questions, bring out points of contention, and review the evidence such as it is. My goal is to give the reader a sense of where things stand on these issues and to suggest to scholars some interesting research directions. Since little evidence is available on these issues, the reader is forewarned that what follows is leavened with a healthy measure of my personal reflections and intuitions. In this sense, the last two chapters represent a departure from the rest of the book, which tries not to stray far beyond the bounds of what can be empirically documented.

This chapter begins by considering the problem of majority tyranny and then examines how the initiative meshes with the Constitutional principles of American democracy. The final chapter contains some reflections on the initiative process as an approach to delegation problems and as a way to increase political competition.

The Danger of Majority Tyranny

As we have seen, the initiative process promotes majority rule, a core principle of American democracy. Yet an equally important principle is that all people have certain fundamental rights that cannot be violated even if a majority wishes to do so. The institutions of American government are designed to prevent the many from "tyrannizing" the few. To repeat an oft-cited passage from *Federalist* no. 51:

> It is of great importance in a republic, not only to guard the society against the oppression of its rulers; but to guard one part of the society against the injustice of the other parts. Different interests necessarily exist in different classes of citizens. If a majority be united by a common interest, the rights of the minority will be insecure.

An important question is then: does the initiative, by empowering the majority, undermine the rights of numerical minorities?

Much has been written on this question, mostly in the last thirty years, and many opinions have been expressed both for and against the initiative (see Cronin 1989, and Bowler, Donovan, and Tolbert 1998 for a summaries). Perhaps the most important thing to note is that these opinions rest on intuition, not on convincing, systematic evidence. No one has gone to the data and actually measured how the initiative affects minority rights.[1]

Let me briefly describe what has been done. By far the most common approach is anecdotal. Typically, an author singles out a handful of laws involving the civil rights of minorities, studies how they came about in some detail, and then generalizes from his or her specific examples to the initiative process as a whole. There is nothing wrong with this approach to a point; anecdotes certainly provide useful information and help flesh out the picture. The problem is that we do not know if a particular anecdote is representative of a general pattern or is simply a special case, an exception to the rule. There is little justification for inferring general tendencies from a handful of anecdotes.

The other complication is that the performance of the initiative has to be compared to the alternative, which is lawmaking by elected legislatures. It is not enough to show that initiatives have occasionally undermined minority rights, since no form of government known to man provides ironclad protection of minorities. Legislatures also have violated the civil rights of minorities. Indeed, for every blatant instance of initiative failure, we can readily identify a similar example where minority rights were undercut by a legislature. Take Jim Crow laws, for example: in Oklahoma, an initiative was approved in 1910 that disenfranchised black citizens; in the other southern states, similar laws were passed by state legislatures. Another example: in California, an initiative was approved in 1920 that restricted the property rights of Japanese; the internment of Japanese-American citizens during World War II came about through the actions of elected officials.[2] A listing of anecdotes like this is useful to remind of us the dangers of democracy, but it only tells us that no form of government is perfect. It does not tell us if the overall record of initiatives is *worse* than that of legislatures.

Several recent studies attempt to go beyond anecdotes by collecting broad samples and subjecting them to statistical analyses. These studies compare the passage rate of civil rights measures to the passage rate of all other measures. They assume that if antiminority initiatives pass more often than other initiatives, the initiative process is a threat to minority rights. The evidence points in no particular direction. Gamble (1997) found that antiminority measures were more likely to pass than other measures in a sample dominated by local initiatives, while Donovan and Bowler (1998) and Frey and Goette (1998) found *lower* passage rates for antiminority measures in samples of state ballot propositions in the United States and national and local ballot propositions in Switzerland (respectively).

Yet none of these studies compared initiative lawmaking to legislative lawmaking, and we know that legislatures sometimes pass antiminority laws, too. Even if their findings had agreed, these studies would not tell us whether the initiative increases or reduces the risk to minority rights. The impact of the initiative on minority rights cannot be discerned by comparing how often voters approve antiminority initiatives to how often they approve other initiatives.[3] If, for example, voters approve 60 percent of the antiminority initiatives that come before them, while city councils approve 80 percent of the antiminority measures that come before them, then one could argue that city councils are the more serious threat to minority rights. The ratio of the passage rate of antiminority to other initiatives has no bearing on the conclusion.[4] The unavoidable fact is that the only way to compare how the initiative process treats minorities with how legislatures treat them is to look at data from initiatives *and legislatures.* None of the existing studies, however, examined the performance of legislatures on civil rights issues; they only looked at initiatives. I believe these studies are to be commended for moving the discussion beyond the level of anecdotes, and their evidence does give a sense of how often initiatives threaten minority rights. But they shed no light on the question of interest: how much of a threat does the initiative process pose to minority rights *compared to the legislative process?*

Another unresolved issue in the literature is how to distinguish "majority rule" from "majority tyranny." It will not do to classify every issue where the majority prevails as an instance of tyranny. If we did, then majority-rule democracy would be tyranny by definition. What we need is to identify a set of basic human rights that are essential to a free society, such as life, personal liberty, and political equality. Laws that violate these basic rights are out of bounds even if favored by a majority, and their approval would constitute "majority tyranny." Most people would put slavery, Jim Crow, and the internment of Japanese Americans into this category. Laws that work against the interest of minorities but do not infringe on their basic human rights should be considered the normal stuff of politics, examples of majority *rule.* The problem is that the line between a "right" and an "interest" is gray and highly subjective. Consider, for example, two California initiatives from the 1980s. Proposition 63 made English the state's official language, without spelling out exactly what that meant. Proposition 96 mandated AIDS testing for persons charged with sexual offenses or assaults if bodily fluids were transferred. According to Gamble (1997), both measures were instances of "majority tyranny" (the first violated the civil rights of language minorities and the second the civil rights of people with AIDS) rather than legitimate exercises of majority rule. Not every reader would agree with her classification, I suspect. The point here is not to criticize Gamble's classification—she had to draw a line somewhere—but to highlight a fundamental difficulty in evaluating the initiative.[5] We want to assess how the initiative affects minority rights, but we do not know exactly what these rights are.

In short, we simply do not have compelling evidence yet on whether initiatives or legislatures pose a greater threat to minority rights, or even if there is a difference. The most defensible position is one of agnosticism: pending more evidence, we just don't know. Fortunately, the question seems amenable to empirical analysis. It should not be too difficult to collect data on civil rights legislation and compare the outcomes under both forms of government. Given the increasing interest in the issue of majority tyranny, I feel reasonably optimistic that in the next few years we will start to see evidence that addresses the limitations of previous work.

Now let me move from what is known to what I suspect. If I had to guess what the evidence ultimately will show, it would be that the initiative process is *not* a greater threat to minority rights than legislatures. I say this primarily because opinion data consistently show that racial and ethnic minorities themselves do not consider ballot propositions dangerous. According to several Field polls, large majorities of blacks, Latinos, and Asians believe that "statewide ballot propositions are a good thing" (see table 8.1).[6] The numbers vary somewhat over time, but even in 1997 after a series of racially charged initiatives, strong majorities of each minority group still supported the process. And the number that considered the initiative process to be a "bad thing" is minuscule, typically less than 5 percent. Evidently, most members of these minority groups do not view the initiative process as a threat to their well being. It is possible that people are ignorant of the danger they face; that is, they mistakenly approve of the initiative process (and that is one reason we need data on the actual effects). But given a century of experience with the initiative process, and the constant attention paid to civil rights issues by elites of these groups, I would find it surprising if a significant threat existed that the survey respondents had simply failed to appreciate.

Now in a way, this creates something of a puzzle. The evidence in this book shows that the initiative promotes the interests of the many not the few. I studied fiscal policies not civil rights laws, but I cannot see an obvious reason to expect the pro-majority feature of the initiative to be confined to taxes and spending. Thus, I would expect that when the interests of the majority collide with those of a minority on social policy, the majority

Table 8.1 Support for Ballot Propositions by Racial/Ethnic Groups

"Do you think that statewide ballot proposition elections are a good thing for California, a bad thing, or don't you think they make much difference?"

	Percentage responding "good thing" and "bad thing"							
	Asians		Blacks		Latinos		Whites	
Year	Good	Bad	Good	Bad	Good	Bad	Good	Bad
1979	80.0	3.3	60.0	12.9	83.2	1.1	87.2	4.2
1982	78.1	3.1	69.2	6.2	83.2	5.6	84.8	5.2
1997	76.9	1.9	56.9	8.6	72.8	3.3	72.6	11.5

will win more often when the initiative is available. Why then would minorities express such strong support for the initiative process?

One possible explanation is that blacks, Latinos, and Asian Americans do not view themselves as minorities on most of the important policy questions that have to be decided. Rather they perceive the "minority" (the group that loses to the majority) to be someone else. We have some evidence on this. Hajnal, Gerber, and Louch (2002) studied fifty-one California ballot propositions and found that black, Latino, and Asian American voters were only about 1 percent less likely than white voters to be on the winning side of the vote. Essentially the same pattern emerged even when they focused on measures where minorities voted cohesively or on issues that minorities said they cared most about. Perhaps minorities expect to be disadvantaged by the initiative when it comes to issues that divide along racial lines, but they anticipate making up for these losses and then some by being on the winning side of most other issues. English as the official state language might be an acceptable price to pay for having lower taxes, for example. Such a calculus does not seem entirely unreasonable. Racial and ethnic minorities enjoy significant Constitutional protection stemming from the Equal Protection Clause, and the courts have been fairly aggressive in enforcing these rights for the last thirty years. I find it hard to imagine an initiative that seriously undermined minority rights surviving judicial scrutiny given the current state of jurisprudence.

Finally, this line of reasoning suggests to me that the literature might not be looking for the right kind of majority tyranny. Majority tyranny may be more of a threat to numerical minorities who do not enjoy clear Constitutional protection and the favor of the courts, such as business groups, people who live in certain geographic areas, people who enjoy activities the majority disapproves of, such as smoking, drinking, and hunting, and so on. Although it has become a mantra in the literature to cite the *Federalist* papers on the dangers of majority tyranny, it is seldom noted that the concern there was primarily about the rights of *economic* interests (*Federalist* no. 10):

> But the most common and durable source of factions, has been the various and unequal distribution of property. Those who hold, and those who are without property, have ever formed distinct interests in society. Those who are creditors, and those who are debtors, fall under a like discrimination. A landed interest, a manufacturing interest, a mercantile interest, a monied interest, with many lesser interests, grow up of necessity in civilized nations, and divide them into different classes,

> actuated by different sentiments and views. The regulation of these various and interfering interests forms the principal task of modern Legislation.

We might do well to take this argument more seriously and investigate how the initiative process impacts the interests of unpopular, numerically small economic groups. For example, are cigarette taxes higher—that is, are tobacco companies asked to provide a larger share of government revenue—with initiatives or legislatures? This aspect of the majority tyranny issue, so far ignored in the literature, constitutes yet another important unresolved question concerning the initiative and minority rights.

The Initiative, the Constitution, and the Foundations of American Democracy

The U.S. Constitution established a representative democracy, not a direct democracy. This was not by accident. The Founders were deeply skeptical of direct democracy. As James Madison put it in another oft-cited passage of the *Federalist* no. 10:

> A pure democracy, by which I mean, a society, consisting of a small number of citizens, who assemble and administer the government in person, can admit of no cure for the mischiefs of faction. . . . Democracies have ever been spectacles of turbulence and contention; have ever been found incompatible with personal security, or the rights of property; and have in general been as short in their lives, as they have been violent in their deaths. Theoretic politicians, who have patronized this species of government, have erroneously supposed, that by reducing mankind to a perfect equality in their political rights, they would, at the same time, be perfectly equalized and assimilated in their possessions, their opinions, and their passions.
>
> A republic, by which I mean a government in which the scheme of representation takes place, opens a different prospect, and promises the cure for which we are seeking.

The initiative process is not exactly what Madison had in mind by a "pure democracy," but it is surely a step away from the "pure" representative government he envisioned. The institutions of American government have served the country well for more than two hundred years and should not be tampered with lightly. An important question is whether the initiative departs so far from the Constitutional scheme that it undermines the foundations of American democracy.

Much has been written on this question but the answer is elusive. As a matter of law, the answer is clear: the initiative process *is* constitutional. Article IV, section 4 of the U.S. Constitution "guarantee[s] to every state in this union a republican form of government." In the early twentieth century, the initiative process was challenged as a violation of this so-called Guarantee Clause. The Supreme Court declined to consider the merits of the case, holding that it was for the Congress not the courts to decide whether a state's government was "republican" or not.[7] When Congress admits a state with the initiative process to the Union (as happened with Oklahoma and Alaska) or accepts the representatives of an initiative state, or when the President recognizes a government under powers delegated to him by Congress, that state is thereby presumed to have a republican form of government. The initiative has thus been accepted as constitutional by the proper authorities for more than one hundred years now.

Although the constitutionality of the initiative process is settled for practical purposes, the underlying issue is not. Serious critics still contend that the initiative is incompatible with the principles of American government. In the dire words of David Broder (2000, 1), the process is "alien to the spirit of the Constitution" and a threat to "subvert the American system of government." What follows is a brief overview of the main arguments, and my view of where things stand.

What Would the Founders Say?

A natural starting point for understanding how the initiative process might affect the Constitutional machinery is the writings of the Founders. Unfortunately, nothing like the initiative process was on the table when the Constitution was framed, so the best we can do is speculate what the Founders would have thought had they considered it.

One approach has been to focus on the meaning of the phrase "republican government," since it is clear that the Founders sought to establish a "republic." "Republican government" clearly entails some form of popular participation, but exactly what forms are included is vague, and it is doubtful the Founders would have agreed on the particulars. In *Federalist* no. 10, as just noted, Madison defined a republic narrowly as government by representatives, contrasting it with "pure democracy," by which he had in mind something like a town meeting. It would be quite a stretch to fit the initiative process into his notion of a republic. Thomas Jefferson's definition, on the other hand, was broader, and could easily accommodate the initiative process:

> Action by the citizens in person, in affairs within their reach and competence, and in all others by representatives, chosen immediately, and removable by themselves, constitutes the essence of a republic. . . . All governments are more or less republican in proportion as this principle enters more or less into their composition.[8]

John Adams simply noted that he "never understood" what a republic meant, and "no other man ever did or ever will."[9]

A second approach to determining the Founders' intent is to examine the initiative process in light of the underlying *theory* of government in the Constitution. The emphasis here again has been on the celebrated *Federalist* no. 10, in which Madison laid out the argument for representation and against pure democracy. It is worth quoting at length:

> The two great points of difference between a democracy and a republic are, first, the delegation of the government, in the latter, to a small number of citizens elected by the rest: secondly, the greater number of citizens, and greater sphere of country, over which the latter may be extended.
>
> The effect of the first difference is, on the one hand to refine and enlarge the public views, by passing them through the medium of a chosen body of citizens, whose wisdom may best discern the true interest of their country, and whose patriotism and love of justice, will be least likely to sacrifice it to temporary or partial considerations. Under such a regulation, it may well happen that the public voice pronounced by the representatives of the people, will be more consonant to the public good, than if pronounced by the people themselves convened for the purpose. On the other hand, the effect may be inverted. Men of factious tempers, or local prejudices, or of sinister designs, may by intrigue, by corruption or by other means, first obtain the suffrages, and then betray the interests of the people. . . .
>
> The other point of difference is, the greater number of citizens and extent of territory which may be brought within the compass of republican, than of democratic government; and it is this circumstance principally which renders factious combinations less to be dreaded in the former, than in the latter. The smaller the society, the fewer probably will be the distinct parties and interests composing it; the fewer the distinct

> parties and interests, the more frequently will a majority be found of the same party; and the smaller the number of individuals composing a majority, and the smaller the compass within which they are placed, the more easily will they concert and execute their plans of oppression. Extend the sphere, and you take in a greater variety of parties and interests; you make it less probable that a majority of the whole will have a common motive to invade the rights of other citizens; or if such a common motive exists, it will be more difficult for all who feel it to discover their own strength, and to act in unison with each other.

Modern commentators have tended to focus on the first of Madison's arguments, the potential for representatives to "refine and enlarge" the public views. However, that was not the decisive point for Madison. Indeed, he observes that representatives can "betray the interests of the people."[10] Thomas Jefferson expressed an even greater skepticism toward delegated power: "The mass of citizens is the safest depository of their own rights; . . . the evils flowing from the duperies of the people are less injurious than those from the egoism of their agents."[11]

In fact, the key advantage of a republic over a democracy from Madison's perspective is that a representative democracy can function over a wider expanse of territory and a larger population than a pure democracy. The strength of representative democracy comes from the counterbalancing interests that are encompassed by a government that extends over a large population and territory, not from the superior virtue of representatives or the give and take of their deliberations.

It helps to understand the context of Madison's argument. Madison's immediate purpose was to persuade the citizens of New York to adopt the federal Constitution. As such, his purpose was not so much to argue against direct democracy—there were no serious proposals to move the United States in that direction. Rather, he was trying to defuse the antifederalist argument that the new Constitution concentrated too much unchecked power in the hands of the central government. It was generally accepted in the late eighteenth century that popular rule had been a failure throughout history (the classical Greek city states were favorite examples). Given this, the antifederalists argued that the power of the central government had to be limited (as in the Articles of Confederation, which gave veto rights to individual states) or the people's rights would be endangered. Madison accepted the premise of the antifederalist argument—that democracies historically were unstable—but then argued that the problem could be cured by extending the government over a sufficiently large population and territory. Previous attempts at popular government failed, in his view, because they had not been applied on a large enough scale. The Constitution would cure the problem of pure democracy—its limited scope—by working through representatives instead of directly through the people. The important point here is that the main problem with pure democracy is its limited scope, not its lack of representation. Madison was not alone in this view: "A democracy [is] the only pure republic, but impracticable beyond the limits of a town," wrote Jefferson.[12]

Federalist no. 10 never reaches the question: Would pure democracy be acceptable if it could be established over a large population and territory? As such, it is not clear how far the argument against "pure" democracy extends to the initiative process. The initiative process can be applied over a large population and area (the population of California alone is now more than ten times the population of the entire United States in 1787), so it should enjoy the same benefits from encompassing multiple competing interests that Madison used to justify representative democracy. The case against the initiative process, then, would seem to rest primarily on the alleged ability of representatives to refine the public views, but as we have seen, even Madison viewed this argument with skepticism.

Another important ingredient of the Constitution is the system of checks and balances. The Constitution deliberately fragmented power between the legislative, executive, and judicial branches, following principles laid down by Montesquieu (1989, book 10, chap. 6) and widely accepted by the Founders: "All would be lost if the same man or the same body of principal men, either of nobles, or of the people, exercised these three powers: that of making the laws, that of executing public resolutions, and that of judging the crimes or the disputes of individuals." In broad terms, separation of powers is preserved when the initiative process is available. The voters have the power to legislate, but they do not administer, execute, or judge the laws. And as Gerber et al. (2001) have shown, the power of the other branches to check direct legislation is real: many initiatives approved by the voters are subsequently blocked by judicial decisions or the failure of the executive to enforce them.

However, the Constitution incorporated two additional counterbalancing features that the initiative process overrides: the division of legislative power into two houses, and the executive veto over legislation. Both of these devices again followed Montesquieu, although he envisioned an upper house of hereditary nobles and a monarchical executive. While a bicameral legislature and executive veto were considered desirable by most of the Founders, it is not clear whether they viewed these checks as fundamental to the new Constitution. Three American states in the late eighteenth century did not have bicameral legislatures (Georgia, Pennsylvania, Vermont), and all but three states (Massachusetts, New York, and South Carolina) excluded the executive veto from their first constitutions.[13] These states were not considered to be in violation of republican principles as far as we know.[14]

Some time ago, Charles Beard, who was generally sympathetic to the initiative process, concluded from his survey of the Founders' views that "no one has any warrant for assuming that the founders of our federal system would have shown the slightest countenance to a system of initiative and referendum applied either to state or local affairs. If some state had possessed such a system at that time, it is questionable whether they would have been willing to have compromised with it, as they did with the slave states, in order to secure its adherence to the Union" (Beard and Shulz [1912] 1970, 29). I think the case is not so cut and dried, as I have tried to explain here. The Founders were deeply distrustful of legislatures, much like modern-day initiative proponents, and at least some of them had faith in the public at large to vote its interest. Moreover, the Founders were not uniformly hostile to direct democracy in the forms that existed at the time, such as New England town meetings, nor were they opposed to periodic popular lawmaking via referendums. Massachusetts held a statewide referendum in 1778 on a post-independence constitution, and New Hampshire held a series of constitutional referendums (working through town meetings) in 1778, 1781, and 1783. It seems clear the Founders would have objected to a national town-meeting form of government as proposed by some modern direct democracy advocates. How they would have felt about the initiative process—a grafting of periodic citizen-initiated referendums onto a predominantly representative government—is not so obvious.[15]

It Comes Down to Evidence Again?

The writings of the Founders give valuable insight into how the pieces of the Constitution fit together, but they do not incorporate the experiences of the last two hundred years. Yet it is the historical record that holds the most promise for understanding how the machinery of American government works. Indeed, the Founders probably would have viewed the parsing of their words in search of answers (as I just did above, and many others have done elsewhere) somewhat skeptically. "Forty years of experience in government is worth a century of book-reading," wrote Thomas

Jefferson in 1816, and this the Founders "would say themselves were they to rise from the dead."[16] The men who set up the American federal system were thoughtful empiricists. They sought practical solutions for governance problems from historical experience, not in the writings of authorities. Our approach should be the same: the answer to whether the initiative undermines American government must be found in the data.

Empirical research has only begun to seriously engage this question. The difficulty is not in determining whether the Constitution has served the country well. It has. Rather, the problem is identifying what *parts* of the Constitutional scheme are important and which are not. It is clear that not everything established in 1787 is essential. The Constitution has been modified without damaging its essential features many times over the last two centuries. Most would agree that some changes have improved on the original plan and brought American democracy closer to its true principles, such as the ending of slavery, the granting of voting rights to blacks, women, and those without property, and the direct election of U.S. senators. Yet we can also conceive of modifications that would have a pernicious effect. There is no shortage of opinions about why American government works, but these are at best informed hunches. The truth is that we simply do not have much of an empirical basis at present for saying that one part of the Constitutional scheme is important and another is not. Consequently, there is not much factual ground to stand on when assessing whether the initiative is harmful to the core principles of American government.[17]

Although definitive answers await serious empirical research, an impressionistic look at the historical record does not give much reason to be concerned about the initiative process. The initiative has been part of American government for more than a century now. While it is not obvious exactly how to measure "quality of government," casual observation suggests that initiative states have done just as well as noninitiative states using the more obvious metrics: initiative states seem to be just as free, prosperous, and nice places to live as noninitiative states. There is no heavy migration of citizens from initiative states to noninitiative states as would be expected if the initiative was a serious threat to life, liberty, and the pursuit of happiness. Indeed, many states that are typically viewed as attractive places to live—for example, California, Florida, Massachusetts, and Washington—happen to be initiative states. I am not claiming that the initiative caused any of this (although I would not foreclose the possibility, either), only pointing out that the initiative has not caused things to go horribly awry. Whatever its demerits may be, the initiative does not cause the Constitutional sky to fall.

The few pieces of modern empirical research that are designed to assess how the initiative affects the quality of governance point in the same direction. One purpose of government is to promote (or at least not hinder) economic prosperity. Evidence from two recent studies suggests that if anything the initiative process is good for the economy. One study documented that output per worker was higher in initiative states than in noninitiative states, and imputed that noninitiative states "wasted" 20 percent more of their government spending than initiative states (Blomberg, Hess, and Weerapana 2001). The other study found that output per capita was higher in Swiss cantons (roughly the same as American states) with the initiative than in cantons without the initiative, after controlling for the physical and human capital stock (Feld and Savioz 1997). One interpretation of this evidence is that the initiative process causes governments to choose policies that are more favorable for economic growth. For example, the initiative might be used to direct public funds into valuable infrastructure instead of pork barrel projects. This interpretation is reinforced by another study of Switzerland: an analysis of municipal trash collection found greater efficiency in cities with the initiative than cities without the initiative (Pommerehne 1983). A more general measure of government performance might be the "happiness" of the citizens. Happiness is notoriously difficult to measure, but a recent study of Switzerland found that citizens who lived in cantons where the initiative is available reported higher levels of subjective well-being ("happiness") than those living in cantons where the initiative is unavailable, after controlling for a large number of demographic and economic variables (Frey and Stutzer 2000). I should say that I have some methodological misgivings about much of this evidence, so I take it as only suggestive. Robustness needs to be established and other metrics of government performance need to be investigated. It is notable, however, that to this point there does not appear to be a single empirical study that finds the initiative process reduces the quality of government, however measured.

CHAPTER 9 

Delegation, Information, and Competition

Although this book refutes the most common criticism of the initiative—that it allows special interests to subvert the policy process—it does not claim the initiative is a good (or bad) feature of American democracy. The evidence shows that the initiative promotes majority rule, which is for the most part desirable, but questions remain whether the process threatens the rights of minorities or undermines the Constitution. As discussed in the preceding chapter, the evidence currently available on "majority tyranny" and the Constitution does not give much cause to worry, but definitive answers await more empirical research. For what it is worth, the evidence has left me sympathetic to the process, but still willing to be persuaded by new evidence.

Be that as it may, I suspect that arguments over whether direct democracy is a good or bad thing will become irrelevant in the not too distant future, much like questions about whether democracy itself is a good or bad thing. The initiative and other forms of direct democracy are here to stay, and in all likelihood will grow in importance. The electorate is increasingly educated and sophisticated, and the revolution in communication technology (internet, satellites, etc.) has made more information accessible to more people than at any time in human history. Ordinary citizens can now become as knowledgeable as their representatives. It is difficult to imagine the American people one day deciding to cut off their participation in policymaking and turn it over entirely to politicians.

As direct democracy continues to spread, interest will fade in whether it should be done away with altogether, and will turn instead to understanding how direct democracy interacts with the other institutions of American democracy, and how the various institutions can be made to work together productively. Answering these questions will require development of new frameworks and theories concerning the function of the initiative process in a (primarily) representative democracy. This concluding chapter outlines three such approaches—I call them the delegation, information, and competition views—that I believe have some promise. The three views are not incompatible and are not offered as competing theories but rather as frameworks that allow us to focus on different aspects of the same problem. At this point, I can only offer sketches, brief appraisals, and speculation, but my hope is there is enough content to stimulate further research and thinking about the role of the initiative process.

The Prevailing View: Delegation

The conventional way of thinking about the initiative is in terms of a delegation model of democracy. Democracy, from a delegation perspective, is a relationship between principals (voters) and their agents (representatives). The principals appoint agents to make policy and run the government on their behalf. Delegation allows the principals to take advantage of the expertise of policymaking professionals, and spares the principals from having to become policy experts themselves. The downside of delegation is that the agents might not act in the interests of the principals. The initiative, seen from this perspective, is a tool that allows the principals to override their agents when the agents misbehave.

The Logic of Delegation: Specialization versus Agency Costs

Principal-agent relationships are a ubiquitous feature of modern life. Managers delegate decisions to their subordinates, litigants delegate decisions to their lawyers, congressmen delegate decisions to bureaucratic agencies, and so on. The logic of delegation is fairly well understood.[1] The narrow benefit of delegation is that it allows a nonspecialist to take advantage of the knowledge of experts. More broadly, delegation facilitates specialization. Each person becomes an expert in a narrow set of tasks and delegates the rest of his decisions to experts in the other tasks. My expertise is in college education, and students learn economics from me, but I rely on the expertise of others for my medical and dental care, to repair my car, to manage my retirement fund, and to teach my young children how to read. A central lesson of economics since Adam Smith is that economic specialization leads to economic prosperity. An economy populated by experts who trade with each other across specializations is much wealthier than an economy in which each person is a jack-of-all-trades, or a Robinson Crusoe who provides everything for himself. Representative government is a form of specialization like any other: one group of people specializes in making public decisions and administering the government, freeing everyone else to specialize in developing software, building cars, making movies, teaching college students, raising children, and so on.

The cost of delegation is that agents might misuse their authority. Government officials might take actions that harm the citizens or fail to take actions that would help. This possibility is more than theoretical. Popular support for the initiative process is founded on the belief that elected officials do not always act in the public interest. Opinion surveys make it clear that Americans do not trust their representatives to do the right thing, and have much more confidence in the electorate at large. For example, table 9.1 reports a survey in which, by 3-to-1 margins, respondents expressed more confidence in decision-making by the public than by legislators.

There are two main ways of controlling agency problems. First, the principals can try to get the agents to make the right decisions by careful screening and design of incentives. For example, in the private sector managers try to hire employees who admire the firm's products and goals (screening), and firms offer profit-sharing plans, stock ownership, and promotion based on performance (incentives). In the political sphere, voters try to select agents who they believe share their values and goals (screening) and they use the possibility of reelection to provide incentives: incumbents who do a good job are given another term in office and unsatisfactory representatives are thrown out (Peltzman 1998).

A second way to control agency problems is for the principals to reserve the right to overrule their agents. In the private sector, the principal

Table 9.1 Confidence in the Legislature versus the Voters

	Percentage of respondents giving each answer			
	Legislature	Voters	Same	Not sure
All things being equal, which do you think is more likely to produce laws that are in the public interest: when the law is adopted by the legislature or when the law is adopted by the voters?	20.4	65.5	NA	13.6
If an organization supported a measure that would *improve* the way government works, which group would be more *receptive* to the idea: the legislature or the voters?	13.5	59.6	17.7	8.8
If an organization supported a measure that would *harm* your state, which group would be more receptive to arguments *against* the measure: the legislature or the voters?	20.6	61.5	12.6	4.8

Note: "Same" means the respondent expected the legislature and voters to be equally receptive. The "same" response was not available for the first question. The fraction of respondents who declined to answer, never more than half a percent, is not reported.

almost always retains this right. When a manager delegates decisions to subordinates, it is understood that he or she can step in if the decision is unsatisfactory. The initiative is the political version of the principal's right to overrule the agent. If elected officials behave unfaithfully, the voters can intercede and implement their desired policies directly.

One argument against the initiative process is that voters already have the means to control their representatives by refusing to reelect them if they perform poorly. This boils down to an assertion that candidate elections provide a perfect solution to agency problems. This is clearly not the case. If it were, there would be no reason for our entire Constitutional system with its multitude of checks and balances. We would simply elect our representatives and let them go about their business unencumbered by anything but the prospect of having to win reelection. The argument is analogous to saying that managers should never retain the right to overrule their subordinates because they can simply fire and replace subordinates who make bad decisions.

It seems likely, therefore, that the initiative will increase the principals' control of agency problems beyond what can be accomplished by candidate elections alone. However, the initiative process requires voters to become engaged in policymaking, and thereby sacrifice some of the benefits of delegation. Whether the initiative is desirable from a delegation perspective depends on whether the mitigation of agency costs outweighs the reduced specialization benefits.

Half a Theory

My purpose here is not to work out the delegation view in any detail, but some of the more direct implications and limitations are worth noting. The essence of the theory is that the value of the initiative depends on how the benefits of expertise compare to the agency costs of delegation. We can speculate on the future of the initiative, then, by considering how the benefits and costs of delegation are likely to evolve over time. On the benefit side, it seems likely that in an increasingly complex world, the benefits of specialization will grow. Efficiency will call for continued if not increasing involvement of governance experts in public decisions. It will not be efficient for ordinary citizens to develop the expertise required to actively participate in governing on a continuous basis. Many governance experts will hold office, but increasing specialization will probably swell the ranks of governance experts outside the government, in think tanks, universities, the media, and organized interest groups. To the extent that these out-of-government experts provide information cues to voters in direct democracy elections, it may be possible to enjoy some of the fruits of specialization without having to delegate authority to agents. The use of information cues would be practical only for broad questions of policy, however, so one can imagine increasing public involvement in formulating the general principles of public policy and decreasing involvement in the daily business of government. On the cost side, as more and more public decisions are delegated to governance specialists, the scope for misbehavior will increase. This could lead to an increased reliance on mechanisms to control agency problems such as initiatives and referendums.

Several other less speculative implications of the delegation view emerge from studies that use the tools of modern game theory to model the initiative process.[2] The models proceed by assuming that legislators choose an initial policy, not necessarily in the interest of their constituents, and then outsiders (such as an interest group) have the option of paying a cost to put a competing proposal (initiative) before the voters. An immediate implication is that the initiative is only useful when representatives misbehave. When representatives faithfully pursue the public interest, an initiative would be counterproductive because legislators have a superior ability to identify good policies.

A second implication of these models is that voters are never worse off when the initiative is available and can be better off. If the outsider's proposal is worse than the legislature's policy, the voters stick with the status quo; if the outsider's proposal improves on the status quo, the voters adopt the initiative and are better off. It follows that the initiative process pushes policy closer to the position of the median voter. The evidence in this book, especially chapters 3 and 4, shows this is in fact what seems to happen when it comes to taxes and spending. Gerber (1996, 1999) presents evidence suggesting it is also what happens for capital punishment and parental notification of abortion policies.

But there is a problem: the models imply that voters are *always* better off (or never worse off) having the initiative process available. If so, then why do only half of the states and cities in the country have it? Why isn't the initiative process nearly universal if it can never make the voters worse off? A partial explanation might be that elected officials in many jurisdictions simply refuse to allow voters the option of adopting the initiative. But this cannot be the full explanation because voters have rejected proposals to make the initiative process available on occasion.

The most likely explanation for why the initiative is not universal would seem to be that it has some cost that is not incorporated in the delegation model as currently formulated. The cost cannot be simply the principals' lost time from being involved in the decision (or, more generally, the productivity decline from less specialization). Even if the principals pay a time cost to participate, the models suggest they are still better off having the *right* to intervene since they can simply not exercise the right in situations where it is too costly. The cost must be related to a factor excluded from the standard model.

Work has only begun in understanding what the cost might be. In two recent papers, my co-authors and I extended the model to incorporate incomplete information, and showed how the initiative process in theory might work to the disadvantage of voters. If legislators are unsure about the preferences of voters, availability of the initiative can cause them to accommodate extreme interests more than they would if the initiative was unavailable (Matsusaka and McCarty 2001). If voters are unsure about the consequences of certain government programs, availability of the initiative process can cause legislators to choose inefficient projects in order to mislead voters about the projects' merits (Marino and Matsusaka forthcoming). Both papers report some evidence consistent with the idea that incomplete information is important for understanding the costs of the initiative process, but the situations they identify where the initiative hurts rather than helps seem like special cases.

To summarize, the most common way of thinking about the initiative process is in terms of delegated power: representatives are the agents of voters, and voters reserve the right to overrule policy decisions that are not in their interest. Some progress has been made in developing formal models of the initiative along this line. Three implications emerge from the theoretical literature. First, the initiative is valuable only when the legislators misbehave. Second, the initiative brings policy closer to what the majority wants, consistent with the evidence in this book. But third, the initiative has no downside; voters can utilize the process when it is beneficial, and ignore it otherwise. This last implication runs up against the stubborn fact that half of the states and cities in the United States have not adopted the initiative process. It is hard to believe so many states and cities would not have availed themselves of a process with no downside. Until the costs are better understood, the delegation view would seem to be only half a theory.

The Information View

The delegation view is such an ingrained part of conventional thinking about democracy that you might wonder what other view there could be. I will discuss two. The first differs from the delegation view in only one respect, but an important one. It concerns the nature of political information. The delegation view implicitly assumes that a small group of experts (legislators) are capable of knowing or collecting the information necessary to choose the "right" policy. Elections serve to select this group and keep them honest, but otherwise the people have nothing to contribute to policymaking. As Schumpeter (1950, 295) put it:

> The voters . . . must understand that, once they have elected an individual, political action is his business and not theirs. This means they must refrain from instructing him about what he is to do. . . . Not only instructions as formal as those French *cahiers* but also less formal attempts at restricting the freedom of action of members of parliament—the practice of bombarding them with letters and telegrams for instance—ought to come under the same ban.

Schumpeter's position may be a bit extreme, but it captures an important theme of the delegation view: representatives know best when it comes to policymaking. The knowledge and preferences of ordinary citizens are not particularly useful for making wise policy decisions. The experts are capable of making the right decisions themselves, or in consultation with other experts.

However, it is not so obvious that good policy depends only on the information of experts. We can imagine situations where the "right" policy primarily depends instead on the values of the members of the community, or where the accumulated knowledge of everyday citizens would be more useful than the knowledge of experts. What I call the information view emphasizes the dispersed information and preferences of the population instead of the knowledge of experts.[3] The fundamental challenge for democracy, seen from the information perspective, is finding a way to bring this dispersed information to bear on the formulation of policy.

To give a concrete example, whether or not a particular business regulation is desirable depends on how it will affect the profitability of businesses, the welfare of employees, the prices and choices offered to consumers, and so on. A great deal of useful information about these effects is inside the heads of managers, employees, customers, and so on, and it would be difficult for a legislator to discover more than a tiny fraction of it on his own. George McGovern, a U.S. Senator with a fondness for regulation while in office, lost his regulatory zeal after he left office and became the owner of a small business that went bankrupt:

> [One] lesson I learned by owning the Stratford Inn is that legislators and government regulators must more carefully consider the economic and management burdens we have been imposing on U.S. business. As an innkeeper, I wanted excellent safeguards against a fire. But I was startled to be told that our two-story structure, which had large sliding doors opening from every guest room to all-concrete decks, required us to meet fire regulations more appropriate to the Waldorf-Astoria. A costly automatic sprinkler system and new exit doors were items that helped sink the Stratford Inn—items I was convinced added little to the safety of our guests and employees.[4]

The importance of dispersed information may be even more important for "social" issues. For example, the decision whether or not to allow physician-assisted suicide is not really something where an expert has an advantage. Such a decision is largely a matter of the people defining what sort of community they want to live in, and the key inputs to that decision are the values and preferences of the community members themselves.

In short, from the perspective of the information view, good policy cannot be formulated by appealing only to abstract principles, the opinions of experts, or other centralizable information. It also requires tapping the dispersed information and preferences of ordinary citizens. The initiative can be seen as a way of tapping that information. One thing that allows the initiative to aggregate information better than legislatures is the law of large numbers. To take an example from Lupia (2001) by way of Condorcet, suppose a public decision must be made in which there are two possible outcomes. Suppose further that one of the policies is unambiguously better than the other, but that each person has only a 51 percent chance of knowing which is the better and which is the worse policy. That is, each person's knowledge about policy is not much better than just flipping a coin. Even though individuals are not well informed, if one million people cast votes for one of the two policies based on their information, the probability that the "better" option would win is approximately 100 percent. Because of the law of large numbers, randomness will cancel out in the aggregate, leaving a very clear picture of which policy is better. Legislatures, which involve the input of many fewer people, might end up doing a worse job aggregating information even if individual legislators are more informed than individual voters.

The issue-bundling problem in candidate elections is another obstacle to collecting information in representative government. Candidates take positions on a huge number of issues. Exactly what the voter thinks about a particular issue is difficult to determine from his vote in a candidate election. Did the incumbent win because voters agreed with his position on education, or taxes, or affirmative action, or . . . ? The initiative solves the bundling problem by stripping out a particular issue, resulting in a much clearer picture of voter opinion on that issue.

From the delegation perspective, the initiative is useful only when representatives are unfaithful; or to put it the other way, when representatives are faithful, the initiative is not valuable. One implication of the information view is that the initiative can be valuable even if representatives are faithful and competent. An important part of a representative's job, according to the information view, is to discover the knowledge and preferences of his or her constituents. The initiative may be complementary to that endeavor. Another implication of the information view, at least as formalized in Matsusaka and McCarty 2001, is that the initiative can sometimes make the voters worse off. The argument is rather technical and may not be robust, but it suggests that consideration of dispersed information may be one way to fill in the "other half" of the delegation theory (what are the costs of the initiative).

The utility of the information view has yet to be demonstrated empirically. There is some evidence in Matsusaka 1992 and Matsusaka and McCarty 2001, but it is only suggestive. The information view does make it easy to understand some patterns of initiative and referendum use. For example, a common practice is to hold local referendums to decide whether a community will allow liquor to be sold within its borders. The explanation in terms of the information view is that the "right" liquor policy for a community depends primarily on the community's values not expert knowledge, and the best way to determine community values is to ask the people to vote. Another example is that initiatives are used to resolve "moral" issues and issues having to do with the distribution of income much more often than they are used to resolve technical issues such as the organization of courts and legal procedures. The knowledge and values of the population at large are more likely to be important for moral and distributional issues than technical issues.[5]

There is another empirical regularity, not widely known, that may be worth mentioning here. It concerns the prevalence of the initiative in cities. As figure 9.1 shows, cities are increasingly likely to make the initiative available as they become larger. The information view suggests one way to explain the pattern: good policymaking depends on the local

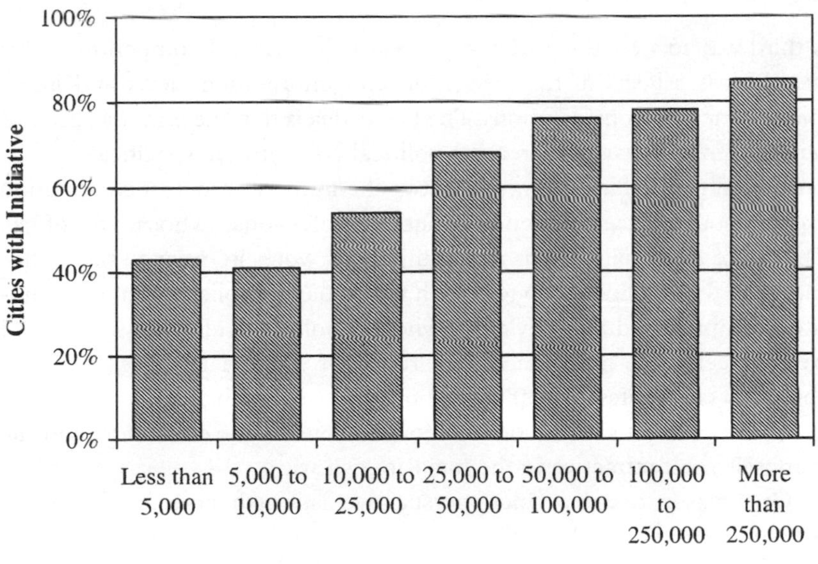

Figure 9.1 Initiative Availability and City Size.
Note: This figure reports the percentage of cities that provide the initiative by size of city as of 1986.

information of ordinary citizens, and local information is more difficult for representatives to ascertain in large cities because the number of constituents is so much larger. The initiative is an especially valuable way to fill the gap in large cities by allowing citizens to register their preferences when representatives have a difficult time figuring them out.[6]

To summarize, I am not arguing that the information view is superior to the delegation view, nor am I arguing that the information view "fills in" the missing half of the delegation view. Rather I am making the more modest suggestion that the information view may capture some consequences of the initiative process that are not captured by the delegation view. It may be productive to ask what information is really important for good policy decisions, the centralizable information of experts or the decentralized information of the people, and then inquire how the initiative affects the amount of such information that is brought to bear on public decisions. I offer the information view because it is prima facie plausible, and because it challenges some of the lessons of the delegation view. In particular, while the delegation view implies that the initiative is valuable only when representatives misbehave, the information view suggests the initiative may useful even when representatives are faithful.

The Competition View

A third way to view the initiative process is in terms of competition. This view blends aspects of the delegation and information views and introduces some new considerations. The basic idea is that the initiative process can be seen as a way of increasing political competition, specifically, competition in the making of laws. Without the initiative process, competition over laws takes place between the political professionals who run for office. They state their policy goals and compete for votes in order to take office and push their policies through. With the initiative, policies can be formulated and proposed by individuals who are not political professionals and are not seeking to hold office. Regardless of whether new laws are proposed by candidates for office or policy entrepreneurs not running for office, the proposals must compete for the votes of the electorate, and the proposals most attractive to the majority will win.

One reason a competition perspective is worth entertaining is the growing interest in the idea of competition itself. Competition has emerged at the dawn of the twenty-first century as an important organizing principle of human societies. Much of the history of the twentieth century can be seen a contest between two organizing principles, monopoly and competition. In the economic sphere, the debate was whether monopolies and centrally planned economies (such as in the Soviet Union or Cuba) or economies with competing firms (such as the United States) would lead to more prosperity. A parallel debate took place in the political sphere between advocates of governments monopolized by a single party (such as the Communist or Nazi Party) and advocates of governments where parties are free to compete for office. The contestants are still skirmishing, but the war is over and competition is the clear winner in the court of public opinion.[7]

The other reason for considering a competition view is that we already understand a great deal about competition in economic and political markets. If we view the initiative through the lens of competition, we can exploit principles that have been discovered about those other forms of competition. And thinking about parallels in the arguments may lead us to new insights about the initiative itself. This section reviews some of the main lessons concerning competition between firms, parties, and governments, and then discusses what these lessons might mean for thinking about the initiative process. Since, as far as I know, the idea of competition has never been linked to the initiative process before, I provide a bit more background here than in previous sections. Again, the point is not that the competition view is superior to the delegation and information views, but that a competition view may lead to insights and questions about the initiative process that are not revealed by the other approaches.

Competition between Firms, Parties, and Governments

Competition between firms is the bread and butter of modern economics. Economic theory recognizes two benefits of competition. The first is a static benefit: given the available resources and technologies, competition results in the most efficient possible production arrangements (generally called the First Fundamental Theorem of Welfare Economics). The result holds in an environment of atomistic profit-maximizing firms that are individually unable to influence the market price. In the jargon of economics, when firms take the market price as given, profit maximization leads to all firms having the same marginal cost, and marginal rates of substitution across inputs are equalized in all uses, the technical conditions for efficiency. Less technically, one can think of competition driving out high-cost firms, leaving only the most efficient producers (and production plans) in the market.

There is also a more subtle benefit of competition: prices incorporate and reflect the information of individual consumers and suppliers about the value of products they buy and the cost of things they produce. Prices thus serve as information transmitters that allow economic activity to be coordinated between people who do not know each other. It is the information-transmitting property of prices that makes market economies more productive than centrally planned economies (Hayek 1945). In a centrally planned or monopolized market, prices do not reflect all available information and it is impossible to organize production efficiently.[8]

Competition also has a dynamic benefit: it creates a fertile environment for innovation, which fuels economic growth. Firms in competitive markets continually seek to improve the quality of their goods and services, production processes, and forms of organization. They do this in search of profits. Competition allows firms to experiment, and rewards those experiments that satisfy the wants of consumers or increase the efficiency of production. Decentralized decision-making allows numerous individuals to bring their own particular knowledge to bear in a way that would not be possible under monopoly.

Competition does not always lead to efficiency, however. A number of situations are known to cause problems. Chief among them is a market with "externalities," costs imposed on third parties when a transaction takes place (such as medical expenses incurred by people who live near a polluting factory). Intuitively, when market participants do not pay the full costs of their actions, prices will not incorporate relevant information and a static inefficiency will arise. Another problem for competition is markets in which there are significant fixed costs, such as for power generation. The efficient scale in such a market might require only a single firm, creating a tension between competition and efficiency. Competition may also suffer dynamic inefficiencies. If firms can copy the innovations of each other at low cost, no one may want to be the first mover who makes the initial investment that leads to a discovery. As a result, a competitive market might underinvest in innovation. Alternatively, if there are large gains to making the initial discovery, there may be overinvestment in innovation.

The most important type of political competition is the competition between political parties for votes. Votes are the currency that allows parties to hold elected office and set policy. The most celebrated result on party competition is the median voter theorem of Hotelling (1929) and Downs (1957), which shows that competition for votes leads parties to adopt centrist positions that appeal to a majority of the electorate. There is something to be said for pleasing the majority and not adopting extreme policies, but good policymaking sometimes involves more than that;

"compromise" is not always a virtue, especially when an issue touches on fundamental liberties.

The benefits of party competition are easier to see by analogy with market competition. First, party competition pushes government in the direction of efficient policies. If a single party has monopoly power, it can divert a fraction of the society's resources to the ruler's friends, family, or Swiss bank account. Resources can still be expropriated in a multiparty system, but a party that promises to divert fewer resources will be favored by the voters. In equilibrium, competition will push the parties toward minimal diversion of resources. Much like a high-cost firm that cannot survive in a competitive market, a political party that imposes high costs on a majority of the voters will be voted out in competitive elections. Although my example here focuses on outright theft by government officials, the point is more general: politicians can divert resources to their associates in the form of government contracts, favorable regulation, tax breaks, and so on.[9]

Party competition also facilitates the revelation of information about citizen preferences, which is useful in making policy responsive to the voter's interests. Despite serious investments of time and money, parties and pollsters are never certain about the electorate's policy preferences. When parties take different positions, elections provide a way for voters to signal their preferences. Thus, competitive elections transmit information to policymakers in much the same way as prices transmit information in competitive markets. With a single party, voters cannot use elections to signal their opinions about alternative policies, so less information is revealed and brought to bear on policy formation.

Party competition can also lead to undesirable outcomes. One of the thorniest problems is cycling: under certain conditions, such as when the issue space is multidimensional, any given set of policies can be defeated by at least one other set of policies. Since no set of policies is clearly favored by the majority, public policy could bounce around unpredictably over time as one set of policies after another is adopted. Policy instability makes it difficult for businesses and individuals to plan, creating economic inefficiencies. In practice, democratic government does not appear to exhibit the instability predicted by these models, perhaps because the assumptions for stability are approximately true (for example, Poole and Rosenthal [1991] argued that the policy space is essentially one-dimensional) or because other institutions are in place that induce stability (such as procedural rules; Shepsle and Weingast 1981). In a different vein, Buchanan and Tullock (1962) suggested that competition for votes might cause elected officials to spend public funds inefficiently. Legislators might try to buy the votes of their constituents by approving local pork barrel projects, and paying for them out of general revenue. Such appropriations help local voters in a narrow sense—they get the benefits but share the costs with other taxpayers—but when every legislator plays the game, it results in an inefficiently high level of overall spending. This view finds some support in the data.[10]

Another form of political competition takes place between governments. At the subnational level, it is referred to as Tiebout competition. The idea is that governments—cities are the best example—compete with each to attract and retain residents (or businesses). They compete by offering menus of public goods and taxes. Individuals take into account the tax and spending policies of the surrounding cities, and "vote with their feet" by settling in the cities with the most attractive and efficient policies. Tiebout competition puts pressure on governments to adopt efficient policies, much like price competition in markets pushes firms to produce at low cost. Tiebout competition also facilitates information revelation by allowing people to signal their policy preferences. A danger of Tiebout competition is that it might trigger a "race to the bottom" as cities fight to attract industry and allow their environment to be degraded. However, the evidence suggests that if anything the reverse is true: there is a race to the top (Fischel 2001).

Economic historians have focused on competition between national governments (Bernholz, Streit, and Vaubel 1998). A general theme is that competition fosters innovation. For example, North (1981, 1998) attributes the rise of the Western world between the tenth and eighteenth centuries in part to the fact that Europe contained numerous small states. Without the centralized political control typical at that time in China and the Islamic states, Europeans were able to experiment with a variety of legal, political, and economic institutions. This creative atmosphere led to a burst of innovation. Competition between states also put pressure on rulers to limit the amount of resources they expropriated and to grant certain property rights and other liberties to their subjects.

The Initiative as a Form of Competition

The preceding discussion highlights some of the better known consequences of competition between firms, parties, and governments. Let us here turn to the idea that the initiative is a form of competition, specifically competition in the lawmaking process, and explore the parallels between this type of competition and other types of competition.

A first observation from the competition perspective is that by allowing "free entry" into the lawmaking process, the initiative puts pressure on "suppliers" of laws to adopt policies favored by the voters. This is just another way of stating the main result of the book: the initiative causes governments to adopt policies that are favored by the many rather than the few. This implication is also central to the delegation view.

A second and less obvious consequence of introducing competition into the lawmaking process is that it increases the revelation of information, which may lead to better policymaking. Voting is an important way citizens signal their policy preferences; for many it is the only way. To convey a preference, a voter must have a choice in the ballot box. The initiative provides a choice: vote for the proposal or reject it in favor of the status quo. Candidate elections do not always provide a choice. Indeed, competition in candidate elections is likely to lead to an *absence* of choices as Downsian parties converge on the same policies. The convergence of candidates, a fact continually bemoaned by ordinary citizens, has some desirable properties if they converge in the vicinity of the median voter. However, if the parties perceive the position of the median voter incorrectly, they might converge on the wrong point, and there is nothing in the electoral process that would self-correct. The initiative offers a way to break the gridlock of Downsian competition because it allows proposals to reach the voters outside the milieu of party competition. The fact that even seemingly crazy and hopeless proposals can be placed before the voters by a determined petitioner is particularly important, because these are the proposals that are unlikely be brought before the public under party competition. The possibility that a "crazy" proposal might turn out to enjoy majority support is more than theoretical: Proposition 13, for example, was dismissed by leaders of both parties and most expert opinion before its overwhelming victory.

Third, the initiative process is likely to promote policy innovation by allowing "policy entrepreneurs" to enter the "market" at lower cost. Without the initiative, a policy entrepreneur must convince an elected official to take up his cause, or run for office himself. With the initiative, those options are still available, but the entrepreneur can also go directly to the voters. Over time, we would expect to see individuals specialize in being initiative policy entrepreneurs, and they would develop capabilities to detect policies that the people want but are not being delivered by the established parties.[11] As the number of proposals rise, the likelihood of good new ideas being discovered goes up. Thus, the initiative is likely to create a more innovative policymaking environment. The problem of too little innovation is likely to be especially acute when parties are highly competitive, because Downsian pressures will make elected officials and candidates hesitant to embrace policies that are far from the perceived median.

On the downside, from a competition perspective the initiative process may exacerbate cycling problems. It is possible that legislators can solve cycling problems with procedural rules or repeated play, but it is more difficult to see how such solutions could be implemented for initiative elections. Another risk is that there may be too many resources devoted to making new laws. If there are first-mover advantages, policy entrepreneurs may invest too much in creating new laws. Rapid changes in policy, even if each change represents a marginal improvement in some sense, could be costly because it makes it difficult for individuals and agents to make long-term plans.

As should be apparent, these observations are speculative. There is no research from the competition perspective that works out how the initiative process might change American government. By listing some implications that seem to follow from studying other types of competition, I hope to suggest that something can be learned from studying the initiative as a form of competition.

Conclusion

This chapter outlines three frameworks for thinking about the role of the initiative process in American democracy: the delegation, information, and competition views. In the delegation view, the initiative provides voters a way to control the misbehavior of their representatives. In the information view, the initiative provides a way to collect the dispersed information of ordinary citizens and bring it to bear on policy. In the competition view, the initiative allows nonpoliticians to compete against professional politicians in proposing new policies. I have tried to suggest that each view may be useful in shedding light on how the initiative process changes American government, and in particular what might be the benefits and costs of having ordinary citizens directly involved in the proposal and passage of laws.

The purpose of this chapter, as with the entire book, is not to argue for or against the initiative process. The preponderance of the book is devoted to rigorous statistical evidence about the consequences of the initiative process. Most of the book focused on a particularly important argument—

that the initiative process allows special interests to subvert the policy process—and showed that the argument is inconsistent with the evidence. But there are other arguments for and against the initiative process that have to evaluated with hard evidence before any strong conclusions about the overall merits of the process are justified. The initiative serves the many and not the few, but whether that is a good or bad thing will require a great deal more empirical evidence to determine.

APPENDIX 1 

Initiative Provisions in States, 1898–2003

This appendix reports the state-level legal provisions for the initiative process. One purpose is to provide an accurate description of the state-level initiative procedures currently (August 2003) in place in the United States. That information appears in tables A1.1 and A1.2. Similar information is available in other books, but the information tends to become outdated as time passes and provisions are changed.

The second purpose of this appendix is to make available to researchers a reasonably accurate summary of initiative provisions across time. Table A1.3 lists the changes that each state has made in its initiative provisions over time. As can be seen, initiative provisions are not static. One of the obstacles to empirical research using state panel data is the difficulty of determining what the exact initiative provisions were in each state in the sample of years. By comparing tables A1.1, A1.2, and A1.3, the researcher should be able to establish the precise provisions (such as signature requirement) that were in effect in any given state in any given year. The historical information in table A1.3 is incomplete; there are some changes I have not been able to identify so far. Updates of all three tables will be available on the web page of the Initiative and Referendum Institute (www.iandrinstitute.org).

Researchers should be aware that errors (possibly typographical) seem to have crept into the main published sources for information on initiative provisions, including Magleby 1984, Schmidt 1989, Dubois and Feeney 1998, and Waters 2003. I have made every effort to ensure that the information in this appendix is accurate and complete, primarily by basing the tables on readings of state constitutions and statutes, but also by comparing my conclusions with information listed on official web sites and published in Dubois and Feeney 1998 and Waters 2003. Historical information was assembled by reading the original amendments and statutes in Beard and Shulz 1912, the histories in Plott 2003, and miscellaneous articles and monographs. Where the information in this appendix disagrees with Magleby, Schmidt, Dubois and Feeney, or Waters, I consulted the original documents to verify the accuracy of the information in tables A1.1, A1.2, and A1.3. For more information, I recommend Dubois and Feeney 1998 and especially the *Initiative and Referendum Almanac* by M. Dane Waters (2003), far and away the most comprehensive collection of information on the initiative process ever published.

Table A1.1 Initiative Provision, Signature Collection, Approval, and Amendment Provisions as of 2003

State	Type	Signature Requirement				Approval	Amendment by Legislature
		Total	Geographic	Basis	Time		
Alaska	S(I)	10%	1 signature from 2/3 state house districts*	E	1 Y	M*	Amend any time, repeal after two years, both with majority vote
Arizona	S	10%	—	G	20 M	M	3/4 vote each house and only to further purpose of measure
	C	15%	—	G	20 M	M	—
Arkansas	S	8%	4% from 15 counties	G	UL	M	Any time with 2/3 vote each house
	C	10%	5% from 15 counties	G	UL	M	—
California	S	5%	—	G	150 D	M	Prohibited, amendment only by vote of people
	C	8%	—	G	150 D	M	—
Colorado	S	5%	—	S	6 M	M	Standard
	C	5%	—	S	6 M	M	—
Florida	C	8%	8% from 1/2 congressional districts	P	UL*	M	—
Idaho	S	6%	—	R	18 M	M	Standard
Illinois	C	8%	—	G	18 M	60% or 50% B	—
Maine	S(I)	10%	—	G	1 Y	M*	Standard

Continued

Table A1.1 continued

State	Type	Signature Requirement: Total	Geographic	Basis	Time	Approval	Amendment by Legislature
Massachusetts	S(I)	3% + 1/2%	No more than 1/4 signatures from 1 county	G	64 D	M and 30% B*	Standard
	C(I)	3%	No more than 1/4 signatures from 1 county	G	64 D	M and 30% B*	—
Michigan	S(I)	8%	—	G	4Y*	M*	Any time with 3/4 vote each house
	C	10%	—	G	4Y*	M	—
Mississippi	C(I)	12%	No more than 1/5 signatures from 1 congressional district	G	12 M	M and 40% B*	—
Missouri	S	3 1/3%*	5% from 2/3 congressional districts	G	18 M	M	Standard
	C	5 1/3%*	8% from 2/3 congressional districts	G	18 M	M	—
Montana	S	5%	5% from 1/2 counties	G	1Y	M	Standard
	C	10%	10% from 40 state legislative districts	G	1Y	M	—
Nebraska	S	7%	5% from 2/5 counties	R	1Y	M and 35% B	Standard
	C	10%	5% from 2/5 counties	R	1Y	M and 35% B	—

Nevada	S(I)	10%	10% from 3/4 counties	E	10 M	M*	After 3 years with majority vote
	C	10%	10% from 3/4 counties	E	11 M	M in 2 consecutive elections	—
North Dakota	S	2%	—	N	1 Y	M	2/3 vote each house in first 7 years, standard thereafter
	C	4%	—	N	1 Y	M	—
Ohio	S(I)	3% + 3%	1.5% + 1.5% from 44 (of 88) counties	G	UL	M*	Standard
	C	10%	5% from 44 counties	G	UL	M	—
	C(I)	10%	5% from 44 counties	R	UL	M*	—
Oklahoma	S	8%	—	H	90 D	M	Standard
	C	15%	—	H	90 D	M	—
Oregon	S	6%	—	G	2 Y	M	Standard
	C	8%	—	G	2 Y	M	—
South Dakota	S	5%	—	G	1 Y	M	Standard
	C	10%	—	G	1 Y	M	—
Utah	S	10%	—	G	UL	M*	Standard
	S(I)	5% + 5%	—	G	UL	M*	Standard
Washington	S	8%	—	G	6 M	M*	2/3 vote each house for 2 years, then standard
	S(I)	8%	—	G	10 M	M*	2/3 vote each house for 2 years then standard

Continued

Table A1.1 continued

State	Type	Signature Requirement				Approval	Amendment by Legislature
		Total	Geographic	Basis	Time		
Wyoming	S(I)	15%	15% from 2/3 counties	E	18 M	50% B*	Amend any time, repeal after 2 years, majority vote

*See note below under column heading for elaboration.

Type: Type of initiative available. S = statutory initiative, C = constitutional amendment initiative. Measures go directly to the voters (direct initiative) unless indicated with "(I)", in which case the legislature has the option to approve the measure without sending it to the voters (indirect initiative).

Signature Requirement: Number of signatures required to place a measure on the ballot.

Total: Total number of signatures required, expressed as percent (of votes cast in previous election, registered voters, etc.; see Basis). For indirect initiatives, "X% + Y%" means that X% is required to place a measure before the legislature, and an additional Y% is required to place the measure before the voters if the legislature does not approve it. Missouri does not have a total signature requirement; the reported numbers are imputed from the distribution requirement.

Geographic: "X% from Y districts" means that signatures must be collected from X% of the voters in *each* of Y districts. Alaska has a trivial requirement of 1 signature (not 1%) in each of 2/3 of state house districts.

Basis: Signature percentage calculated in terms of G = votes cast in the preceding gubernatorial election, E = ballots cast in preceding general election, P = votes cast in preceding presidential election, S = votes cast in preceding secretary of state election, R = registered voters, N = population, and H = votes received by state office receiving the highest number of votes in last general election.

Time: The amount of time that petitioners are given to collect signatures before having to start over, expressed in D = days, M = months, Y = years, UL = unlimited time. Florida petitions can circulate indefinitely, but the signatures become invalid four years after they are signed. Michigan petitions can circulate for four years but signature are (rebuttably) presumed to expire after 180 days.

Approval: M means approval requires 50% + 1 of the votes cast on the measure. "X% B" means approval requires votes in excess of X% of all ballots cast (which may include ballots that abstained on the measure). Utah requires 2/3 approval for measures involving wildlife. Washington requires 60% approval for gambling measures. In indirect initiative states, the legislature can adopt the measure after signatures are collected, and the proposal will not go to the voters. In Alaska and Wyoming, the measure does not go the voters if the legislature adopts "substantially the same" measure. In Massachusetts, a measure does not go to the voters unless it receives 1/4 of the votes in the legislature for two consecutive sessions or if the legislature fails to vote on it.

Amendment by Legislature: Indicates when and under what condition the legislature can amend a statute. "Standard" means the legislature can amend or repeal the measure at any time with a majority vote of each house. Otherwise, amendment typically requires a supermajority in both houses of the legislature. Constitutional amendments can only be amended by a vote of the people.

Table A1.2 Initiative Restrictions as of 2003

State	Type	Subject Limits	Waiting Period
Alaska	S(I)	May not "dedicate revenues, make or repeal appropriations, create courts, define the jurisdiction of courts or prescribe their rules, or enact local or special legislation."	—
Arizona	S, C	—	—
Arkansas	S, C	—	—
California	S, C	Prohibits measure that "names any individual to hold any office, or names or identifies any private corporation to perform any function or to have any power or duty."	—
Colorado	S, C	—	—
Florida	C	—	—
Idaho	S	—	—
Illinois	C	May only amend Article IV of Illinois Constitution, which has to do with the election, organization, and procedures of the state legislature.	—
Maine	S(I)	—	—
Massachusetts	S(I), C(I)	Prohibits measures related to "religion, religious practices or religious institutions, or to the appointment, qualification, tenure, removal, recall, or compensation of judges; or to the reversal of judicial decisions; or to the powers, creation, or abolition of courts; or the operation of which is restricted to a particular town, city, or other political division or to particular districts or localities of the commonwealth; or that makes a specific appropriation of money from the treasury of the commonwealth" and measures inconsistent with "the right to receive compensation for private property appropriated to public use; the right of access to and protection in courts of justice; the right of trial by jury; protection from unreasonable search, unreasonable bail and the law martial; freedom of the press; freedom of speech; freedom of elections; and the right of peaceable assembly." Also prohibits measures related to initiative process itself.	4 years

Continued

Table A1.2 Continued

State	Type	Subject Limits	Waiting Period
Michigan	S(I), C	—	—
Mississippi	C(I)	May not be used to change the state Bill of Rights, provisions relating to the Mississippi Public Employees' Retirement System, the initiative process, or "the right of any person to work (regardless) of membership or nonmembership in any labor union or organization."	2 years
Missouri	S, C	May not be used "for the appropriation of money other than of new revenues created and provided for (by the initiative)."	—
Montana	S, C	May not be used for "appropriations of money and local or special laws."	—
Nebraska	S	May not interfere with legislative prerogative that "the necessary revenue of the state and its governmental subdivisions shall be raised by taxation in the manner as the legislature may direct."	3 years
	C	—	3 years
Nevada	S(I)	Prohibits any measure that "makes an appropriation or otherwise requires the expenditure of money, unless such statute or amendment also imposes a sufficient tax . . . or otherwise constitutionally provides for raising the necessary revenue."	—
	C	—	—
North Dakota	S, C	—	*
Ohio	S(I), C, C(I)	Prohibits measures "authorizing any classification of property for the purpose of levying different rates of taxation thereon or of authorizing the levy of any single tax on land or land values or land sites at a higher rate or by a different rule than is or may be applied to improvements theron or to personal property" (i.e. prohibits the "single tax").	—
Oklahoma	S, C	—	3 years*
Oregon	S, C	—	—

South Dakota	S, C	—	—
Utah	S, S(I)	—	—
Washington	S, S(I)	—	—
Wyoming	S(I)	May not be used "to dedicate revenues, make or repeal appropriations, create courts, define the jurisdiction of courts or prescribe their rules, (or) enact local or special legislation."	5 years

* See note below under column heading for elaboration.

Type: Type of initiative available. S = statutory initiative, C = constitutional amendment initiative. Measures go directly to the voters (direct initiative) unless indicated with "(I)", in which case the legislature has the option to approve the measure without sending it to the voters (indirect initiative).

Subject Limits: Content that may not appear on an initiative. Most states have single subject rules, sometimes explicit and sometimes implied by general legislative procedures, but they are enforced unevenly across states. I have not attempted to list the extent to which single subject rules bind because it is largely a subjective exercise (Dubois and Feeney (1998) provide one classification.) Florida's single subject rule explicitly excludes measures that limit the power of the government to raise revenue. Many states also prohibit initiatives that concern matters prohibited to the legislature. Because such restrictions are sometimes subjective and not always explicit, I have not attempted to list them. (Dubois and Feeney (1998) provide a list.)

Waiting Period: How much time must pass before an essentially similar measure can be placed on the ballot. North Dakota prohibits the same issue from appearing on the ballot more than twice in twelve months. In Oklahoma, the three year waiting period can be ignored if signatures of 25% of electors are collected.

Miscellaneous note: Mississippi allows only five initiatives on the ballot in any election.

Table A1.3 Changes in Initiative Provisions over Time

State	Type	Adopted	Changes and Year of Change
Alaska	S	1956	—
Arizona	S	1911	1914: Provision adopted requiring legislative supermajorities (3/4 of each house) to amend measures approved by voters (previously could be amended by simple majorities).
	C	1911	—
Arkansas	S	1910	—
	C	1910	1920: Provision repealed that limited to three the number of amendments that could appear on the ballot in any two year period. 1925: Requirement that a measure receive the votes of half of all ballots cast eliminated.
California	S	1911	Initially, both direct and indirect initiatives were available, with signature requirements of 8% and 5%, respectively. 1966: Indirect initiative repealed. Signature requirement for direct initiative reduced from 8% to 5%.
	C	1911	—
Colorado	S, C	1910	—
Florida	C	1968	1972: Single subject rule adopted. 1994: Tax limitation measures exempted from single subject rule.
Idaho	S	1912	Constitution does not specify signature requirement so initiative could not be used until legislature established a signature requirement. 1933: Legislature established signature requirement (initiative could not be used before this). 1997: Signature requirement reduced from 10% to 6%. Distribution requirement of 6% in every county added. 2001: Distribution requirement struck down by federal district court.
Illinois	C	1970	—
Maine	S	1908	1951: Signature requirement changed from a flat 12,000 to 10%. 1981: Circulation period changed from unlimited to one year.

Massachusetts	S	1918	1950: Waiting period increased from 2–3 years to 4 years. Signature requirement changed from 25,000 + 5,000 to 3% + 1/2%.
	C	1918	1950: Signature requirement changed from 25,000 to 3%.
Michigan	S	1913	—
	C	1908	Initially, only indirect initiative was available. The legislature could prevent a measure from reaching the voters by majority vote of each house. 1913: Indirect initiative replaced with direct initiative. Signature requirement changed from 20% of votes received in previous secretary of state election to 10% of votes received in previous gubernatorial election. Requirement that a measure receive votes of 1/3 of all ballots cast eliminated. Requirement that signatures be collected only at regular election and registration locations eliminated.
Mississippi	C	1992	Both statutory and constitutional amendment initiatives were adopted in 1914. State supreme court struck them down in 1922
Missouri	S, C	1908	—
Montana	S	1906	Original signature requirement was 8%, at some point changed to 5%. Original distribution requirement was 8% in each of 2/5 of the counties. 1972?: Distribution requirement changed to 1/3 of districts. 2000: Current distribution requirement adopted.
	C	1972	2000: Distribution requirement changed from 1/3 of districts to current.
Nebraska	S	1912	1920: Signature requirement changed from 10% to 7%.
	C	1912	1920: Signature requirement changed from 15% to 10%.
Nevada	S	1912	1958: Distribution requirement added.
	C	1912	Initially, only indirect initiative was available. 1958: Distribution requirement added. 1962: Indirect initiative replaced with direct initiative and requirement that a measure be approved in two consecutive elections.
North Dakota	S	1914	Original signature requirement was 10% of voters in half of counties. Initiative was indirect. 1918: Indirect initiative changed to direct initiative. Signature requirement changed to a flat 10,000. 1978: Signature requirement changed to 2%.

Continued

Table A1.3 Continued

State	Type	Adopted	Changes and Year of Change
	C	1914	Original signature requirement was 25% of voters in half of counties. After voter approval, measure had to be approved a second time, either by voters again or by legislature. 1918: Second approval requirement eliminated. Signature requirement changed to flat 20,000. 1978: Signature requirement changed to 4%.
Ohio	S, C	1912	—
Oklahoma	S, C	1907	1974: Requirement that a measure receive the votes of half of all ballots cast eliminated
Oregon	S	1902	Original signature requirement was 8% of votes cast for justice of supreme court. 1968: Signature requirement changed to 6% of votes cast for governor.
	C	1902	Original signature requirement was 8% of votes cast for justice of supreme court. 1954: Signature requirement increased to 10%. 1968: Signature requirement changed to 8% of votes cast for governor.
South Dakota	S	1898	—
	C	1972	—
Utah	S	1900	Initiative could not be used until legislature enacted implementing legislation. 1917: Implementing legislation enacted (previously the initiative could not be used). Signatures had to be collected in the office and presence of an officer competent to administer oaths. Post WWII: Requirement to collect signatures in official locations removed. 1998: Distribution requirement changed from 15 of 29 counties to 20 of 29 counties. 2000: 2/3 supermajority requirement for wildlife measures adopted. 2001: Distribution requirement struck down by Utah Supreme Court.
Washington	S	1912	1952: Provision adopted allowing legislature to amend/repeal in first two years with 2/3 vote of each house (previously the legislature could not amend/repeal in first two years.) 1956: Signature requirement changed from 10% or a flat 50,000 (whichever leads to a smaller number of signatures) to 8%. 1972: 60% supermajority requirement for gambling measures adopted.
Wyoming	S	1968	—

Type: Type of initiative available. S = statutory initiative, C = constitutional amendment initiative.

APPENDIX 2 Initiative Provisions in the Twenty Largest Cities, 2000

This appendix reports the legal provisions for the initiative process in the twenty largest American cities as of 2000. The information was collected from city charters, municipal codes, state constitutions, state statutes, city web pages, and communications with city election officials. Cities are ranked by population according to the 2000 census. See Matsusaka 2003 for more information on cities.

Table A2.1 Initiative Provisions in the Twenty Largest Cities, 2000

	Type	Signature Requirement			Prohibited Subjects	Source
		Total	Basis	Time		
1. New York, NY	A	50,000	—	120 D	Anything but changes in "manner of voting" and offices available	Charter §40
2. Los Angeles, CA	A	15%	M	200 D	—	Charter §450–55, 460–64; CA Elections Code Div. 9 Ch. 3
	O	15%	M	120 D	—	
3. Chicago, IL	—	—	—	—	—	—
4. Houston, TX	A	20,000	—	—	—	Charter VII-b, §1–3, TX Local Govt. Code 9.004
	O	15%	*	—	—	
5. Philadelphia, PA	—	—	—	—	—	—
6. Phoenix, AZ	A	15%	M	6 M	—	City Code XV, XVI; AZ Constitution IV Part 1 §1(8), AZ Stats. 19–141 to 19–143
	O	15%	M	6 M	—	
7. San Diego, CA	A	15%	R	200 D	—	Charter §23; City Code Art. 2 Divs. 10, 11, 28; CA Elections Code Div. 9 Ch. 3
	O	10%	R	180 D	—	
8. Dallas, TX	A	20,000	—	—	—	Charter Ch. XVIII §11–15; TX Local Govt. Code 9.004
	O	10%	R	60 D	—	
9. San Antonio, TX	A	20,000	—		Appropriations, tax levies, franchises, utility rates, zoning	Charter IV §34–44; TX Local Govt. Code 9.004
	O	10%	R		Appropriations, tax levies, franchises, utility rates, zoning	
10. Detroit, MI	A	5%	M	1 Y	Appropriations	Charter Art. 12; MI Statutes 117.21–117.25
	O	3%	M	6 M	Appropriations	
11. San Jose, CA	A	15%	R	200 D	—	City Charter §1603; CA Elections Code Div. 9 Ch. 3
	O	5%	R	180 D	—	

12. Indianapolis, IN	—	—	—	—	—	—
13. San Francisco, CA	A	10%	M	200 D	—	Charter Art. 14; CA Elections Code Div. 9 Ch. 3
	O	5%	M	180 D	—	
14. Jacksonville, FL	A	5%	R	—	—	Charter §18.05
15. Columbus, OH	A	10%	R	—	—	Charter §41–55, OH Constitution XVIII §9
	O	5%	R	—	—	
16. Austin, TX	A	20,000	—	—	Appropriations, tax levies	Charter Art. IV; TX Local Govt. Code 9.004
	O	10%	R	—	Appropriations, tax levies	
17. Baltimore, MD	A	10,000	—	—	—	MD Constitution Art. XI-A
18. Memphis, TN	—	—	—	—	—	
19. Milwaukee, WI	A	15%	G	60 D	—	WI Statutes 9.20, 66.0101
	O	15%	G	60 D	—	
20. Boston, MA	—	—	—	—	—	

*See note below under column heading for elaboration.

Type: Type of initiative available, if any. S = statutory (ordinance) initiative, A = charter amendment initiative. If blank, then the city does not provide any form of the initiative. When an initiative proposing an ordinance qualifies for the ballot, the city council (or equivalent) has the option to approve the measure without sending it to the voters, except in San Francisco.

Total: Number of signatures required to qualify a measure for the ballot, expressed either as an absolute number or as a percentage (of registered voters, votes cast in previous mayoral election, etc.; see Basis.)

Basis: Signature percentage calculated in terms of R = number of registered voters, M = votes cast in previous mayoral election, G = votes cast in previous gubernatorial election. In Houston, the percentage for an ordinance is in terms of the number of votes cast in the preceding Democratic primary for the nomination of mayor and commissioners.

Time: Amount of time petitioners are permitted to collect signatures, expressed as D = days, M = months, Y = years. When no limit on the circulation period could be found, the entry is left blank.

Prohibited Subjects: Content that may not appear on an initiative. Also, initiative law is usually interpreted as prohibiting proposals that are "administrative" rather than "legislative" in character.

APPENDIX 3 

Data Definitions and Sources

Rather than scatter data sources and definitions throughout the text, I have consolidated them all in this appendix, arranged by chapter.

Chapter 1

Number of Americans living in a city or state with the initiative: 1986 numbers were calculated by assuming that in noninitiative states 79 percent of the population lived in a metropolitan area (the national average), and that 58 percent of these people had access to the initiative (the average for noninitiative states in the 1986 ICMA survey). For 2003, the estimated fraction of people living in initiative states or cities in 1986 (70 percent) was multiplied by the 2003 population of the United States. Population numbers throughout were taken from the Census Bureau.

Spending for ballot propositions from Garrett and Gerber 2001; other numbers from the Federal Elections Commission web site.

Figure 1.1: From information in Appendix 1.

Figure 1.2: From data in *Initiative and Referendum Almanac* (Waters 2003).

Figure 1.3: Calculated using ICMA *Form of Government Survey, 1986.* Although more recent, the 1991 and 1996 surveys do not distinguish non-initiative cities from cities that simply failed to complete the survey (Matsusaka 2003).

Table 1.1: From information in Appendix 2.

Chapter 3

Number of initiatives and bills during 1999–2000 from Jeff Jacoby, "A Jewel in the Crown of American Self-Government," *Boston Globe,* June 7, 2001, and *Initiative and Referendum Almanac* (Waters 2003).

Total government spending in 2000 was calculated as $1.788 trillion (federal outlays, from *Statistical Abstract of the United States, 2002*) –$0.248 trillion (federal aid to state and local governments, from *Statistical Abstract of the United States,* 2002) + $1.747 trillion (state and local direct expenditure, from *Government Finances, 1999–2000*). GDP of $9.191 trillion from National Income and Product Accounts, table 1.2.

Figure 3.1. From information in *Statistical Abstract of the United States, 2000,* table 494.

Tables 3.1, 3.2, 3.4, 3.7, and figure 3.2: Government finance numbers (total spending, total revenue, federal aid, state spending, local spending, taxes, and charges) and state income, except where noted, from yearly editions of *Governmental Finances* and its successor *Government Finances,* published by the Census Bureau. General revenue from own sources is all revenue except intergovernmental aid and revenue from liquor stores, utilities, and trusts. Direct general expenditure is all spending except for intergovernmental aid and expenditure on liquor stores, utilities, and trusts. Revenue for 1957 imputed from numbers in *Statistical Abstract of the United States, 1959.* Federal aid for 1957 from *Statistical Abstract of the United States, 1959,* table 515. Income for 2000 from *Statistical Abstract of the United States, 2001,* table 651. Metropolitan population numbers for 1960 from *State and Metropolitan Area Data Book, 1986;* for 1970, 1980, 1990 from *State and Metropolitan Area Book, 1991;* for 1994 from *State and Metropolitan Area Data Book, 1997–98;* for 1998 from *Statistical Abstract of the United States, 2000,* table 33; and for 2000 from *Statistical Abstract of the United States, 2001,* table 30. Metropolitan population for all other years interpolated assuming a constant growth rate. Population numbers (usually as of July 1) from

Census Bureau web site. Southern states: Alabama, Arkansas, Florida, Georgia, Louisiana, Mississippi, North Carolina, South Carolina, Tennessee, Texas, and Virginia. Western states: Alaska, Arizona, California, Colorado, Hawaii, Idaho, Montana, Nevada, New Mexico, Oregon, Utah, Washington, and Wyoming. Summary statistics in table A3.1.

Initiative dummy was equal to 1 if a state allowed any sort of initiative (statutory or constitutional amendment, direct or indirect) according to appendix 1. Illinois was coded as a noninitiative state, as discussed in chapter 2. Signature requirement was the percentage required. I did not adjust for the denominator. If the state had different signature requirements for different types of initiatives, I chose the lowest. The results are virtually the same if I use the highest signature requirement, just the statutory signature requirement, or just the constitutional amendment signature requirement. North Dakota changed its signature requirement from a flat 10,000 to 2 percent in 1978. I coded the signature requirement as 2 percent for the pre-1978 period as well.

Tables 3.2, 3.3, 3.4, 3.7, and figure 3.3: NOMINATE variable is first dimension DW-NOMINATE score averaged across all of the state's senators. Since each senator is assigned only one score per congress, and a congress sits for two years, the numbers vary only every other year.

Table A3.1 Summary Statistics for State and Local Regressions, Chapter 3

Variable	Mean	S. D.	Minimum	Maximum	N
Revenue	3,186	822	1,486	6,172	1,488
Expenditure	3,867	935	2,011	7,598	1,488
State expenditure	1,790	649	761	5,318	1,488
Local expenditure	2,101	630	805	5,560	1,488
Centralization, %	46	9	23	81	1,488
Taxes	2,280	590	1,109	4,689	1,488
Charges	593	183	241	1,101	1,104
Taxes/Revenue, %	80	5	66	91	1,104
Income	21,486	4,673	11,349	40,878	1,488
Federal aid	795	217	291	1,756	1,488
Population, millions	4.9	5.2	0.4	34.0	1,488
Metropolitan population, %	66	21	16	100	1,488
Growth of population, previous 5 years, %	5.8	5.6	−6.3	32.3	1,488
Ideology 1: NOMINATE for U.S. senators, average	−0.04	0.30	−0.66	0.78	1,488
Ideology 2: "Citizen Ideology" from Berry et al. (1998)	49	23	0	98	1,440
Ideology 3: "Liberal/conservative" thermometer from NES, median	51	4	39	72	472

Note: This table reports summary statistics for the data used in tables 3.1, 3.2, 3.4, 3.7, and figure 3.2. Revenue, expenditure (total, state, local), taxes, charges, income, and federal aid are expressed in year-2000 dollars per capita. N is the number of observations.

Table 3.2, 3.3, and figure 3.3: Citizen Ideology is "Revised 1960–1999 citizen ideology series" from *Measuring Citizen and Government Ideology in the United States* (ICPSR Study 1208). Series ends in 1999. Liberal/Conservative Thermometer based on variable CF0801, "Liberal-Conservative Thermometer Index," in *American National Election Studies Cumulative Data File, 1948–1998* (ICPSR Study 8475).

Table 3.3 and figure 3.3: Polling numbers provided by Robert Erikson, who collected them for his book *Statehouse Democracy* (Erikson, Wright, and McIver 1993).

Tables 3.5, 3.8: Initiative status from ICMA *Form of Government Survey* in 1981, 1986, 1991, 1996. All other data from Census Bureau: Income and population for the 1980s from *County and City Data Book, 1988;* for the 1990s from *County and City Data Book, 1994.* Fiscal data for 1982 from *Census of Governments, 1982: Finance Summary Statistics* (ICPSR 8394); for 1987 from *Census of Governments, 1987: Finance Statistics* (ICPSR Study 9484); for 1992 from *Census of Governments, 1992: Finance Statistics;* for *1997 from Census of Governments, 1997: Finance Statistics.* I truncated observations where the fiscal or income variables

Table A3.2 Summary Statistics for City Regressions, Chapter 3

Variable	Mean	S. D.	Minimum	Maximum	N
		Panel A: 1980s			
Revenue	524	333	97	2,394	5,493
Expenditure	686	414	145	2,892	5,505
Taxes	277	169	45	1,221	5,505
Charges	122	151	0	1,371	5,534
Taxes/Revenue, %	72	17	15	100	5,433
Income	17,299	5,203	9,101	46,716	5,505
Federal aid	39	68	0	527	5,505
State aid	110	116	0	858	5,505
Local aid	19	37	0	263	5,505
Population	26,450	99,817	2,170	3,259,340	5,505
		Panel B: 1990s			
Revenue	721	479	117	3,434	8,077
Expenditure	986	677	163	4,565	8,078
Income	19,887	7,945	9,375	64,671	8,078
Federal aid	17	36	0	258	8,078
State aid	150	167	0	1,104	8,078
Local aid	25	48	0	304	8,078
Population	24,180	94,679	2,507	3,485,398	8,078

Note: This table reports summary statistics for the data used in tables 3.5 and 3.8. Revenue, expenditure, taxes, charges, income, and aid (federal, state, local) are expressed in year-2000 dollars per capita. N is the number of observations. Statistics are calculated for the truncated samples used in the regressions. Explanatory variable statistics are only reported for the samples used in the expenditure regressions, that is, columns (2) and (4) of table 3.5.

were in the top or bottom 1 percent of the distribution. For the 1980s, 50 percent of cities in the sample had the initiative and 45 percent of cities in the sample were in initiative states. For the 1990s, the corresponding numbers were 39 percent and 41 percent. Other summary statistics are in table A3.2.

Table 3.6: Based on information in *Government Finances in 1996–97.*

Number of initiatives in Wyoming and North Dakota, 1968–92, from *Initiative and Referendum Almanac* (Waters 2003).

For all tables, I adopted the convention of reporting numbers smaller in magnitude than 0.005 as 0.00 to reduce clutter in the tables. I retained the sign, however, so a coefficient of –0.00 means the actual value was between 0 and –0.005.

Chapter 4

ACIR: From summaries published in various issues of *Changing Public Attitudes on Governments and Taxes.* The publication was titled *Public Opinion and Taxes* in 1972, and *Revenue Sharing and Taxes: Survey of Public Attitudes* in 1973. All were published by Advisory Council on Intergovernmental Relations, Washington, D.C.

NES: From the *American National Election Studies Cumulative Data File, 1948–1998* (ICPSR Study 8475).

Figure 4.2. From various years of ACIR.

Figure 4.3. From *Los Angeles Times* Poll nos. 366 and 463.

Figure 4.4: Based on question VCF0839 from NES. I used the weighting variable VCF0009A to correct for under- and oversampling. This is stretching the survey a bit beyond its purpose since the weights are intended to make the national sample representative, not the initiative and initiative subsamples.

Figure 4.5: Data for 1972–93 are from the ACIR. The 1999 data are from Bruskin/Goldring Research as reported in Shaw and Reinhart 2001. "Don't know/no opinion" responses are not reported.

Figure 4.6: From ACIR, 1988.

Figure 4.7: Reports the average percentage giving each response for six polls: Gallup 1975, 1994, 1996, 1998, and Hart and Teeter Research Companies 1995, 1997, as reported in Shaw and Reinhart 2001.

Figure 4.8: Based on questions CF0651 and CF0652 in NES.

Table 4.1: From ACIR 1987 and 1988. For Panel A, the wording was somewhat different in 1987: "If your local government decided to raise a small amount of additional revenue to help meet costs and improve services, which one of these would you prefer? (1) A local income or wage tax, or an increase in existing local income or wage tax rates, (2) A local sales tax, or an increase in the existing local sales tax, (3) An increase in property tax rates, (4) An increase in user fees or charges for things like the use of local parks and swimming pools, parking, library use, garbage pick-up, or ambulance service, or (5) Don't know."

April 2002 Internet Survey: Survey administered by R. Michael Alvarez and Robert Sherman, available online at web site for USC/Caltech Center for the Study of Law and Politics.

Chapter 5

Table 5.1 and figure 5.1: Fiscal data from *State and Local Government: Sources and Uses of Funds: Twentieth Century Census Statistics* (ICPSR Study 6304), by Richard E. Sylla, John B. Legler, and John Wallis. Sylla, Legler, and Wallis collected the information from hardbound copies of the Censuses of 1902, 1913, 1932, and 1942. In describing the data here, parentheses indicate terms taken directly from the ICPSR documentation by Sylla, Legler, and Wallis (SLW). The label "ISO" indicates a classification code in SLW.

There are idiosyncratic features of the data in each year. In 1902, combined state and local numbers are those classified as TGG in SLW. This double counts state aid to local governments, but there is no simple way around the problem. In 1913, state-only numbers correspond to SSS in SLW. Local numbers were calculated by summing "Counties" (CCC) and "Incorporated Places over 2,500" (L11) and multiplying by the 1902 ratio of LTT/(LTT–L03). This corrects for the fact that the 1913 Census did not include local governments with populations less than 2,500. Combined state and local numbers were calculated by adding the state and local numbers, then subtracting state apportionments for education (ISO 3931) and other state apportionments (ISO 3932). State aid to local governments was subtracted from the total to avoid double counting. In 1932, combined state and local numbers correspond to TGG in SLW. This double counts state aid to local governments, but again there is not a simple way around the problem. In 1942, combined numbers are those classified as TGN. "Provision for Debt Repayment" (ISO 4100) was subtracted from expenditure to make the numbers comparable to the other years. Federal aid was subtracted from revenue. Revenue from federal government was constructed in the same way as the fiscal data. For 1902, 1913, and 1932, the numbers are "Subventions and Grants" (ISO 2300). For 1942, the category is ISO 2350, revenue "From Federal Government."

Table A3.3 Summary Statistics for Chapter 5

Variable	Mean	S. D.	Minimum	Maximum
Revenue	563	341	66	1,458
Expenditure	620	372	79	1,666
Income	6,027	2,391	1,617	12,559
Federal Aid	62	67	1	416
Population, millions	2.3	2.3	0.05	13.7
Urban population, %	41	20	8	92
Growth of population, previous 5 years, %	10.8	11.3	–2.4	62.0

Note. This table reports summary statistics for the data used in table 5.1 and figure 5.1. Revenue, expenditure, income, and federal aid are expressed in year-2000 dollars per capita. There are 192 observations.

Personal income per capita for each state in 1900 and 1920 came from the Census. Values for 1930 and 1940 came from *Survey of Current Business.* Numbers for 1910 were interpolated so that the twenty-year change was allocated proportionally to the change in nominal GNP. The numbers were then interpolated geometrically to find per capita income in the sample years. Lawrence Kenny and John Wallis provided the data by decades. Population and rural population for each state in years ending in "0" were taken from the Census and provided by John Wallis. Lawrence Kenny provided rural population data, taken from the Census. Values for sample years were calculated by geometric interpolation.

The initiative dummy is equal to 1 if the state had adopted the initiative by the year preceding the fiscal data. Adoption dates were coded using information in appendix 1. Utah was coded as a noninitiative state because its legislature did not pass workable implementing legislation until after World War II.

Summary statistics are in table A3.3.

Chapter 6

Figure 6.1: From a regression of spending on the usual control variables (regression [3] in table 3.1) and 44 year-specific initiative dummies. The reported numbers are coefficients on the initiative dummies. Data are described under chapter 3.

Chapter 7

Figure 7.1: Urban areas are defined as incorporated places (cities, towns, villages) with 2,500 or more people. Data from Census Bureau.

Figure 7.2. From *Government Finances* as described under chapter 3.

Figure 7.3: Election returns from *Statement of Vote,* published by California Secretary of State.

Figure 7.4: Public opinion is from Stimson 1999. I used updated numbers that run through 2000, available on James Stimson's web site at the University of North Carolina. Numbers are rescaled to make them comparable to the spending numbers. I believe the units have no intrinsic meaning, although Stimson in his book argues that they do.

Tables 7.1 and 7.2: From *Initiative and Referendum Almanac* (Waters 2003), supplemented by miscellaneous materials describing ballot propositions.

New York apportionment in 1930: From Eagles 1990.

Chapter 8

Table 8.1. Original data collected by the Field Institute, California Polls 7904, 8206, and 9703. I thank Zoltan Hajnal for providing the raw data.

Chapter 9

Figure 9.1: Calculated from ICMA *Form of Government Survey, 1986,* and information in Appendix 2.

Table 9.1: Adapted from opinion survey in 1991 by the Initiative & Referendum Institute, reported in *Initiative and Referendum Almanac* (Waters 2003).

APPENDIX 4 

Critical Notes on the Empirical Literature

In the process of writing this book, I discovered what appear to be errors in several related articles, errors that lead to results that sometimes seem to contradict my findings. This appendix describes the apparent errors in order to help the reader assess the literature. I do not go into great detail, but provide enough information to guide researchers who want to dig deeper on their own.

Fiscal Effects

A main finding of this book (chapter 3) is that the initiative cut state spending and taxes over the last several decades. The estimates reported here are the most comprehensive to date and, as discussed in the text, are robust to variations in specification. Many other studies have found that the initiative cut state spending and taxes during the sample period (Matsusaka 1995a; Gilligan and Matsusaka 1995; Rueben 1996; Merrifield 2000; Bails and Tieslau 2000; Matsusaka and McCarty 2001;

Besley and Case 2003; Primo 2003). The only exception that I am aware of is Zax 1989, which reported a positive relation between state spending and the initiative. The discrepancy almost certainly is due to the fact that Zax did not delete Alaska from his sample. In 1980, the single year Zax studied, Alaska was so flush with revenue from oil taxes that its spending was $8,171 per capita (year-2000 dollars here and throughout), more than six standard deviations above the mean of $1,622; spending in the other 49 states ranged from $863 to $3,244 per capita. I do not have access to the same control variables as Zax used, but to illustrate the problem I regressed state spending on income and population, controls we both use, for a sample containing all 50 states in 1980. Consistent with Zax, the coefficient on the initiative dummy was positive: +$53.86. However, the coefficient changes sign to –$111.36 if Alaska is deleted from the sample. This suggests that the initiative dummy in Zax's regression is actually capturing an Alaska effect not an initiative effect.

Camobreco 1998 is sometimes cited as finding a positive effect of the initiative on spending and taxes. This is a misreading of his results. Camobreco, like Zax, studied only a single year, 1990. He estimated a cross-sectional regression (his model 1b):

$$T_i = 171.4 \times I_i - 17.0 \times I_i \times L_i + \ldots,$$

where T_i is state taxes per capita, I_i is an initiative dummy, L_i is a measure of the liberalism of the electorate, *i* indexes the states, and the ellipses indicate an intercept and four other control variables that are not important here. It is sometimes mistakenly claimed that the coefficient of 171.4 on I_i means that the initiative increased taxes. In fact, the effect of the initiative (difference in spending between initiative and noninitiative states) implied by the regression is $T_i (I_i = 1) - T_i (I_i = 0) = 171.4 - 17.0 \times L_i$. If we calculate this for the mean value of L_i (which appears to be about 15 based on figures 1, 2, and 3 in the Camobreco paper), the implied effect of the initiative works out to be –$83.6, which is in the vicinity of what I find. The same calculation for his expenditure regression (his model 2b) indicates an initiative effect of –$159.9 per capita when it comes to spending, again consistent with what I find. In short, Camobreco's evidence reveals a negative relation between state spending and taxes and the initiative, consistent with the rest of the literature.

In sum, the literature almost uniformly shows a negative relation between state taxes and spending over the last several decades. To claim that the evidence is mixed, as some have done, is a misreading of the literature.

Responsiveness

Another central finding of the book is that the initiative process makes policy more responsive to the will of the majority. Lascher et al. 1996 and Camobreco 1998 (hence L&C) are statistical studies that claim to find no relation: policies are no more or less responsive to public opinion in initiative states. Now, as discussed in chapter 4, I believe that some of my evidence could be viewed as consistent with the same conclusion—no more or less responsiveness—although such an interpretation feels forced to me. However, the L&C evidence itself should not be viewed as supporting that conclusion because the studies rely on a flawed methodology. I explain the problem in detail elsewhere (Matsusaka 2001), so here I will only give an example. L&C estimate regressions of the form:

$$T_i = a + b \times I_i + c \times I_i \times P_i + d \times P_i + \dots,$$

where T_i is taxes (or some other policy), I_i is a dummy variable equal to 1 for initiative states, P_i is a measure of public opinion in initiative states, i indexes a state, a, b, c, and d are coefficients to be estimated, and the ellipses indicate other terms that are not essential for this discussion. The coefficient d represents the marginal effect of a change in P on T in noninitiative states ($\partial T / \partial P|_{I=0}$), and $c + d$ represents the marginal effect of P on T in initiative states ($\partial T / \partial P|_{I=1}$). Therefore, c is the difference in marginal effects between initiative and noninitiative states. L&C test and generally cannot reject $c = 0$ along several policy dimensions, and conclude that policy is equally responsive in initiative and noninitiative states.

Here is a simple example why their conclusion does not follow from their evidence. It is easiest to explain after re-expressing the L&C equation as follows:

$$T_i = a + c_I \times I_i \times P_i + c_N \times N_i \times P_i + \dots,$$

where N_i is a dummy variable equal to 1 for noninitiative states. The equation estimates the marginal sensitivities directly for initiative and noninitiative states: $c_N = \partial T / \partial P\,|_{N=1,\,I=0} = d$ and $c_I = \partial T / \partial P\,|_{I=1,\,N=0} = c + d$. In this setup, L&C's critical test is $c_I = c_N$.

The policy desired by the people cannot be observed by the researcher, but suppose the true relation was that a state with opinion P wanted taxes $T = 100 + 10P$. Now suppose we estimate $T_i = 100 + 10P_i + \dots$ in initiative states ($c_I = 10$) and $T_i = 120 + 10\,P_i + \dots$ in noninitiative states ($c_N = 10$). Then initiative states are giving the people exactly the policy they want while noninitiative states are delivering too much T, that is, initiative states are fully responsive and noninitiative states are not. L&C would observe that $c_I = c_N$ (or $c = 0$ in their original specification) and incorrectly conclude that initiative and noninitiative states are equally responsive to public opinion. The problem, as the example suggests, is that responsiveness (in the relevant sense) cannot be inferred from the slope, $\partial T / \partial P$, alone. My example here works through different intercepts in initiative and noninitiative states although L&C do not allow for different intercepts in their regressions (their scatterplots and the related literature suggest they should). This does not invalidate the criticism but points to possible misspecification in their model. In any case, although I made the point in this example by allowing the intercepts to vary, the point is more general: examples can be constructed by allowing any coefficient in the regression (say, the coefficient on state income) to vary between initiative and noninitiative states. Unless the researcher knows the exact functional form of the relation between desired policies and preferences, there is no obvious way to get around this problem.

In a response to my critique, Hagen et al. (2001) appear to misunderstand the nature of the problem. They work through about eleven lines of algebra to show that it is possible to test whether $c_I = c_N$ (or $c = 0$ in terms of their original model, relabeled β_{IG}) under the belief that "the parameter of primary interest is . . . the difference in responsiveness [defined as the slope coefficients] between initiative and noninitiative states" (1260). They are correct that it is possible to compare the slope coefficients, but the problem (as the example above shows) is that responsiveness cannot be measured from the slope coefficient alone.[1]

Finally, a comment on the evidence in Gerber 1996 and 1999. Gerber frames her analysis in terms of explaining how policy deviates from the median—see equation (1) on page 128 of Gerber 1999—which is a very attractive approach. However, what she ends up estimating in equation (2) or (3) on pages 129–30 is a variation of the L&C methodology. Her equation (2) is not a re-expression of (1), contrary to what the text claims; it is (approximately) a re-expression of (1) *without the absolute value operator*, which is something else entirely. Although her estimates would seem to be subject to the same criticism as L&C, I nevertheless believe her conclusions are sound. What differentiates Gerber's study from L&C is that Gerber has direct information on policy preferences, so she does not face the problem of not knowing the relation between desired policy and preferences. I looked at the unpublished raw opinion data she used for her studies, and in every state it appears that the median voter was in favor of parental consent for minors to have an abortion and the death penalty.

Her estimates show (less transparently than I would like) that initiative states were more likely to adopt these policies than noninitiative states (tables 7.4 and 7.6 in Gerber 1999). These two facts alone (that is, without getting into the meaning of the slope coefficient) indicate that initiative states were more responsive to opinion than noninitiative states. In short, Gerber's evidence does indicate that initiative states are more responsive than noninitiative states, but the support does not come from the slope coefficient.

To summarize, the evidence to date shows that initiative states are more responsive to opinion than noninitiative states when it comes to fiscal policy (this book), parental consent (Gerber), and the death penalty (Gerber). It is also clear that initiative states are more responsive to public opinion about term limits. There is no valid evidence along any policy dimension that initiative states are less (or equally) responsive to opinion than noninitiative states. The only view that is currently supported by scientific evidence is that the initiative makes policy more responsive to public opinion.

NOTES

Chapter One

1. See Bradford 1911, Oberholzer 1912, and Crouch 1943 for the early history of the initiative in cities. Matsusaka 2003 provides an overview of current initiative provisions in cities.

2. This information is difficult to ascertain. My search of the post-Soviet constitutions indicated that the following republics allow initiatives: Latvia, Lithuania, Kirhgizia, Moldavia, Turkmenistan, and Ukraine.

3. For nontechnical but somewhat dated discussions of the main issues, see Magleby 1984 and Cronin 1989. Lupia and McCubbins 1998 is an outstanding study of information cues using modern theory and empirical techniques, and should be considered essential reading on the issue. Popkin 1991 is also valuable, and Downs 1957 contains the first rigorous theoretical study of the problem.

4. At first blush, the use of information shortcuts might seem a shirking of citizen duty. However, I would argue instead that it represents a responsible and economical way for citizens to register their opinions about public policy, which is the purpose of voting in the first place. It is not irresponsible to rely on the opinions of others; we do it for a great many of our everyday decisions, even the most important. Even professional legislators rely on information shortcuts: their decisions to support or oppose a bill often are based on the advice of fellow legislators, trusted aids, etc., not on a detailed reading of the text.

5. There is more evidence than what I discuss in this paragraph. See Lupia and McCubbins 1998, Bowler and Donovan 1998, and Gerber and Lewis 2002.

6. Despite the scholarly debate, the fact that 49 of 50 states require popular approval by referendum for amendments to their constitutions—apparently without controversy—suggests that there is actually a broad consensus that ordinary citizens are capable of voting on issues. The point of contention would seem to be whether to allow ordinary citizens to make proposals or to reserve this right to the legislature.

7. They reach the conclusion by slightly different avenues, however. Broder seems to suggest that money can buy legislation directly by qualifying measures for the ballot and getting them approved. Gerber is more pessimistic about the direct effect of money, but suggests it matters indirectly, by allowing wealthy groups to veto changes in the status quo and by providing a way to put pressure on legislators.

8. The term "special interest" is inherently ambiguous; in some sense we are all special interests. Throughout I operationalize the term to mean a group comprised of less than a majority of the electorate. I realize one could define the majority to be a special interest as well, but that would make the entire notion of special interest subversion vacuous.

Chapter Two

1. A useful elaboration of the theory incorporating modern developments in game theory is Lohmann 1998, although curiously she seems unaware of the huge body of preexisting work. Matsusaka 1995b develops the link between information and abstention.

2. Agency problems—the failure of agents to pursue the interests of those they represent—are the most common justification for the initiative process. Whether and to what extent legislators actually ignore constituent interests is the subject of the large and contentious "shirking" literature. Important contributions include Kau and Rubin 1979, Kalt and Zupan 1984, and Peltzman 1984. The special 1993 issue of *Public Choice* provides a good introduction to the issues and evidence.

3. Matsusaka 1992 is the first systematic treatment of the role of the initiative in correcting "honest mistakes." Matsusaka and McCarty (2001) develop the argument that extreme interest groups might use an initiative threat to cause the legislature to take a more extreme position. Kessler (forthcoming) develops the idea that initiatives might reduce information acquisition by elected officials.

4. Buchanan and Tullock 1962, and Weingast, Shepsle, and Johnsen 1981 contain important formal analyses of logrolling.

5. Besley and Coate 2000 is the only model of the bundling problem applied to initiatives. Bundling is related to the well-known problem of cycling in spatial voting models, although it is difficult to see what the cycling results would imply for the initiative process. For an overview, see Mueller 2003.

6. Many have made this argument. Perhaps the clearest exposition of the idea appears in Gerber 1996. Gerber 1998 gives examples where initiative threats appear to have influenced the legislature. Gerber also points out other indirect effects; for example, a failed initiative might signal unexpected support for a policy change, and garner a legislative response.

Chapter Three

1. For a review of the limited evidence currently available, see my entry under "Initiative and Referendum" in the *Encyclopedia of Public Choice* (2003). Rather than

being a model of the profound influence of the initiative, Proposition 13 is a good example of how tricky it is to convincingly identify initiative effects. The difficulty can be seen by noting that California ranked third among continental states in overall spending per capita in 1977, the year before Proposition 13 passed, but had fallen only to fourth place in 1987, ten years later. This is not to say that Proposition 13 was unimportant, but it illustrates that *demonstrating* its importance is not as easy as it might seem. For a careful attempt to discern the effects of Proposition 13, see Gerber et al. 2001, especially chap. 15.

2. The distinction between federal, state, and local spending is somewhat subjective. In the numbers used here, expenditure is attributed to the level of government that makes the final disbursement (so called "direct expenditure"). State aid to a local school district will show up as a local government expenditure, not a state expenditure. I consider alternative definitions below when it is material to the analysis.

3. For more systematic evidence on the relation between direct democracy and borrowing, see Matsusaka 1995a and Kiewiet and Szakaly 1996.

4. Matsusaka and McCarty (2001) report systematic evidence on the relation between initiative use and signature requirements, collection periods, and geographic dispersion requirements. As shown in appendix 1, states differ in how they define the "electorate" when calculating the signature requirement.

5. If a is the coefficient on the initiative dummy and b is the coefficient on the signature requirement, then the full effect of the initiative in a state with a signature requirement of S is $a + bS$. An F-statistic indicates if the effect is significantly different from zero.

6. I also ran exploratory regressions that included the actual number of initiatives on the ballot instead of the signature requirement. The number of initiatives turns out to be a significant correlate of tax and spending cuts as well.

7. One might question whether senators actually vote the interests of their constituents. Reasonable scholars disagree on this, but I find the evidence in Peltzman 1984 persuasive: Constituent interests explain most of the variation in their representatives' votes, especially for high-profile issues such as taxes and spending. For the purposes of table 3.2, we do not need senators to follow constituent ideology slavishly; we only need a correlation or general tendency in that direction.

8. I also tried the "government ideology" variable of Berry et al., with similar results.

9. I also ran the regressions using the mean values and tried deleting states with fewer than ten respondents, none of which affected the results in a material way. I am slightly abusing the NES data here because the surveys are not designed to be representative at the state level.

10. The initiative was also promoted by organized labor, especially the AFL-CIO, and the socialists. Initiative and referendum provisions appeared in the national and state platforms of the American Socialist Party.

11. As another approach to endogeneity problems, I estimated the regressions using instrumental variables (not reported) where the instrument for the initiative dummy was the availability of the initiative process in 1920. This follows Poterba (1995) and is based on the idea that institutions are difficult to change. The estimated initiative effects were, if anything, larger in magnitude.

12. Voters might also care about the mix between state and local government because they care about the mix of services provided by government. If voters like the services provided by local governments (such as police and fire) more than those provided by state

government, they might want to shift money to local governments independent of any considerations relating to centralization. The precise reasons for decentralization are not important for my analysis.

13. I also estimated the state-only regressions for a subset of years using general expenditure, which includes intergovernmental transfers, instead of direct general expenditure. The estimated effects are similar, but generally larger in magnitude.

14. Local government in the United States is fragmented between counties, cities, school districts, and special districts, with each accounting for a large chunk of spending. Municipalities and counties each account for about a quarter of local government spending. I focus on cities primarily because of data availability.

15. See Matsusaka 2003 for a detailed description of the ICMA survey and a discussion of the problems with the survey questions and organization.

16. Alaska and Wyoming are deleted as usual. All financial variables are expressed in year-2000 dollars. I deleted observations with values of the financial variables (revenue, expenditure, income, aid) in the top or bottom 1 percent. In many cases, these were obvious coding errors. The standard errors are adjusted for clustering by city in the 1980s sample but not in the 1990s sample (there was no straightforward way to match cities over time.)

17. The sample for regressions (2) and (3) runs from 1978 to 2000 because the data sources do not report charge revenue separately from miscellaneous revenue prior to 1978. I also estimated these regressions with charges + miscellaneous revenue as the dependent variable, and the results are about the same. See also Matsusaka 1995a.

18. The main problem was that the initiative coefficients changed sign and significance depending on exactly what regional variables were included. Because there is not a compelling reason to prefer one specification to the other, I thought it would only muddy the waters to choose one or two for presentation. For the benefit of a skeptical reader, I note that initiative cities can show *increased* reliance on taxes relative to fees for some specifications.

Chapter Four

1. I know of only five studies that the treat the questions as empirical propositions and try to resolve them directly using modern empirical methods (Gerber 1996, 1999, Gerber and Hug 2002, Lascher et al. 1995, Camobreco 1998). All of the studies have methodological problems, in the last two cases fatal. Appendix 4 contains a detailed discussion of the studies and their problems.

2. See Hansen 1998 for evidence that opinions on broad fiscal matters are generally coherent.

3. My definition of "special interest" has no normative content. In casual conversation, the term is sometimes used normatively to mean an interest opposed to the (purely subjective) "public interest." Because such a definition is entirely subjective, it is unsuitable for scientific analysis.

4. To avoid introducing theoretical jargon here, I have tolerated some imprecision. This note goes into a bit more detail for the technical reader. We are trying to learn from figure 4.2 the views of the median voter. Suppose citizens are defined by a desired change in spending, S, and there are two cutoff values, $S_H > 0$ and $S_L < 0$, that determine how people respond to polls. Citizens with $S \geq S_H$ say they want to increase spending, citizens with $S \leq S_L$ say they want to cut spending, and citizens with $S_L < S < S_H$ say they want to keep spending "about where it is." It is clear from figure 4.2 that the

median voter (S_{med}) is in the group that wants services to be kept about the same, that is, $S_L < S_{med} < S_H$. This in itself does not tell us much: the median voter could have $S_{med} > 0$ or $S_{med} = 0$ or $S_{med} < 0$. However, it is easy to show that if the distribution of S is symmetric around the median, the median S cannot be positive, and if the distribution is atomistic, the median S must be negative. There is no reasonable assumption that would have the median voter in favor of spending increases.

5. Nothing rides on this as far as the subversion hypothesis goes. We would reject the hypothesis even if a majority favored the status quo: If the initiative allows special interests to subvert the public will, we should see a majority *opposed* to prevailing policies in initiative states.

6. To give just one other example, a January 19, 2001 CBS News Poll asked, "If you had to choose, would you rather have a smaller government providing fewer services, or a bigger government providing more services." The responses were 51 percent for smaller government and 36 percent for larger government, similar in substance to the ACIR and LAT/ABC results.

7. All of the differences discussed in this paragraph are statistically significant, primarily because there are 14,000+ observations.

8. Niemi, Stanley, and Vogel (1995) essentially find the same pattern as Peltzman—voters punish governors who raise taxes—in a study focusing on a single year, 1986.

9. In 1990, the ACIR asked respondents to rate the performance of state and local governments from "excellent" to "failing." Again, local government did better, although the differences were less pronounced than in figures 4.6 and 4.7.

10. The terminal phrase "for the country as a whole" is unfortunate and muddies the waters a bit.

11. If we assume ratings are distributed continuously and symmetrically around the median, then the argument used in the previous section would imply that a majority viewed local government as more efficient.

12. Asked whether state and local spending and taxes should be decreased, kept the same, or increased, 59 percent favored cuts, 18 percent favored the status quo, and 6 percent wanted more spending. In comparison, the *Los Angeles Times* survey in 2001 found 54 percent in favor of cuts and 31 percent in favor of increases.

13. Two potential sources of bias come to mind that probably work in opposite directions. First, the question mentions that revenue would be used for "services" rather than transfers. This may lead to a bias toward the "charges" response since charges are more naturally associated with services. Second, the respondents are offered a menu of three different taxes but only a single charge category. This may exaggerate the number of tax responses.

14. But see the evidence in Gerber 1996 and 1999, which suggests that death penalty and abortion policies are closer to the majority position in initiative states than noninitiative states.

15. This phrase is a homage to Lapalombara and Hagan (1951), who long ago called for initiative students to base their opinions more firmly on empirical evidence.

Chapter Five

1. This view is common in the political science literature, but based on examination of the subject matter of ballot measures, not on evidence of the actual policy effects of the initiative (for example, Cronin 1989).

2. See Higgs 1987 and Wallis 2000 for general discussions of the growth of government since 1900.

3. Tullock (1959) and Buchanan and Tullock (1962) first formulated this idea. Weingast, Shepsle, and Johnsen (1981) developed a useful formal model.

4. Niskanen 1971 and 1975 is the pioneering work.

Chapter Six

1. The median voter result only holds under certain conditions, a one-dimensional issue space, single-peaked preferences, candidates who care only about holding office and not about policy, etc. I brush over all of these extensions since many lead to cycling, which would not help to explain the facts at hand.

2. It may be worth restating that the "leviathan" theories, such as the fiscal commons theory of Buchanan and Tullock (1962) and the bureaucracy theory of Niskanen (1971), do not seem to explain the facts either, particularly the higher spending by initiative states in the early twentieth century. See chapter 5.

3. The view of representatives as "trustees" rather than "agents" of the voters has also enjoyed something of a revival recently among legal scholars. See "Symposium: The Republican Civic Tradition," *Yale Law Journal*, 1988.

4. A vast empirical literature is testimony to the broad appeal of the shirking idea. Kau and Rubin 1979, Kalt and Zupan 1984, and Peltzman 1984 are important early empirical studies. Peltzman 1984 and Stratmann 1991, 1995, and 2002 are careful studies of the role of campaign contributions. Bender and Lott 1996 and Ansolobehere et al. 2003 are good surveys.

5. Whether a significant amount of shirking actually takes place is an open question. My reading of the evidence—following and based on Peltzman 1984, Kau and Rubin 1993, and Bender and Lott 1996—is that ideological shirking is less frequent than we have been led to believe. The answer is not material for my purposes, however, since I will argue that the twentieth-century evidence can be understood without relying on shirking by legislators. Adams and Kenny (1989) provide evidence that elections do provide some discipline.

6. This is not intended as a comprehensive list of factors that allow ideologues to survive in office. For example, Wittman (1983) and Ingberman and Villani (1993) develop spatial models showing that median voter outcomes need not attain when candidates/parties have policy preferences. Calvert 1985 is an interesting contrast. Besley and Coate (2000) provide a model where divergences between initiative and noninitiative states can arise for three distinct reasons, although their model would seem more applicable to explaining divergences along secondary policy dimensions, not fiscal policy.

7. Matsusaka 1992 and Matsusaka and McCarty 2001 develop theories based on this idea and provide some empirical tests.

8. For a simple overview of the theory of gerrymandering, see Gilligan and Matsusaka 2003.

9. Higgs 1987 contains a good discussion of how preferences (he calls them "ideologies") might evolve in response to changes in the economic and political environment.

10. The comprehensive (covering most of the twentieth century) studies of Peltzman (1984, 1985, 1990) and Erikson, Wright, and McIver (1993) use completely different methodologies and data yet reach the same conclusions. Peltzman

(1985, 656) examines congressional voting: "Profound changes in congressional voting patterns over the course of the twentieth century can be traced mainly to corresponding changes in the economic interests of their constituents." Erikson, Wright, and McIver (1993, 245) investigate the relation between public opinion and policy in the states throughout the twentieth century: "State politics does exactly what it is supposed to do in theory—faithfully translate public preferences into broad patterns of policy."

Chapter Seven

1. Higgs 1971 is a useful overview that speaks to some of the issues raised in this chapter.

2. In the figure, an urban area is defined as an incorporated place with more than 2,500 residents. The massive migration from the country to the cities shows up using all kinds of alternative definitions, such as population in large cities and number of large cities.

3. See Higgs 1971. Costa (1995) studied voting patterns on California referendums and found that urban voters were more likely to support state health insurance programs than rural voters.

4. Becker (1981) discusses this in more depth. See also Schultz (1975), who argued that education provides general skills that enhance a person's ability to work productively in a changing economy. Higgs (1971) discusses the economics of education in rural areas at the turn of the nineteenth century.

5. *Baker v. Carr* (1962) made representation issues justiciable, and *Reynolds v. Sims* (1964) applied the one person, one vote rule to the states. *Wesberry v. Sanders* (1964) and *Avery v. Midland County* (1968) required congressional districting and local governments, respectively, to conform to the rule.

6. The quote is reported in Boyle 1912, 41–42, but there is no other information about the speaker.

7. My emphasis here on urban/rural conflicts as a way to understand early twentieth century politics follows a long tradition among historians (Eagles 1990).

8. This argument should not be pushed too far. As discussed earlier, the initiative can influence policy even without measures appearing on the ballot.

9. To put the numbers in perspective, note that almost 900 initiatives in total went before the voters from 1902 to 1949. The table begins with 1910 because there were no initiatives on these subjects prior to 1910.

10. I have not attempted to separate the "revenue neutral" measures that primarily dedicated the use of gas tax revenues for one type of road project rather than raising new funds.

11. The basic facts can be found in any British history book (for example, Havighurst 1985), although not necessarily with this interpretation. Tuchman 1962 provides a colorful history of the Parliament Bill.

12. The discussion owes a significant debt to Sears and Citrin 1985 and Schmidt 1989.

13. Stimson calculated another measure of opinion that focuses on the "size of government" (rather than "liberalness" in general, which presumably encompasses social and international as well as fiscal issues). Although "size of government" is closer to what we want to measure, I report "liberalness" because it is available for a longer

period and the two series move together when both are available. I enthusiastically recommend Stimson 1999 to anyone interested in the evolution of popular opinion and how we measure it.

14. The shift of opinion against government spending in the 1990s is also apparent in figure 4.3.

Chapter Eight

1. This may be about to change. As I write this chapter, a working paper by Gerber and Hug (2002) is circulating that attempts a systematic comparison of civil rights laws in initiative and noninitiative states.

2. Cronin 1989 contains a good discussion of these cases.

3. Curiously, Donovan and Bowler (1998) and Frey and Goette (1998) both seem aware of the problem, the former describing the methodology as "a potential logical fallacy" (1021), and Gamble (1997, 262) admits that "direct democracy must be compared with the representative system."

4. Actually, even this inference is problematic since we have no information on how often antiminority measures come before voters and city councils. For example, suppose that both voters and city councils approve 60 percent of the antiminority measures they face, but that such laws are proposed much more often in noninitiative cities. Then the noninitiative cities would end up with more "majority tyranny" even though approval rates are the same.

5. I don't mean to entirely absolve previous research, however. I think there has been a tendency to define majority tyranny far too broadly. For example, if California's Proposition 38 for English-only ballots was really majority tyranny, why did 52 percent of Latinos support it (Hajnal, Gerber, and Louch 2002)? A partial solution would be for researchers to report their results using several different definitions. Every study should also explicitly state what definition is being used, as Goette and Frey (1998) did.

6. This table was inspired by a similar table in Hajnal, Gerber, and Louch 2002.

7. The key decision is *Pacific States Telephone and Telegraph Company v. Oregon,* 223 U.S. 118 (1912), which essentially applied the principle established in *Luther v. Borden,* 42 U.S. 1 (1849), that the Guarantee Clause is nonjusticiable.

8. Letter from Thomas Jefferson to Pierre Samuel Dupont de Nemours, 1816. Thomas Jefferson Digital Archive, University of Virginia, etext.lib.virginia.edu/jefferson. Other letters cited below are also available through the archive.

9. As quoted in Wood 1998, 48.

10. In his letter to Jefferson on October 24, 1787, explaining the Constitutional Convention, Madison did not even bother to list the "refine and enlarge" argument for representative government, focusing entirely on the scope argument.

11. Letter from Thomas Jefferson to John Taylor, 1816.

12. Letter from Thomas Jefferson to Isaac H. Tiffany, 1816.

13. Moreover, the New Jersey Plan introduced at the Constitutional Convention by delegates from Connecticut, Delaware, Maryland, New Jersey, and New York provided for a unicameral legislature. Executive veto information comes from Fairlie 1917.

14. A recent trend in political economy has been to view legal institutions in terms of creating "veto players," individuals or bodies who can slow down or

prevent an action from taking place. For example, Hammond and Miller (1987) develop a model of the U.S. Constitution that interprets the checks and balances as creating veto players in order to induce stability. I believe it is incomplete and somewhat misleading to think of checks and balances in this way, especially when it comes to the Constitution. Stability—too many veto players in the Articles of Confederation—was the *problem* the Founders were trying to solve with the Constitution. Instead, I would argue that fragmentation of power creates a competitive environment where many ideas can flourish and bad ideas rejected. This involves the idea of agenda control, but also information provision and innovation (see chapter 9.)

15. This section draws on Beard and Shultz [1912] 1970, Oberholzer 1912, Ketcham 1957, Diamond 1959, Cronin 1989, and Wood 1998, in addition to the more specific references throughout. The *Federalist* papers and Madison's *Notes of Debates* in the federal convention are essential in understanding how the Founders perceived the Constitution. I also found the *Anti-Federalist* helpful.

16. Letter from Thomas Jefferson to Samuel Kercheval, 1816.

17. Empirical researchers in economics and political science are increasingly interested in understanding how institutions affect the performance of government, so we can hope that a clearer picture will soon emerge. Recent work on the checks and balances of bicameralism and the executive veto is particularly relevant for assessing the initiative process. See, for example, Bradbury and Crain 2001a on bicameralism and McCarty 2000 on executive veto.

Chapter Nine

1. See Kiewiet and McCubbins 1991 and Bendor et al. 2001 for overviews of the theory of delegation as applied to political relations. They do not address the systemwide economic benefits of specialization.

2. The earliest study of the initiative in a delegation model appears to be Denzau, Mackay, and Weaver 1981. I recommend Gerber 1996 as the most transparent treatment. Banks 1990, Lupia 1992, Matsusaka and McCarty 2001, and Marino and Matsusaka forthcoming extend the model to environments of asymmetric information. All of these models use the agenda-setting framework pioneered by Romer and Rosenthal (1979). For a model that does not use the agenda control framework, see Maskin and Tirole 2001.

3. For clarity of discussion, I am drawing a sharp contrast between the delegation and information views, but they are not necessarily incompatible. In many cases, policymaking may benefit from both the information of experts and ordinary citizens.

4. *Inc* magazine, December 1, 1993.

5. Gerber's (1999) finding (from a survey) that businesses use the initiative process primarily to show the legislature that their ideas have popular support can also be understood from an information perspective.

6. The pattern could also be explained in terms of the delegation view: it may be more difficult to monitor representatives (the agency costs are higher) in large cities than small cities. Therefore, the initiative is an increasingly valuable corrective as cities become larger.

7. Miller (1999) discusses other parallels between competition in economic and political markets.

8. This summary of modern economic theory is for the noneconomist. I hope the specialist will forgive me for some imprecision.

9. Becker (1983) shows that competition leads to efficient policies in a model of competition between pressure groups.

10. Gilligan and Matsusaka 1995, 2001; Bradbury and Crain 2001b; Baqir 2002.

11. Howard Jarvis in California and Tim Eyman in Washington could be seen as their forerunners.

Appendix Four

1. Hagen et al. (2001) also raise the question whether trends in public opinion (conservative in the 1970s, liberal in the 1980s, conservative in the 1990s) together with estimated initiative effects are consistent with what would be expected if the initiative was responding to public opinion. I think the evidence in chapter 7 on the 1960s, 1970s, and 1980s, answers that question in the affirmative.

REFERENCES

Adams, James D., and Lawrence W. Kenny. 1989. The retention of state governors. *Public Choice* 62: 1–13.

Ansolobehere, Stephen D., John M. de Figueiredo, and James M. Snyder. 2003. Why is there so little money in politics? *Journal of Economic Perspectives* 17, no. 1: 105–30.

Bails, Dale, and Margie A. Tieslau. 2000. The impact of fiscal constraints on state and local expenditures. *Cato Journal* 20, no. 2: 255–77.

Banks, Jeffrey S. 1990. Monopoly agenda control and asymmetric information. *Quarterly Journal of Economics* 105: 445–64.

Baqir, Reza. 2002. Districting and government overspending. *Journal of Political Economy* 110, no. 6: 1318–54.

Beard, Charles A., and Birl E. Shulz. [1912] 1970. *Documents on the State-Wide Initiative, Referendum, and Recall.* 1st ed., 1912; rpt. New York: De Capo Press.

Becker, Gary S. 1981. *A Treatise on the Family,* Cambridge, Mass.: Harvard University Press.

———. 1983. A theory of competition among pressure groups for political influence. *Quarterly Journal of Economics* 98: 371–400.

Bender, Bruce, and John R. Lott Jr. 1996. Legislator voting and shirking: A critical review of the literature. *Public Choice* 87: 67–100.

Bendor, J., A. Glazer, and T. Hammond. 2001. Theories of delegation. *Annual Review of Political Science* 4: 235–69.

Benz, Matthias, and Alois Stutzer. Forthcoming. Are voters better informed when they have a larger say in politics? Evidence from the European Union and Switzerland. *Public Choice.*

Bernholz, Peter, Manfred E. Streit, and Roland Vaubel, eds. 1998. *Political Competition, Innovation, and Growth: A Historical Analysis.* Berlin: Springer.

Berry, William D., Evan J. Ringquist, Richard C. Fording, and Russell L. Hanson. 1998. Measuring citizen and government ideology in the American states, 1960–93. *American Journal of Political Science* 42, no. 1: 327–48.

Besley, Timothy, and Anne Case. 2003. Political institutions and policy choices: Evidence from the United States. *Journal of Economic Literature* 41. no. 1: 7–73.

Besley, Timothy, and Stephen Coate. 2000. Issue unbundling by voter initiatives. Working paper, LSE and Cornell University.

Blomberg, S. Brock, Gregory D. Hess, and Akila Weerapana. 2001. The impact of voter initiatives on economic activity. Working paper, Wellesley College.

Bowler, Shaun, and Todd Donovan. 1998. *Demanding Choices: Opinion, Voting, and Direct Democracy.* Ann Arbor: The University of Michigan Press.

Bowler, Shaun, Todd Donovan, and Caroline J. Tolbert, eds. 1998. *Citizens as Legislators: Direct Democracy in the United States.* Columbus: The Ohio State University Press.

Boyle, James. 1912. *The Initiative and Referendum: Its Folly, Fallacies, and Failure.* Columbus, Ohio: A. H. Smythe.

Bradbury, John Charles, and W. Mark Crain. 2001a. Bicameral legislatures and political compromise. *Southern Economic Journal* 68, no. 3: 646–59.

———. 2001b. Legislative organization and government spending: Cross country evidence. *Journal of Public Economics* 82: 309–25.

Bradford, Ernest S. 1911. *Commission Government in American Cities,* New York: The Macmillian Company.

Broder, David S. 2000. *Democracy Derailed: Initiative Campaigns and the Power of Money.* New York: Harcourt.

Buchanan, James M., and Gordon Tullock. 1962. *The Calculus of Consent: Logical Foundations of Constitutional Democracy,* Ann Arbor: University of Michigan Press.

Butler, David, and Austin Ranney, eds. 1994. *Referendums around the World: The Growing Use of Direct Democracy.* Washington, D.C.: The American Enterprise Institute Press.

Calvert, Randall L. 1985. Robustness of the multidimensional voting model: Candidate motivations, uncertainty, and convergence. *American Journal of Political Science* 29, no. 1: 69–95.

Camobreco, John F. 1998. Preferences, fiscal policies, and the initiative process. *Journal of Politics* 60: 819–29.

Costa, Dora L. 1995. The political economy of state provided health insurance in the progressive era: Evidence from California. NBER Working Paper 5328.

Cronin, Thomas E. 1989. *Direct Democracy: The Politics of Initiative, Referendum, and Recall.* Cambridge, Mass.: Harvard University Press.

Crouch, Winston W. 1943. Municipal affairs: The initiative and referendum in cities. *American Political Science Review* 37, no. 3: 491–504.

Denzau, Arthur T., Robert J. Mackay, and Carolyn L. Weaver. 1981. On the initiative-referendum option and the control of monopoly government. In *Tax and Expenditure Limits,* edited by Helen F. Ladd and T. Nicolaus Tideman, 191–222. Washington, D.C.: The Urban Institute Press.

Diamond, Martin. 1959. Democracy and the Federalist: A reconsideration of the Framers' intent. *American Political Science Review* 53, no. 1: 52–68.

Donovan, Todd, and Shaun Bowler. 1998. Direct democracy and minority rights: An extension. *American Journal of Political Science* 42, no. 3: 1020–24.

Downs, Anthony. 1957. *An Economic Theory of Democracy.* New York: Harper and Row.

Dubois, Philip L., and Floyd Feeney. 1998. *Lawmaking by Initiative: Issues, Options and Comparisons.* New York: Agathon Press.

Eagles, Charles W. 1990. *Democracy Delayed: Congressional Reapportionment and Urban–Rural Conflict in the 1920s.* Athens: The University of Georgia Press.

Erikson, Robert S., Gerald C. Wright, and John P. McIver. 1993. *Statehouse Democracy: Public Opinion and Policy in the American States.* New York: Cambridge University Press.

Fairlie, John A. 1917. The veto power of the state governor. *American Political Science Review* 11, no. 3: 473–93.

Feld, Lars P., and John G. Matsusaka. 2003. Budget referendums and government spending: Evidence from Swiss cantons. *Journal of Public Economics* 87: 2703–24.

Feld, Lars P., and Marcel R. Savioz. 1997. Direct democracy matters for economic performance: An empirical investigation. *Kyklos* 50, no. 4: 507–38.

Filer, John E., and Lawrence W. Kenny. 1980. Voter reaction to city-county consolidation referenda. *Journal of Law and Economics* 23: 179–90.

Fischel, William A. 2001. *The Homevoter Hypothesis: How Home Values Influence Local Government Taxation, School Finance, and Land-Use Policies.* Cambridge, Mass.: Harvard University Press.

Frey, Bruno S., and Lorenz Goette. 1998. Does the popular vote destroy civil rights? *American Journal of Political Science* 42, no. 4: 1343–48.

Frey, Bruno S., and Alois Stutzer. 2000. Happiness, economy and institutions. *Economic Journal* 110: 918–38.

Gamble, Barbara S. 1997. Putting civil rights to a popular vote. *American Journal of Political Science* 41, no. 1: 245–69.

Garrett, Elizabeth, and Elisabeth R. Gerber. 2001. Money in the initiative and referendum process: Evidence of its effects and prospects for reform. In *The Battle Over Citizen Lawmaking: A Collection of Essays,* edited by M. Dane Waters, 73–95. Durham, N.C.: Carolina Academic Press.

Gerber, Elisabeth R. 1996. Legislative response to the threat of popular initiatives. *American Journal of Political Science* 40, no. 1: 99–128.

———. 1998. Pressuring legislatures through the use of initiatives: Two forms of indirect influence. In *Citizens as Legislators: Direct Democracy in the United States,* edited by Shaun Bowler, Todd Donovan, and Caroline J. Tolbert. Columbus: Ohio State University Press.

———. 1999. *The Populist Paradox: Interest Group Influence and the Promise of Direct Legislation.* Princeton, N.J.: Princeton University Press.

Gerber, Elisabeth R., and Simon Hug. 2002. Minority rights and direct legislation: Theory, methods, and evidence. Working paper, University of Michigan.

Gerber, Elisabeth R., and Jeffrey B. Lewis. 2002. Voting in low information elections: bundling and non-independence of voter choice. Working paper, University of Michigan and UCLA.

Gerber, Elisabeth R., Arthur Lupia, Mathew D. McCubbins, and D. Roderick Kiewiet. 2001. *Stealing the Initiative: How State Government Responds to Direct Democracy.* Upper Saddle River, N.J.: Prentice Hall.

Gilligan, Thomas W., and John G. Matsusaka. 1995. Systematic deviations from constituent interests: The role of legislative structure and political parties in the states. *Economic Inquiry* 33: 383–401.

———. 2001. Fiscal policy, legislature size, and political parties: Evidence from the first half of the twentieth century. *National Tax Journal* 54: 57–82.

———. 2003. A simple theory of redistricting with applications to voting rights law. Working paper, University of Southern California.

Hagen, Michael G., Edward L. Lascher Jr., and John F. Camobreco. 2001. Response to Matsusaka: Estimating the effect of ballot initiatives on policy responsiveness. *Journal of Politics* 63, no. 4: 1257–63.

Hajnal, Zoltan L., Elisabeth R. Gerber, and Hugh Louch. 2002. Minorities and direct legislation: Evidence from California ballot proposition elections. *Journal of Politics* 64, no. 1: 154–77.

Hamilton, Alexander, James Madison, and John Jay. [1787–88] 1961. *The Federalist.* Edited by Jacob E. Cooke. Middletown, Conn.: Wesleyan University Press.

Hammond, Thomas H., and Gary J. Miller. 1987. The core of the Constitution. *American Political Science Review* 81, no. 4: 1155–74.

Hansen, John Mark. 1998. Individuals, institutions, and public preferences over public finance. *American Political Science Review* 92, no. 3: 513–31.

Havighurst, Alfred F. 1985. *Britain in Transition: The Twentieth Century,* Chicago: The University of Chicago Press.

Hayek, F.A. 1945. The use of knowledge in society. *American Economic Review* 35, no. 4: 519–30.

Higgs, Robert. 1971. *The Transformation of the American Economy, 1865–1914: An Essay in Interpretation.* New York: John Wiley and Sons.

———. 1987. *Crisis and Leviathan: Critical Episodes in the Growth of American Government.* New York: Oxford University Press.

Hotelling, Harold. 1929. Stability in competition. *Economic Journal* 39: 41–57.

Ingberman, Daniel, and John Villani. 1993. An institutional theory of divided government and party polarization. *American Journal of Political Science* 37, no. 2: 429–71.

Kahn, Matthew E. 2002. Demographic change and the demand for environmental regulation. *Journal of Policy Analysis and Management* 21, no. 1: 45–62.

Kahn, Matthew E., and John G. Matsusaka. 1997. Demand for environmental goods: Evidence from voting patterns on California initiatives. *Journal of Law and Economics* 40: 137–73

Kalt, Joseph P., and Mark A. Zupan. 1984. Capture and ideology in the economic theory of politics. *American Economic Review* 74: 279–300.

Kau, James B., and Paul H. Rubin. 1979. Self-interest, ideology, and logrolling in congressional voting. *Journal of Law and Economics* 22: 365–84.

———. 1993. Ideology, voting, and shirking. *Public Choice* 76: 151–72.

Kessler, Anke S. Forthcoming. Representative versus direct democracy: The role of information asymmetries. *Public Choice.*

Ketcham, Ralph L. 1957. Notes on James Madison's sources for the Tenth Federalist Paper. *Midwest Journal of Political Science* 1, no. 1: 20–25.

Kiewiet, D. Roderick, and Mathew D. McCubbins. 1991. *The Logic of Delegation: Congressional Parties and the Appropriations Process.* Chicago: The University of Chicago Press.

Kiewiet, D. Roderick, and Kristin Szakaly. 1996. Constitutional limitations on borrowing: An analysis of state bonded indebtedness. *Journal of Law, Economics, and Organization* 12, no. 1: 62–97.

Lapalombara, Joseph G., and Charles B. Hagan. 1951. Direct legislation: An appraisal and a suggestion. *American Political Science Review* 45: 400–21.

Lascher, Edward L. Jr., Michael G. Hagen, and Steven A. Rochlin. 1996. Gun behind the door? Ballot initiatives, state policies, and public opinion. *Journal of Politics* 58: 760–75.

Lohmann, Susanne. 1998. An information rationale for the power of special interests. *American Political Science Review* 92, no. 4: 809–27.

Lupia, Arthur. 1992. Busy voters, agenda control, and the power of information. *American Political Science Review* 86: 390–404.

———. 1994. Shortcuts versus encyclopedias: Information and voting behavior in California insurance reform elections. *American Political Science Review* 88: 63–76.

———. 2001. Dumber than chimps? An assessment of direct democracy voters. In *Dangerous Democracy? The Battle over Ballot Initiatives in America,* edited by Larry J. Sabato, Howard R. Ernst, and Bruce A. Larson. Lanham, Md.: Rowman and Littlefield Publishers.

Lupia, Arthur, and Mathew D. McCubbins. 1998. *The Democratic Dilemma: Can Citizens Learn What They Need to Know?* New York: Cambridge University Press.

Magleby, David B. 1984. *Direct Legislation: Voting on Ballot Propositions in the United States.* Baltimore: Johns Hopkins University Press.

Marino, Anthony M., and John G. Matsusaka. Forthcoming. Decision processes, agency problems, and information: An economic analysis of capital budgeting procedures. *Review of Financial Studies.*

Maskin, Eric, and Jean Tirole. 2001. The politician and the judge: Accountability in government. Working paper, Princeton University and MIT.

Matsusaka, John G. 1992. Economics of direct legislation. *Quarterly Journal of Economics* 107: 541–71.

———. 1995a. Fiscal effects of the voter initiative: Evidence from the last 30 years. *Journal of Political Economy* 103: 587–623.

———. 1995b. Explaining voter turnout patterns: An information theory. *Public Choice* 84: 91–117.

———. 2000. Fiscal effects of the voter initiative in the first half of the 20th century. *Journal of Law and Economics* 43: 619–48.

———. 2001. Problems with a methodology used to test the responsiveness of policy to public opinion in initiative states. *Journal of Politics* 63, no. 4: 1250–56.

———. 2003. I&R in American cities: Basic patterns. In *Initiative and Referendum Almanac,* edited by M. Dane Waters, 31–36. Durham, N.C.: Carolina Academic Press.

Matsusaka, John G., and Nolan M. McCarty. 2001. Political resource allocation: Benefits and costs of voter initiatives. *Journal of Law, Economics, and Organization* 17: 413–48.

Mayer, William G. 1992. *The Changing American Mind: How and Why American Public Opinion Changed between 1960 and 1980.* Ann Arbor: University of Michigan Press.

McCarty, Nolan. 2000. Proposal rights, veto rights, and political bargaining. *American Journal of Political Science* 44, no. 3: 506–22.

Merrifield, John. 2000. State government expenditure determinants and tax revenue determinants revisited. *Public Choice* 102: 25–50.

Miller, James C. III. 1999. *Monopoly Politics.* Stanford, Calif.: Hoover Institution Press.

Montesquieu, Charles. 1989. *The Spirit of the Laws,* edited by Anne M. Cohler, Basia C. Miller, and Harold S. Stone. New York: Cambridge University Press.

Moulton, Brent R. 1986. Random group effects and the precision of regression estimates. *Journal of Econometrics* 32: 385–97.

Mueller, Dennis C. 2003. *Public Choice III.* New York: Cambridge University Press.

Niemi, Richard G., Harold W. Stanley, and Ronald J. Vogel. 1995. State economics and state taxes: Do voters hold governors accountable? *American Journal of Political Science* 39, no. 4: 936–57.

Niskanen, William A. 1971. *Bureaucracy and Representative Government,* Chicago: Aldine-Atherton.

———. 1975. Bureaucrats and politicians. *Journal of Law and Economics* 18: 617–43.

North, Douglass C. 1981. *Structure and Change in Economic History.* New York: Norton.

———. 1998. The rise of the Western world. In *Political Competition, Innovation and Growth: A Historical Analysis,* edited by Peter Bernholz, Manfred E. Streit, and Roland Vaubel, 13–28. Berlin: Springer.

Oberholzer, Ellis Paxson. 1912. *The Referendum in America.* Rev. ed. New York: Charles Scribner's Sons.

Parsons, Frank. 1900. *Direct Legislation: The Veto Power in the Hands of the People.* Philadelphia: C. F. Taylor.

Peltzman, Sam. 1976. Toward a more general theory of regulation. *Journal of Law and Economics* 19: 211–40.

———. 1984. Constituent interest and congressional voting. *Journal of Law and Economics* 27: 181–210.

———. 1985. An economic interpretation of the history of congressional voting in the twentieth century. *American Economic Review* 75, no. 4: 656–75.

———. 1990. How efficient is the voting market? *Journal of Law and Economics* 33: 27–63.

———. 1992. Voters as fiscal conservatives. *Quarterly Journal of Economics* 107: 327–61.

———. 1998. *Political Participation and Government Regulation.* Chicago: The University of Chicago Press.

Plott, Steven L. 2003. *Giving Voters a Voice: The Origins of the Initiative and Referendum in America.* Columbia: University of Missouri Press.

Pommerehne, Werner W. 1983. Private versus öffentliche Müllabfuhr: Nochmals betrachtet. *Finanzarchiv* 41: 466–75.

Poole, Keith T., and Howard Rosenthal. 1991. Patterns of congressional voting, *American Journal of Political Science* 35: 228–78.

Popkin, Samuel L. 1991. *The Reasoning Voter.* Chicago: The University of Chicago Press.

Poterba, James M. 1995. Capital budgets, borrowing rules, and state capital spending. *Journal of Public Economics* 56: 165–87.

Primo, David. 2003. Stop us before we spend again: Institutional constraints on U.S. state spending. Working paper, University of Rochester.

Roberts, Brian E. 1990. Political institutions, policy expectations, and the 1980 election: A financial market perspective. *American Journal of Political Science* 34, no. 2: 289–310.

Romer, Thomas, and Howard Rosenthal. 1979. Bureaucrats versus voters: On the political economy of resource allocation by direct democracy. *Quarterly Journal of Economics* 93: 563–87.

Rowley, Charles Kershaw, and Friedrich Schneider, eds. 2003. *Encyclopedia of Public Choice*. Boston, MA: Kluwer Academic Publishers.

Rueben, Kim. 1996. Tax limits and government growth: The effect of state tax and expenditure limits on state and local government. Working paper, Public Policy Institute of California.

Sabato, Larry J., Howard R. Ernst, and Bruce A. Larson, eds. 2001. *Dangerous Democracy? The Battle over Ballot Initiatives in America*, Lanham, Md.: Rowman and Littlefield.

Schmidt, David D. 1989. *Citizen Lawmakers: The Ballot Initiative Revolution*. Philadelphia: Temple University Press.

Schultz, Theodore W. 1975. The value of the ability to deal with disequilibria. *Journal of Economic Literature* 13, no. 3: 827–46.

Schumpeter, Joseph A. 1950. *Capitalism, Socialism, and Democracy*. 3d ed. New York: HarperPerennial.

Sears, David O., and Jack Citrin. 1985. *Tax Revolt: Something for Nothing in California*. Cambridge, Mass.: Harvard University Press.

Shaw, Greg M., and Stephanie L. Reinhart. 2001. The polls—trends: devolution and confidence in government. *Public Opinion Quarterly* 65: 369–88.

Shepsle, Kenneth A. and Barry R. Weingast. 1981. Structure-induced equilibrium and legislative choice. *Public Choice* 36: 221–37.

Stigler, George J. 1971. The theory of economic regulation. *Bell Journal of Economics and Management Science* 2: 3–21.

Stimson, James A. 1999. *Public Opinion in America: Moods, Cycles, and Swings*. 2d ed. Boulder, Colo.: Westview Press.

Stratmann, Thomas. 1991. What do campaign contributions buy? Deciphering causal effects of money and votes. *Southern Economic Journal* 57: 606–20.

———. 1995. Campaign contributions and congressional voting: Does the timing of contributions matter? *Review of Economics and Statistics* 77, no. 1: 127–36.

———. 2002. Can special interests buy congressional votes? Evidence from financial services legislation. *Journal of Law and Economics* 45, no. 2, part 1: 345–73.

Tuchman, Barbara W. 1962. *The Proud Tower: A Portrait of the World before the War, 1890–1914*. New York: Ballantine Books.

Tullock, Gordon. 1959. Problems of majority voting. *Journal of Political Economy* 67: 571–79.

Wallis, John Joseph. 1995. Form and function in the public sector: State and local government in the United States, 1902–1982. Working paper, University of Maryland.

Wallis, John Joseph. 2000. American government finance in the long run: 1790–1990. *Journal of Economic Perspectives* 14, no. 1: 61–82.

Waters, M. Dane. 2003. *Initiative and Referendum Almanac.* Durham, N.C.: Carolina Academic Press.

Weingast, Barry R., Kenneth A. Shepsle, and Christopher Johnsen. 1981. The political economy of benefits and costs: A neoclassical approach to distributive politics. *Journal of Political Economy* 93, no. 4: 642–64.

Wittman, Donald. 1983. Candidate motivation: A synthesis of alternatives. *American Political Science Review* 77: 142–57.

Wood, Gordon S. 1998. *The Creation of the American Republic, 1776–1787.* Chapel Hill: The University of North Carolina Press.

Zax, Jeffrey S. 1989. Initiatives and government expenditures. *Public Choice* 63: 267–77.

INDEX